Death and the Supreme Court

DEATH AND THE SUPREME COURT

Barrett Prettyman, Jr.

New York

Harcourt, Brace & World, Inc.

A Harvest Book

ACKNOWLEDGMENT

The author gratefully acknowledges the permission from Professor Richard H. Field and the *Harvard Law Review* to print the excerpt from "Frankfurter, J., Concurring..." (Copyright © 1957 by The Harvard Law Review Association), which appears on page 40. The author also wishes to express his deep appreciation to the many persons who furnished records, briefs, and other materials so essential to his research, and to the secretaries at Hogan & Hartson who worked so diligently typing and proofreading his various drafts.

Library of Congress Catalog Card Number: 61-12348
Printed in the United States of America

For Ev and Ty

Contents

Death and the Supreme Court

"When the penalty is death, we, like state court judges, are tempted to strain the evidence and even, in close cases, the law in order to give a doubtfully condemned man another chance." Mr. Justice Robert H. Jackson, writing for the Court in *Stein* v. *New York*, 346 U. S. 156 (1953).

Introduction

Most people, otherwise well informed, do not know that the Supreme Court of the United States has its own basketball court. Or that the opinions of the Court are printed in the basement. Or that the "conference room" shown to the public is never used for a conference by the Court. For that matter, most people–including some lawyers–cannot name all nine members of the Court.

Perhaps all this is trivia when compared with what most citizens do not know about the actual work of their highest court–what it accomplishes and how it goes about its business. Despite occasional cautious commentaries by the Justices themselves, even the barebones daily routine involved in hearing cases and reaching decisions seems shrouded in mystery.

This is strange in Washington, where the spotlight follows power. The peculiar power of a Supreme Court Justice cannot be charted, but it can be sensed; it is recognized, though undefined. It is a uniquely American power, since it involves the right to void an act of both the legislative and executive branches. Like all power, it is often misrepresented.

Much of the ignorance about the Court springs from the Justices' self-imposed silence. Unless goaded beyond their patience, the Justices do not publicly answer their critics, whether the attack is against an individual or the Court as an institution. They do not hold press conferences to explain what occurred at private sessions or why they really voted as they did or what that ambiguous phrase in the dissenting opinion was intended to convey.

And this is as it should be. Justice cannot rest on the vagaries of public opinion and public relations. The way to thrash out the knotty problems of cases and controversies lies in open-minded, frank, private, and sometimes brutish discussion, uninhibited by fear of garbled reports to the press after the event. Each judge must feel free to express doubt and confusion, and to change his mind at any point until the decision is finally rendered in open court. The only public utterance of the Court must be its written opinion—agreed to, or concurred in, or dissented from by each Justice voting his own conviction and responsible for his own individual conclusion.

Of necessity, the Court must operate in much the same fashion as a jury. Surely no one believes that jurors should be required to report not only their verdict but who said what and why in the jury room. We do not impose silence because of hokeypokey that cannot be exposed to public gaze but because, as in foreign affairs, honest conclusions are sometimes best reached when not tortured by concern about the public image.

But the self-imposed silence of the Justices must not prevent the rest of us from acquiring as much knowledge as we legitimately can about the most important court in the land. The Supreme Court should be written about and talked about, dissected and analyzed, so that when we come to make up our free minds about it, we act on the basis of fact and not on warped, distorted and biased half-truths.

Those who try to cover the entire work of the Court in a single volume attempt too much. Some columnists to the contrary notwithstanding, the Court's problems are extremely intricate, and judgments or appraisals of even a single term's endeavor become so general as to lose meaning.

This book, then, is an attempt to deal with only one phase of the Court's work—that having to do with cases in which a man's life is at stake. These cases occupy a peculiar place in the Court's business—and to me a most fascinating one. I hope that what follows will show why.

1

Baby

It started on a black night in September, 1948, but no one in Selma realized it at the time. The real terror, the almost hysterical fear that gripped the city, was to come later.

Selma sits like a mud lark beside the Alabama River in the center of the sovereign state of Alabama. Broad Street, the main thoroughfare, shoots like an arrow over the river and through the town to flat country westward. It is a clean and prosperous street, but the dirt roads of the Negro community are only a block away, just as the grand, rambling, proud houses of the elite are street-to-street with Negro shacks and shanties.

It was three thirty in the morning. Mrs. Thelma Manning, covered by a sheet and wearing only a pair of panties, had dropped off to sleep while reading in bed, her bedroom light still on. She was suddenly jolted awake by a rude motion below her waist. Dazed, she opened her eyes to find a Negro sitting on the bed. He had pulled back the sheet and was trying to rip off her panties. She uttered a paralyzing scream that seemed to immobilize the Negro for a moment, and then he scrambled from the bed and ran downstairs and out the front door. Mrs. Manning called the police. They found the prowler's shoes still neatly placed on the front porch, as if a Mohammedan were inside praying.

While the police were investigating Mrs. Manning's complaint, they received a second alarm from only a few blocks away. Mrs. J. M. McLaughlin told them she had just been awakened by a light-skinned Negro trying to pull the sheet off her. When she called for help, the Negro jammed his hand across her mouth in an effort to stifle the sounds and, in doing so, fell across the bed. In the brief struggle that followed, he bit her on the left arm near the shoulder, and then ran from the house.

The police were satisfied that both women had been attacked by the same man. Despite the descriptions they gave and the clue of the abandoned shoes, no subsequent leads developed, and in a few months the manhunt slackened. The night of terror seemed to have been a single, explosive exception to the unruffled routine of Selma's pedestrian existence. Perhaps some crazed traveler had been passing through Selma on his way to more exciting towns—a kind of itinerant rapist. Or perhaps the prowler was the frustrated husband of a domineering, Athenian wife, living on a quiet Selma street and pursuing a shapeless career, suddenly gone berserk for one frantic night, only to return to his normal status the following morning. In any event, the womenfolk of Selma soon relaxed, and the town slumbered on.

Five years passed. In early March, 1953, several families reported to the police that their homes had been broken into. Then, on the night of March 18, a light-skinned Negro entered a drugstore on Broad Street and asked the lady behind the counter for a small bottle of baby oil and a package of prophylactics. She reddened and flounced off to the back of the store to confer with the druggist. The druggist came forward and admonished his customer never to ask a lady for such articles—he should be ashamed of himself. Grudgingly, the druggist made the sale, and the man left.

A few blocks away, Mrs. Delores Stenson, the eighteen-year-old pregnant wife of a sergeant at nearby Craig Air Force Base, had fallen asleep awaiting her husband's return from regular duty at the base. The Stensons rented the front apartment of a one-story clapboard house next door to the Kingdom Hall of Jehovah's Witnesses. The house was surrounded on three sides by a slanting porch laden with antiquated green chairs, a broken swing, and empty flower pots. The front yard was hard, lifeless mud.

At 10:45 P.M., Mrs. Stenson was wrenched into wakefulness by the weight of a body on top of her. She could see only the excited eyes of a Negro—the rest of the face was hidden by a mask and a rag wrapped about his head. He held a knife at her throat. She began sobbing uncontrollably, begging the man to leave her alone. Firmly gripping the knife, the man told her he would kill her if she screamed. Then he shifted the knife, and she felt the point between her legs. If she did not open her legs, he said, he would cut them open. Sobbing, she obeyed, and the man raped her.

When he was through and had gone, Mrs. Stenson's screams roused the landlady and the tenants in the adjoining apartment. The police were called, and Mrs. Stenson was taken to the hospital, where doctors confirmed the fact that she had been raped. The police found an open window in the kitchen, and dirt and type "B" blood on the sheets of her bed. The blood, one of the two most uncommon types, did not match that of either Sergeant or Mrs. Stenson.

The Chief of Police, E. W. Mullen, immediately called every one of his twenty men into active duty, and most of them worked through the night. Bloodhounds were brought to town, but their sniffing around the mud-caked yard of the Stenson home produced nothing but their own disappointed yelps and howls. The police, in an agony of frustration, picked up several Negroes for questioning, but soon released them.

Although her assailant's face had been well covered, Mrs. Stenson ventured a sketchy description of him and said she would know his voice if she were to hear it again. But there was precious little to go on. The intruder had not left a single fingerprint, although Mrs. Stenson was certain he had worn no gloves. The police simply had nowhere to turn.

The news in the Selma *Times-Journal* of the rape struck the town like a thunderclap. The uneasy truce between Negroes and whites had been violated, diplomatic relations were broken, and a siege, just short of open warfare, was tacitly acknowledged on both sides.

But it was not until April 24, over a month later, that near hysteria gripped the town. On that night, the mayor's daughter was attacked.

Mrs. Jean Rockwell was twenty-five years old. She and her husband, a pharmacist, and their two children—a five-week-old infant and sixteen-month-old Chris, the mayor's namesake—had lived in the 800 block of Mabry Street for only two months. They rented an apartment in the back of the house.

On this particular evening, because Mr. Rockwell was still at the drugstore where he worked, Mrs. Rockwell carefully latched the kitchen screen door, locked and chained the kitchen door, and locked the front door leading to the porch. The windows to the bedrooms were closed and the window screens latched. About ten o'clock it began to rain. Mrs. Rockwell put on her pajamas and went to bed. The infant slept beside her; Chris occupied the adjoining bedroom. The lights in the hall to the living room and the parents' bedroom remained on as a welcome to Mr. Rockwell.

Shortly after Mrs. Rockwell had drifted off to sleep, a man slipped around the side of the house and climbed several brick steps which led, inexplicably, to the window of Chris's bedroom. The man cut a small hole in the window screen just above the latch, reached in, and unhooked the latch. Carefully, he opened first the screen and then the window, and climbed over the sill. Seeing the sleeping child, he moved softly out of the room and into the kitchen. He unlocked and opened the kitchen and screen doors, guaranteeing himself an exit route. Picking up a butcher knife that lay on the kitchen table, he walked to the bathroom, put a towel around his head, and passed on to the parents' bedroom.

Mrs. Rockwell woke suddenly and in horror to find a man sitting on top of her. He was slight of build and appeared to be in his twenties. He wore no shirt at all, only an undershirt and a pair of blue jeans, and he held a knife in his left hand, with the edge of the blade at her throat. He told her he was going to kill her if she made a sound.

He had picked on the wrong lady.

Mrs. Rockwell immediately began struggling. In blind desperation and with an instinctive thrust of muscles that surprised both of them, she reacted against him. She flailed and clawed, twisted and turned, pummeled and kicked, trying to clear herself from the weight. He held on, twisting her to get a better grip, while she wrestled, alternately recoiling and counterattacking with all the ingenuity of a trained fighter.

She was making no progress until the baby awoke and screamed in protest at the intrusion on its sleep. The man was momentarily diverted by the sound, and Mrs. Rockwell wrenched free. She dashed for the door of the bedroom. He was behind her at once, grabbing at the pajamas, and so they ran, she in front and he clutching at her from behind, down forty feet of hallway and into the living room. She was screaming all the way, but the sound was muffled by the heavy downpour buffeting the house.

In the living room, the Negro fell over a stool. He had hooked his right hand into her pajamas, and as he fell he carried her down with him. He kept repeating that he would kill her if she did not be quiet, but she continued to scream. He told her "to straighten out," and she knew he meant to rape her on the floor.

He still carried the knife, but with a single, nimble movement, she grabbed at it and twisted it out of his hand. In an instant, the tide had changed, and the attacked had become the attacker. But before she could even strike him, he had jumped up and galloped the length of the living room, down the hall, and out the kitchen door. Mrs. Rockwell ran to the door, locked it, and called the police. The entire battle had lasted about eight minutes.

With a member of the mayor's own family having been attacked, the industry and fervor of the police were unbounded. Officers descended like an avenging horde, trampled the grounds unmercifully, and collected as clues every object on the premises not securely attached. A lineup of suspects was arranged for Mrs. Rockwell, but she failed to find her assailant among them. The calmest man in town was the mayor, who expressed confidence in Chief Mullen and his men—"one of the top-ranking police organizations in the state"—but warned the citizens of Selma to take the simple precautions of locking their doors and pulling their shades.

A week after the Rockwell attack, Mrs. Sally Binford was in bed in her house on Parkman Avenue when she heard a strange noise. She got up and walked toward her bathroom. As she reached the door, she saw the reflection of a face in the bathroom mirror. A Negro was standing in her bathtub. She screamed, and the Negro hastily climbed out the same window through which he had entered, just above the bathtub. Shaken and near collapse, Mrs. Binford called the police. Again, their investigation proved fruitless.

Eleven days passed. On May 12, Dr. Harlan Hollingsworth, a local chiropractor, was awakened shortly after midnight by the sound of someone in his room. He had no sooner begun to gather his senses than he felt a hand on his leg. He grabbed the man, whom he now saw was a thin Negro of medium height, and scuffled with him. Presumably, the Negro had mistaken the doctor for a woman. In any case, the two of them wrestled about for a moment before the Negro shook loose and ran out of the house.

The attacks were now coming at shorter periods. The next victim, only four days later, was a sixty-nine-year-old woman. Mrs. Lilly Little lived in a room near the back of a house on Mechanic Street. Fortunately, her daughter and son-in-law occupied an adjoining apartment. It was late Friday night—after one in the morning, in fact—when she was awakened by the half-knowledge that someone was putting his hands on her. She could not comprehend the phantom confronting her—this man with a cloth around his head and only his eyes showing. He told her to be quiet, but Mrs. Little instinctively screamed. He retaliated immediately by hitting her several times in the face, but the screams had aroused her daughter and son-in-law, and the man could hear them scurrying to his victim's aid. He ran from the room. The police found a screen removed and a window raised at the back of the house.

By now the City of Selma was in a complete state of hysteria. Women did not walk alone after dark; they were locked in at home like harem women, while their menfolk roamed the streets as self-appointed commandos, armed with pistols, knives, pipes, sticks. The slightest disturbance caused a covey of men to come circling in for the kill. The night cries of children brought parents convulsively to their feet. False alarms sometimes poured into the police station too fast to be checked, as nervous women, and even men, for that matter, were terrorized by shadows shifting in the darkness. A teen-age girl claimed she had awakened to find someone pulling on her hand, though no evidence of an intruder could be found. A couple reported tracks around their house, and a lady on Range Street complained that her house had been broken into. Many people reported damaged screens. Selma's supply of window bars, used to seal windows so that they could not be raised, was quickly exhausted; orders were placed in Montgomery and as far away as Mobile, until finally every available window bar in the southern half of the state had been purchased by the nineteen thousand residents of the Selma area.

The attacks were discussed to the exclusion of every other piece of news. Every male Negro, whether tall, short, thin, fat, light, or dark, was an object of suspicion. A thirteen-hundred-dollar reward was offered for the capture of the guilty man, and several Negroes were hopefully jailed, only to be released after their stories were corroborated. In Selma, there was but one municipal purpose, one *raison d'être* that bound the entire community into a straining knot of intent—to find the man responsible for these attacks and to stop him.

The police soon discovered to their horror that some screens were being cut by pranksters. Apparently, making women think the rapist had them in mind struck some people as humorous. But not Chief of Police Mullen. He quickly issued a public warning: someone would be killed if the pranks continued. "People here are on the alert for anyone molesting their homes," he said, "and they are apt to shoot first and investigate later. This kind of joke is never safe, but at this particular time it is flirting with death."

This was the mood of the people—overwrought, apprehensive, explosive—when, at eleven thirty on Saturday night, May 16, a seventeen-year-old high school student named Roland Harris spotted a Negro walking stealthily down an alley that ran by Roland's house. The alley, though only a block and a half from the Negro Masonic Building, was in an all-white neighborhood. Roland, unarmed, followed the Negro for thirty minutes as he prowled the nearby alleys, but finally lost him. There was no doubt in Roland's mind that he had seen the man everyone was looking for, and he called the police.

A few minutes later and not far away, Mr. and Mrs. Jake Youngblood, returning home from a movie, were driving up an alley in back of their house when Mrs. Youngblood noticed a Negro dart across the alley behind the car. She told her husband, and he turned the car around and drove back. Mr. Youngblood got out and questioned the man. His answers were evasive. Youngblood ordered him to walk ahead of the car, and the Negro meekly complied. The strange parade—Negro in front and bright-eyed car trailing slow behind—passed out of the alley to Deason's Service Station on Broad

Street. At eight minutes past twelve, the police were called again.

They arrived to find a slender Negro seated in the back of Youngblood's car beside the gas pumps. He was the same man Roland Harris had seen prowling alleys. A number of white men milled about the car, some of them peering in occasionally at the prisoner. The police quickly took the man into custody and booked him on an open charge of "investigation." The man was William Earl Fikes.

By next morning, the police had gained considerable information about Fikes.

He was not a resident of Selma at all. He lived with his wife and four children in Marion, Alabama, thirty miles away, where he worked at a Pan Am Service Station. In fact, he had been born only five miles from Marion, the youngest of three boys, and during his early years he had helped his father farm a plot of land and direct funerals. Books were not William's particular forte; he entered school at age eight and left eight years later while still in the third grade. On one of his forays from home, while working at a paper mill in Mobile, he met and married a local girl and moved her north to Marion. During World War II, he served in the army for three years, returning to Marion more mature but still a basically quiet lad, responsive only when directly addressed and even then almost inarticulate. He was unlike his friendly, open, talkative father, except that both men were lean in appearance; nor was he like his large, genial mother. She considered him "thickheaded." There had, in fact, been strains of insanity in the family. The uncle and the mother of the elder Fikes had both been declared insane, and both had died in mental institutions. In November, 1949, about a year after the first, seemingly unrelated, attacks on Mrs. Manning and Mrs. McLaughlin, Fikes had been sentenced to six years in prison in connection with the theft of some tires. After serving less than two of the six years, he was released on parole by Governor James E. Folsom in January, 1951, during the last days of Folsom's first term in office.

William Fikes was a slim Negro with a chiseled face, light mustache and strong chin. His hair was black and closely cropped, his nose flat, and his lips full. He was twenty-seven years old, stood five feet eleven, and weighed a hundred and forty pounds, fitting generally the description of the rapist. He did not present a wholly unsatisfactory appearance, except that something was wrong with his eyes. They seemed peculiarly drowsy, and he was slightly walleyed. Or at least the eyes gave that impression. People commented on his eyes but could not put their finger on just what was wrong.

At eleven o'clock on the morning after his arrest, Fikes was brought into the office of the Captain of Police, I. Wilson Baker. Captain Baker was a large man, over six feet tall, and he spoke through thin lips and peered out through slits of eyes and glasses. He was in his early forties, looked almost bald, and showed signs of a double chin. A completely indefatigable worker, he often stayed on a case without rest until it was closed. His record of obtaining confessions was high, the general impression among his contemporaries being that he never used physical force but was stern and gruff and quoted the Bible to great advantage. He had taken a correspondence course in the law to improve his lot as a police officer.

Captain Baker questioned Fikes for two hours about the various housebreakings and attempted rapes that had terrorized Selma. During the questioning, Fikes asked to talk to the county sheriff, who lived in Marion. The sheriff arrived after lunch and conferred with the prisoner. Reluctantly, and yet perhaps with a certain degree of relief, Fikes began to intimate that he had been involved in the housebreakings. The sheriff, Captain Baker, and Chief of Police Mullen placed Fikes in a car and drove him around Selma to several of the houses which had been burglarized. At one of them, Fikes pointed out how he had obtained entry. On their return to the police station, the captain again talked to Fikes for several hours at the end of the day.

The next day, Monday, the captain for the first time wrote out a warrant against Fikes (though for some reason, the warrant was unnumbered and unrecorded). Beginning at 9 A.M., Captain Baker talked with Fikes for about two hours. Fikes now was openly admitting some part in the housebreakings, but his statements were far from conclusive. He mentioned, for example, the two attacks on a single night in 1948, involving Mrs. Manning and Mrs. McLaughlin, but he denied any part in the rape of Mrs. Stenson, the air force sergeant's wife. The police dusted off the shoes that had been found on Mrs. Manning's porch, and, sure enough, they fitted Fikes. He was given a blood test and found to be type "B." He was taken to a lineup, where he was identified by Mrs. Binford as the man she had seen in the bathroom of her home several weeks before.

The owner of the gasoline station where Fikes had worked in Marion visited the boy briefly at the jail, and then, after lunch, Fikes was driven fifty-five miles to Kilby Prison near Montgomery. He was sent there on the orders of a circuit judge and was being held for the custody of the Selma police. Although no specific threats had been made against Fikes, the police guessed from the mood of the town that they had better remove him from the jurisdiction for his own safety. Captain Baker sat in back and talked with him on the way. The sheriff and a police lieutenant sat up front. After their arrival at the prison, Fikes was placed in the "segregation unit," and Captain Baker, a sheriff, an employee of the state toxicologist's office, and a police lieutenant all talked to Fikes for several hours. He was given supper, and then the same group talked to him again. Later that evening, the captain and lieutenant returned to Selma.

The strange world of William Fikes was becoming clearer to the officers now. On the surface, Fikes seemed to have lived out his humdrum days and evenings in Marion—the little town quite proud of its past; the town where General Sam Houston had been married and Woodrow Wilson had walked many times the pathways of historic Marion Military Institute before his elevation to the Presidency. But Fikes was a Jekyll and Hyde. Unbeknownst to those around him, some inexplicable tension kept building up in Fikes to a point he could not endure. His own explanation was that he was not finding sexual satisfaction at home. At any rate, he would feel an urge—a mounting, irresistible urge—to attack a white woman. And so he would climb into his truck and drive past the big white courthouse, past the car cemetery on the edge of town, down the hill to the highway, and along the flat, open, lonely country towards Selma, thirty miles away. He would see an occasional house along the way, badly in need of repair, sitting on short stilts of brick, not deigning to rub its bottom on the orange or red clay beneath. Some patches of land were under shallow water. A few cows, chickens, and emaciated dogs walked the shoulder of the road and skirted the billboards extolling insurance and beer. Finally, he would reach Selma and park his truck beside the Buckeye Oil Mill, where it would not be seen. Then he would begin his search, prowling alleys and peeping in windows. When it was all over, he would climb back into his truck and return to Marion, only to have the tension begin building again—too soon and too urgently. For three months, he had come to Selma almost once a week.

After two days of questioning, Fikes had hinted at most of this, and now, on Tuesday, he rested in prison without visitors. On Wednesday, Captain Baker, the sheriff, and a doctor met at the prison shortly before noon and interrogated Fikes for a short while before lunch and for most of the afternoon and into the early evening. Each man asked questions, but Captain Baker asked the most. The next day was Thursday, May 21. During the day, William's father arrived at the prison, was denied admittance, and drove away. Captain Baker also arrived, carrying a tape recorder belonging to the City of Selma. He and a police lieutenant set up the machine in the chaplain's office and had Fikes brought in. After two periods of interrogation, one lasting about two hours and the second over an hour, the captain put the microphone on a table between Fikes and himself and turned on the machine. First a few preliminaries, and then the captain outlined to Fikes what he wanted.

"Willie, we've only been talking to you about a couple of hours now, haven't we?"

"Yes, sir."

"During this time has anybody cursed you or abused you, beat on you, threatened to beat you or anything, threatened you in any way?"

"No, sir."

"To try to get you to tell us the truth?"

"No, sir."

"Now, William, what we want to do right now is to review everything that we've been over so far, and I want you to tell us the honest to God's truth about everything that you've done so far, you hear?"

"Yes, sir."

"Everything that you've told us so far about these things, breaking in these houses. Have you been breaking into any of the houses in Selma?"

"All that I told you about, I have."

"The ones that you have already told us about?"

"Yes, sir."

The captain asked Fikes specifically about the night the mayor's daughter was attacked. Fikes said he had broken into the house, found a butcher knife, and entered Mrs. Rockwell's room.

"What did you do on that bed with that lady?"

"I started to get on the bed and she woke up and she grabbed me and tussled and stumbled around in there and fell over a stool in the living room, and–"

"And you stumbled out of the bedroom and got down into the living room?"

"Yes, sir."

"And you fell over a stool?"

"Yes, sir."

"Go ahead and tell me now what happened after you fell over the stool, go ahead."

"Fell over the stool. Fell over the stool and fell down in the floor and she tussled the knife out of my hand and got at me and I ran out of there."

"After you fell over the stool and got down on the floor. what did you say to this lady?"

"I told her to open her legs out, I wanted a little."

"Told her to open up her legs, you wanted a little?"

"Yes, sir."

"And she took the knife and you got up and ran out of the door?"

"Yes, sir."

"Now, William, why did you go in this house?"

"I don't know, sir, Captain, just a urge or something. I don't know."

"What kind of urge, William? Just tell in your own words what kind of urge you think it was."

"I don't have any idea, but just–"

"What were you looking for in there?"

"I was looking for some place to have an intercourse."

"Looking for some place to have an intercourse, and you knew white folks lived there, didn't you?"

"Yes, sir."

"And you were trying to have an intercourse with a white lady, is that right?"

"Yes, sir."

With the addition of a few more details, the recorded interview ended.

Friday was another day of rest, but on Saturday the 23rd, a full week after he had been arrested, Fikes was again confronted by questioners. This time they were Captain Baker and Mr. James Hare, the circuit solicitor, who both arrived at the prison shortly after 11:30 A.M., with Mrs. Stenson and her husband. Fikes was brought in, and Mrs. Stenson, after looking closely at his eyes and listening to his voice, identified him as the man who had raped her. An attorney came to the prison to see Fikes during the morning but was turned away, allegedly because he had no authorization to represent the prisoner. Fikes had lunch about 12:30 and dinner about 4:30 P.M., with two officials interrogating him in between, and then a second tape recording was made. The Selma *Times-Journal* in a story the next morning stated that Fikes "broke down at six P.M. yesterday and made his complete confession to Captain Wilson Baker after a nine-hour questioning session," but the reporter subsequently admitted that his reference to nine hours was based largely on surmise.

That Sunday was the first time since his arrest that Fikes saw any member of his family. His father once again drove to the prison and this time was admitted for a talk with his son. No one came to see Fikes on Monday, but on Tuesday the warden, two county solicitors, a police lieutenant, and Captain Baker gathered in the warden's office at the front of the prison and questioned the prisoner for about an hour. The warden's secretary took down two confessions in shorthand and typed them up for Fikes's signature—one dealing with the attack on the mayor's daughter, and the other with the rape of Mrs. Stenson.

The confession as to Mrs. Rockwell closely paralleled the tape recording which Fikes had made five days before. This was the first time, however, that Fikes had admitted either by recording or in writing that he had raped Mrs. Stenson. He told of parking his truck by the Buckeye Oil Mill and buying baby oil and prophylactics in a drugstore. He told of seeing a white lady in bed, breaking in through a back window, and getting on top of her. He had already greased himself with the baby oil, and after he threatened to cut her legs, they had "an intercourse." He asked her where her husband was. She said he would be home any minute. He left, threw away the baby oil, and drove back to Marion. Apparently, he had not used the prophylactics.

The police and prosecutors now had what they wanted. Their cases against Fikes were airtight. The ten-day interrogation period ended, and on June 2, 1953, an Alabama grand jury returned seven separate indictments against Fikes—one for rape, and six for first degree burglary. All seven carried possible death sentences, since capital punishment may be meted out in Alabama for any entry after dark of an occupied dwelling for the purpose of committing a felony—in this case, an entry with the felonious intent of ravishing a woman. Oddly enough, one of the indictments involved an attack on a man, Dr. Hollingsworth, the prosecution's theory being that regardless of the sex of the person Fikes found in bed, he entered the house with the purpose of attacking a woman. The state wanted the death penalty, and it intended to pursue one indictment after the other until it got it. But no one thought more than one trial would be necessary; the Stenson rape case would be tried first, and with Fikes's confession in hand, the prosecution considered a verdict short of death unthinkable.

Two local white attorneys, Hugh (later Judge) Mallory, Jr., and Sam Earle Hobbs, were appointed by the court to defend Fikes against the rape charge. When they looked into their client's background and found such a low degree of intelligence, they arranged to have three Negro psychiatrists from the Veterans Administration Hospital at Tuskegee go to Kilby Prison on June 19. The psychiatrists interviewed Fikes for two hours, and the attorneys were heartened by their report. Fikes pleaded not guilty, and not guilty by reason of insanity.

A near-capacity crowd—one-third Negro and two-thirds white—turned out for the trial of *Alabama v. Fikes* in the Selma courthouse on June 22. The beginning of the trial had to be delayed for five hours because Mallory and Hobbs were in Montgomery, the state capital, petitioning the Alabama Supreme Court to compel an examination of Fikes by a state lunacy commission. Their petition was rejected. As soon as they returned to Selma, they requested the judge to change the venue of the trial, to put the case over to a later date, and to be relieved as Fikes's attorneys—this last request on the ground that they had not had sufficient time to prepare his defense. All three requests were denied, and the trial proceeded. Each day Fikes was driven back and forth from the courthouse to Kilby Prison for safekeeping. There were rumors that men from outside Selma would abduct and lynch Fikes during one of the runs to the prison, but the threat never materialized.

The star witness at the trial, of course, was Mrs. Stenson. The prosecutors, County Solicitor Henry F. Reese and Circuit Solicitor Hare, very much wanted her to make a positive identification of Fikes. Obviously, this was impossible, since her attacker had worn a mask and a rag about his head. Mrs. Stenson, however, was as positive as she could be under the circumstances. She testified that "to the best of my knowledge," she had identified a man at the prison "by his eyes and voice" as her attacker, and she pointed to Fikes as the man whom she had previously identified. She admitted under very careful and gentle handling on cross-examination that Fikes had been the only man brought before her for identification and that her attacker's face had been largely covered, but she nevertheless insisted that Fikes was the culprit.

A doctor testified that he had examined Mrs. Stenson and found definite evidence of male contact, and the druggist swore that Fikes was the customer who had purchased baby oil and prophylactics at his store, but Judge W. E. Callen, a short curly-headed man in his late forties who had definite ideas about what constituted proper evidence, would not allow the prosecution to show that the blood found on Mrs. Stenson's sheets matched Fikes's.

These legal points were dealt with in a perfunctory manner; the real battle developed over the written confession that Fikes had signed on May 26, admitting the rape. Twice, Judge Callen refused its admission on the ground that the police had failed to take Fikes before a committing magistrate promptly after his arrest, so that he could be warned of his rights. Finally, however, over vigorous defense objections, the judge allowed the jury to read the confession after all of the officials involved in obtaining it testified that the police themselves had warned Fikes of his right not to speak and that the confession had been given voluntarily and not as the result of threats, coercion, or force.

Fikes did not take the stand, but his attorneys presented a spirited defense. They brought in witnesses from Marion who testified that Fikes worked long hours and had a good reputation. Each of the three Negro psychiatrists gave his opinion that Fikes was schizophrenic, suffering from dementia praecox. One of them said that when he asked Fikes how he got along with white people, Fikes replied, "They like me. I hate them." On cross-examination, the psychiatrist admitted that Fikes might have known right from wrong, but insisted that this was immaterial because Fikes acted from an uncontrollable impulse. Judge Callen refused to allow a psychiatrist for the state to testify that he had examined Fikes for thirty minutes at the jail and found him sane, because Fikes's attorneys had not been informed of the interview. However, lay witnesses, including the mayor of Marion, were allowed to testify that in their opinion, Fikes was sane.

In his final argument, defense attorney Hobbs stressed that

a Negro with as low an intelligence level as Fikes would certainly have left at least some tell-tale fingerprints in the Stenson house—but none had been found. He also pointed out that Mrs. Stenson, in all that excitement, simply could not have been as sure about her assailant's appearance as she later claimed, particularly since his head had been almost totally covered.

The case went to the jurors—all residents of Selma—at 11:40 P.M. on June 23, the day after the trial began. Every one in town expected a quick decision. But at half past twelve, the jurors returned to ask Judge Callen whether there was a fixed sentence they could impose which the defendant would have to serve. In Alabama, jurors can fix the sentence, but this jury was obviously worried that Fikes might be released from prison early, either on parole or for good behavior. Judge Callen told them that the minimum sentence for rape was ten years, but that he could give no assurance that a defendant would serve any specified period of time. The jurors retired again. At 1:10 in the morning, still deadlocked, they were shepherded by a sheriff to various offices and corridors in one wing of the courthouse, where they spent the night. By the middle of the next morning, the entire town knew that something had gone wrong in the jury room. What could possibly be holding things up? Finally, at 5:45 P.M. on June 24, a full eighteen hours after they had begun their deliberations, the jurors, looking utterly exhausted, filed back into the courtroom. The crowd had grown to two hundred, about half of them Negroes.

"Utter silence" was ordered by Judge Callen. "Any persons making an outbreak or a demonstration of any kind when the verdict is returned will be heavily fined for contempt of court."

The foreman announced without hesitation that the jury found William Earl Fikes guilty of rape. But, he added, ". . . [we] sentence him to ninety-nine years in the state penitentiary." There was shocked silence. The foreman said the jury had a further recommendation: that Fikes never be granted a parole. Judge Callen allowed the recommendation but pointed out that "it in no way has any bearing in this case nor in the future disposition of the prisoner." Fikes, who had sat almost motionless through the trial, received the verdict without any expression whatever.

It did not take long for the enterprising reporters of the Selma *Times-Journal* to discover what had occurred in the jury room. From the outset, the jurors had voted unanimously in favor of a conviction, and eleven to one in favor of the death penalty. The one dissenter said he simply did not believe in capital punishment. His fellow jurors pointed out that he had been questioned on that score when they were being impaneled, and he had failed to reveal his belief. The juror remained adamant. He would not agree to the death penalty, and that was that. The eleven other jurors had no choice but to give in and consent to a life sentence. The recommendation to the court that Fikes not be paroled was an added concession by the single dissenter.

The verdict was not welcome in Selma. Many people pointed out that Fikes had already been paroled from prison once, and the same thing could happen again, notwithstanding the jury's recommendation. The Selma *Times-Journal* commented editorially: "Whether or not you concur in the verdict of the jury at the trial of William Fikes on charges of rape, which the *Times-Journal* emphatically does not, there can be no denial but that the Perry County Negro was given a hearing as fair and as impartial as could have been obtained anywhere."

When one of Fikes's attorneys was asked whether there would be an appeal, he replied, "No comment. The case has too many angles to discuss it at the present time." The most important angle he had in mind was that Fikes had been lucky to escape the death penalty, and if the Alabama Supreme Court were to reverse the case, Fikes might not be so fortunate at a second trial. This tentative conclusion was discussed with the defendant and a definite decision reached: Fikes would not appeal.

The concern of the community that he might some day be released was allayed by an announcement from the circuit solicitor that he intended to prosecute Fikes on the next of the seven indictments. This time, Fikes would be tried for entering the home of the mayor's daughter with an intent to ravish her, also a capital offense.

By now, the plight of the twenty-seven-year-old Negro had reached the attention of the National Association for the Advancement of Colored People. Envelopes were passed out in Negro churches, soliciting money to aid in Fikes's defense. Apparently the drive was successful, because two prominent Negro attorneys, Peter A. Hall and Orzell Billingsley, Jr., soon arrived from Birmingham. Hall was a distinguished-looking man in his late thirties. Like Fikes, he had a light skin and a mustache. Unlike Fikes, he was educated, polished, and articulate. He was, in fact, one of the most sophisticated attorneys Selma had seen in some time. His soft-spoken, polite approach to witnesses—particularly white ones—neatly concealed the alert, aggressive interior of the man. He missed nothing at all that went on in the courtroom. Billingsley was a younger man and acted primarly as Hall's assistant.

Hall's first move was to request Judge Callen to quash the indictment against Fikes, primarily on the ground that Negroes had systematically been excluded from the grand jury panel which indicted him, thus violating his constitutional rights. Surprisingly, Judge Callen granted the motion and quashed the indictment. The jury rolls were promptly revised. This time, a larger number of Negro jurors appeared on the rolls, but again no Negro served on the panel itself. Fikes was re-indicted for the same offense. Hall once again petitioned the court to quash the indictment, pointing out that although the census showed more Negroes than whites living in the county, no Negro had "served on a Dallas County, Alabama, grand jury in modern times." Six days of testimony were taken on this petition, principally from the county jury commissioners. When it was over, the court overruled the objection, and the case proceeded to trial on December 7, 1953. It lasted three days.

The courtroom was again filled almost to capacity, with some two hundred Negroes on one side of the room. Judge Callen again presided. Hare and Reese were joined by a special prosecutor for the state, Thomas G. Gayle.

Mrs. Rockwell, the first witness, told of the attack on her during the rainy night of April 24. She said her assailant had a towel draped over his head so that she saw only "one of his eyes." He was "real thin . . . real slender." She could not positively identify Fikes as the culprit.

The prosecution then proposed to offer evidence that Fikes had committed at least two other similar crimes. A legal hassle immediately developed which the court resolved by instructing the jury that this evidence could be considered for the purpose of showing an intent and motive on Fikes's part to attack Mrs. Rockwell—namely to rape her. As a result of the court's rulings, Mrs. Stenson was allowed to testify that to the best of her knowledge, Fikes was the man who had raped her, and Mrs. Sally Binford swore that Fikes was the man she had seen in her bathtub. The druggist added to these damaging charges by stating again, as he had at the first trial, that Fikes was the man to whom he had sold baby oil and prophylactics before the Stenson attack.

The prosecution offered in evidence Fikes's written confession and one of the two tape recordings, and bolstered its offer by having the police chief testify that he had not grilled Fikes for hours at a time, as alleged in the papers, nor had he threatened or intimidated Fikes into making the confessions. To refute this testimony, Hall sought to put Fikes on the stand, but he wanted it understood that Fikes could be cross-examined *only* about the confessions. The prosecutor objected;

if Fikes took the stand, he would open himself up to questioning on the entire case. It was a ticklish point, but Judge Callen ruled with the prosecutor, and Hall, rather than allow Fikes to be subjected to a full-dress cross-examination, advised his client to keep away from the stand altogether. And so Fikes did not testify, and the confessions were duly admitted into evidence against him.

Again, the three Negro psychiatrists testified that in their opinion Fikes was insane. One of them reminisced about his interview with the prisoner: "I remember his telling me about stealing some automobile tires in '49. He was influenced by a brother, and the brother got the benefit of the tires which fit his car, and the patient—or the man—didn't get any benefit. Then he told of several other events. He did this, even though his wife and mother advised him not to do it. He was easily influenced. And then later on he told of coming from home—I think he lived in Marion—where he was working. He had a good job, security and everything, and he comes to Selma one night—I think he said to get a hamburger sandwich—and while in Selma he said he parked his car on the wrong side of town and got picked up. And when I asked him what happened, he said, 'They put me in jail.' And I said, 'What were you accused of?' And he said, 'I don't know, but I think somebody said something about rape.' And I said, 'Do you know what stealing and rape mean?' And he said, 'Stealing means taking things that don't belong to you.' And I said, 'Do you know what rape means?' And he shook his head. And I said, 'Rape means having sexual relations with a woman under force.' And he said, 'I wouldn't do that, not to go home to face my mama and wife.' " This, said the psychiatrist, was an abnormal reaction.

Fikes's employer and others described the defendant's working habits, pointing out that he could almost always be found at the service station from seven o'clock in the morning until about ten thirty or eleven o'clock at night, and that he often worked late on weekends when traffic was heavy. This was important testimony, because, if true, it meant that Fikes could not have driven to Selma, almost thirty miles away, in time for a number of the attacks, including the one on Mrs. Rockwell, which occurred shortly after ten o'clock on a Friday night. These witnesses also caused some confusion by pointing out that Fikes drove a car and that no one knew he owned a truck, whereas Fikes had claimed in his confessions to have driven a truck to Selma.

Circuit Solicitor Hare, his square jaw and dark, bright eyes aimed squarely at the jury, closed out his case with a rousing argument, which he ended with this admonition: "My only hope is that within you twelve men collectively there is one-half as much fortitude and courage as was manifested by Mrs. Rockwell when she resisted this defendant on the night of April 24. If there is, you can come out of your deliberations only with an honorable verdict—a verdict that William Earl Fikes must burn in the electric chair."

For a second time a jury deliberated the fate of William Fikes. But no member of this jury was squeamish about the death penalty. After only forty minutes of consultation, the foreman announced: "We, the jury, find the defendant guilty of burglary in the first degree as charged in the indictment, and fix his punishment at death." For the first time in over ten years, a Dallas County jury had given the death penalty.

The problem which had bothered Fikes's attorneys after his first trial did not confront Hall and Billingsley; they had nothing to lose by an appeal. And appeal they did, to the Alabama Supreme Court.

By the time the record had been certified, the briefs prepared and printed, the case argued, and the opinions written, a year and a half had passed. The Alabama Supreme Court rendered its decision affirming the conviction on May 12, 1955.

The point that seemed principally to worry the court was

the alleged exclusion of Negroes from the grand jury rolls. The court discussed the matter in detail and quite candidly admitted that prior to October 1953, "Probably they [Negroes] had been systematically left off such rolls on account of race." But the court insisted that the new jury commission had made an honest attempt "to have the negro race fairly represented. . . ." Negroes were not entitled to representation in proportion to their population in the county, because "The evidence shows that a large majority of negroes are ignorant, with little or no education and low moral character, and there is much venereal disease among them and a large percentage of illegitimacy."

As to the confessions introduced against Fikes, the court concluded that all the evidence showed them to have been given voluntarily. The police had not intimidated Fikes; they were not even armed when they questioned him. "He was in prison under protection against possible attack by others. But there was not shown to be threats of violence by the public or unusual excitement. He was not abused, nor questioned at such length and under such conditions as to break his resistance. . . ."

Four justices of the Alabama court joined in this opinion. Two others concurred in the result, stating that they thought it was error not to have allowed Fikes to testify only about the confessions, but under all the circumstances, they saw no reason for reversing the conviction. The seventh justice simply concurred in the result without comment.

Since questions under the United States Constitution were involved, the case was now ripe for appeal to the United States Supreme Court. Mr. Justice Hugo L. Black gave Fikes's attorneys an extension of time in which to prepare their petition, and when the petition was finally filed, the Court granted it, which was the Court's formal way of saying that it would listen to arguments and decide the case. Because Fikes had little or no money, the Court also allowed his attorneys to proceed without the payment of court costs—"*in forma pauperis.*"

Feeling that Hall and Billingsley were primarily trial attorneys and that this case demanded the services of a more experienced appellate lawyer, the NAACP called in Jack Greenberg, the assistant counsel to the NAACP's Legal Defense and Educational Fund, to make the argument before the Supreme Court. Greenberg, though only thirty-two years old, was Thurgood Marshall's chief assistant in New York and had already argued the Delaware school segregation case before the Supreme Court. To oppose Greenberg, the attorney general of Alabama assigned his own special assistant, Robert Straub. A graduate of De Paul University and the University of Alabama Law School, Straub was only a year older than Greenberg, so that the argument presented young and vigorous contemporaries with an opportunity to test their mettle before the highest court in the land.

On December 6, 1956, three years after William Fikes had been sentenced to die, Jack Greenberg rose to his feet in the white mausoleum that houses the United States Supreme Court in Washington, and surveyed the nine alert, far-from-mummified faces before him. To his far right was Mr. Justice William J. Brennan, Jr. Only two months before, Justice Brennan had been sitting on the Supreme Court of New Jersey when he received a sudden call to come to Washington to see President Eisenhower. He was certain that the President wanted to name him chairman of a committee on delays in the courts, and he spent his entire trip to Washington trying to think of how to say "no" to the President of the United States. He was stupefied when Attorney General Herbert Brownell, Jr., met him at Union Station and told him the President wanted to appoint him to fill Mr. Justice Sherman Minton's recently vacated seat on the Supreme Court. But it was a recess appointment, and at the time the Fikes case was argued, Brennan had not yet been confirmed by the Senate. Greenberg must have realized that this case, involving as it did the delicate balance between state and federal power, could not have come at a less opportune time for Brennan, who still had to face the southern members of the Senate Judiciary Committee.

Next to Brennan was Mr. Justice Tom C. Clark, and still further along the bench was Mr. Justice Stanley F. Reed. The "prosecutive" experiences of these two men—one a former Attorney General of the United States and the other a former Solicitor General of the United States—could not have given Greenberg much solace.

Greenberg looked with some trepidation at Mr. Justice Felix Frankfurter, whose head bobbed and weaved impatiently near the top of the bench. The attorney knew he could expect a rash of questions from this, the most persistent interrogator on the Court. But he found a more kindly look —and a more likely vote—from the man at the center of the bench, Earl Warren, fourteenth Chief Justice of the United States. On the Chief Justice's right was a man who had grown up not a hundred miles from Selma. Even now, Mr. Justice Hugo L. Black's Alabama accent stirred rebel souls, though he had long since departed the southerner's philosophy. He still traveled to Clay County, Alabama, though less now than in years past; he may even have known some of the people Greenberg would be talking about.

Near Black was the militant liberal, Mr. Justice William O. Douglas, a man whom few people knew well and even fewer understood. He was a restless man, a fast thinker and a fast worker. By the sheer dint of physical energy, he was carried past and beyond the confines of the Court's work and into totally unrelated fields. He loved the outdoors and described in eloquent language the beauties of nature. He was the closest thing to a Teddy Roosevelt the Court had seen. He loved to travel and to talk to leaders around the world, to express himself on foreign affairs and liberal causes, and to fight for conservation of natural resources. With all this, one would expect in him a fluent, outgoing, almost rakish man; yet one found instead a poor speaker, a man of few close friends, an almost shy man—all in all, an unpolished gem of irregular design. His adherents claimed that he traveled afield not only because of genuine interest but because his brethren on the Court were not his equal, deciding too few cases and working too slowly on those they did decide. His critics replied that Douglas worked so fast because, for him, everything was black or white—the forces of liberalism pitted against the forces of conservatism (evil)—and he failed to understand or appreciate the true nature of the judicial process. Be that as it may, he was a man constantly in the news. At the very time of William Fikes's first trial in Alabama, a House Judiciary Subcommittee was considering a resolution—subsequently abandoned—to impeach Douglas for granting a stay of execution to the condemned spies Julius and Ethel Rosenberg. Greenberg had reason to feel that he had a sympathetic listener in Douglas.

The bench was completed by Mr. Justice Harold H. Burton and Mr. Justice John M. Harlan, both of whom would be hard to sway. Burton approached a criminal case as free from bias as the nature of man can expect, and he would need more proof than argument before he would overturn a conviction. Harlan was a lawyer down to his bootstraps. He loved the law, he loved argument, he loved the courtroom, and he approached it all with wry good humor and a refreshing sense of his own fallibility. He too would need showing.

Like a small-town politician in a close election, Greenberg tallied the votes he could count on and the votes he was sure to lose, and he knew that the result lay somewhere in the hearts of two or three "undecided" voters.

Greenberg had three arguments, all based on the Fourteenth Amendment. First, the confessions used against Fikes had been obtained from him involuntarily. Second, Fikes was unconstitutionally denied an opportunity to testify for the limited purpose of attacking the confessions. And third, Negroes had been systematically excluded from the grand jury which indicted him.

Greenberg's job was to make the circumstances surrounding the confessions as suspicious as possible. The Supreme Court had held many times that it is a violation of the Due Process Clause of the Fourteenth Amendment to convict a man on the basis of a confession which is coerced from him. But what constitutes coercion? The clear case, of course, is one in which a man is beaten until he agrees to write what he is told to write. But there are other methods, equally effective, of making a man perform. Trickery, threats, promises, and a myriad of ruses and pressures can produce startling results. Greenberg had no direct evidence of improper conduct by the police, but he tried to make up for the holes in his case by ticking off the suspicious circumstances surrounding Fikes's capture, extended interrogation, and trial, all of which Greenberg claimed spelled out a case of systematic coercion. He admitted that the Court's decision should not hinge on any arbitrary counting of the hours and days during which the prisoner was held for questioning; there was no magic cut-off point in time, after which the interrogation became unconstitutional. But all of the circumstances here, he said, showed a deliberate attempt to seal off the prisoner from any outside help until his will had been broken.

Greenberg had very tough sledding with his contention that Fikes should have been allowed to take the stand for the limited purpose of testifying about his confessions. The Supreme Court had seemingly ruled to the contrary in another case. As to the exclusion of Negroes from the grand jury, Greenberg contented himself with the argument that despite an attempt by Alabama to make it appear that Negroes were called for service, various methods of exclusion and exemption had still resulted in no Negroes being allowed on the panel which indicted Fikes.

Greenberg sat down and was replaced at the lectern by Robert Straub, representing the State of Alabama. Straub had hardly begun speaking before he was bombarded with questions, and he was so persistently interrogated thereafter that the Chief Justice graciously allowed him extra time to complete his argument.

The Justices—and particularly Brennan—wanted to know why the police had failed to take Fikes before a committing magistrate. An Alabama statute specifically requires the police to take a prisoner "forthwith" before a magistrate, and one of the purposes of the statute is to assure that each prisoner be informed of his constitutional rights, including his right to remain silent, prior to the time he is interrogated at length by the police. Fikes, however, had been questioned for more than a week before he ever saw a committing magistrate. Straub had three answers when the Justices asked him about this. First, the police had testified that they themselves had warned Fikes of his right not to speak. Second, it was not at all unusual in Alabama for a man to be questioned at length before he saw a magistrate, particularly when the police were not sure they had the right man; the police had not singled out Fikes for special or unusual treatment. Third, the Alabama Supreme Court had held several times that even though the statute be violated, the prisoner's confession was not thereby automatically rendered inadmissible.

True, said Brennan, but a violation of the Alabama statute was a circumstance to be considered, along with all the other circumstances surrounding the confession, in determining whether the confession was voluntary or coerced.

Yes, replied Straub, but here the jury and the Alabama Supreme Court had both considered all the circumstances and concluded that Fikes had given his confessions voluntarily.

By the very nature of the case and through no fault of the attorneys, the oral arguments were not completely enlightening, and the Court must have felt a certain degree of frustration in attempting to deal with it. No one really knew for sure—certainly not the lawyers arguing the case—exactly what had occurred during Fikes's incarceration. It was true that the police officers had all testified that no coercion had been used, but police officers are never prone to admit they have violated someone's constitutional rights, and the Justices, from long experience in reviewing criminal cases, were not so naive as to believe that the officers' testimony was totally free from doubt. On the other hand, since Fikes had not been allowed to testify about the confessions, the officers' testimony stood unchallenged and unrefuted in the record. It was a difficult situation, and the Justices, listening to the legal theories of the antagonists before them, looked a bit as if everyone in the room was tilting at tiny, shifting, nebulous windmills.

The argument was over, and the attorneys retired to await the result. The most important function of the Court—the "deciding process"—was now under way. The conference of the Court, at which a preliminary vote would be taken, the assignment and drafting of opinions, and the final casting of votes upon circulation of the opinions—all this would be shut off from public view and even from the view of those who, until now, had been most intimately connected with the case.

These judges, faced with such momentous decisions, are lonely men—not socially, certainly, for they are invited everywhere and lionized when they choose to appear, but lonely by the nature of their job. Like scientists in secret work, they can talk only to their own ilk, and even then must be prudent. On Court business, their confidants consist of their brethren and their own small staffs. Normally, each staff is made up of a secretary and two law clerks, although Mr. Justice Jackson in some years used only one law clerk, Mr. Justice Douglas employs one law clerk and two secretaries, and the Chief Justice, because of extra administrative duties, has two secretaries and three law clerks.

Except for the Chief Justice's suite, which was spread out in a gerrymandered fashion and encompassed the conference and robing rooms, the Justices' chambers were composed of three rooms, less elegant and more narrowly apportioned than those enjoyed by the Court of Appeals, only a few blocks away. Each Justice's office included a handsome fireplace, a large desk, shelves upon shelves of books, and appropriate furniture suiting the particular taste of the Justice. Mr. Justice Harlan, for example, had a long table at one end of the room which he used for writing purposes in preference to his desk. Mr. Justice Frankfurter, because of a back ailment, wrote and dictated in a standing position behind a specially built lectern, similar in all respects to the one used by his idol, Mr. Justice Oliver Wendell Holmes. Mr. Justice Douglas adorned his desks and walls with mementoes of his far-flung travels—a mask from a Buddhist monastery in Tibet, spears from Australia, an Afghan caracal, and a walrus tusk from Alaska. Each chamber reflected, in subtle tones or in garish ornaments, the mood and temperament of the man who occupied it—or perhaps, in some cases, the mood and temperament of the man the Justice would most like to have been.

Each secretary occupied an office shared also by the Justice's messenger. It was large, with file cabinets along one wall and an electric typewriter on a stand next to the desk. Plants, palms, and flowers in some instances adorned the sills of two large windows, and pictures or cartoons from the Justice's past lined the walls. The third room in the suite, occupied by the Justice's law clerks, was a working room, surrounded on two or three sides by shelves of law books and centered by two large desks. Piles of "cert petitions"—briefs asking the Court to hear cases—were usually piled on a table or on the desks, or even on the floor. The clerks typed their own memoranda to their Justice, since the secretary was overwhelmed with answering mail, typing opinions, keeping files, and looking after personal affairs that otherwise would have taken the Justice from more important duties.

Each Justice is master of his own work and has his own work habits. Generally, when there is to be oral argument, a Justice will drive to work, or be driven by his messenger, in time for several hours of study before oral arguments begin. He will enter the Court through the garage in the basement and ride an elevator two flights to the main floor of the building. From the elevator to his office, he will be "behind gates"—that is, cut off from the public part of the building by heavy, swinging gates. As soon as he reaches his desk, he will attempt to clear away the most important part of the mail his secretary will have prepared for him, perhaps confer with his law clerks, and then devote himself to a study of the briefs dealing with the cases to be argued that day. Most of the law books he needs in studying these briefs will be at hand in his own office; others can be gotten quickly from the library on the third floor or from the Library of Congress across the street.

On argument days, the Court sat, in 1956, from noon until two and from two thirty until four thirty, allowing only a half hour for the Justices to join together in their dining room for a bite to eat, or to return to their own chambers to dine alone. The rest of the day was devoted to talks with other Justices, conferences with law clerks about pending cases, drafting opinions, and, when it could not be avoided, seeing visitors. During the weeks when the Court did not hear arguments, the routine was much the same except that more time could be devoted to drafting and reading opinions and to deciding which cases the Court would consider. More often than not, a Justice would have to take his work home with him.

It was a schedule that left little time for socializing—for some Justices, an almost Spartan existence.

Five weeks after the Fikes argument—a relatively brief period, considering the intervention of the Christmas recess—

the Court rendered its decision. Chief Justice Warren wrote the majority opinion and was able to garner the supporting votes of five other Justices—Black, Frankfurter, Douglas, Clark, and Brennan—although Justices Frankfurter and Brennan deemed it necessary to add a few words of their own to what the Chief Justice wrote.

Warren discussed only the legality of the confessions, because the conviction was reversed on that ground and it thus became unnecessary to cover Greenberg's other arguments. For Warren and the Justices he carried with him, the question of due process rested not only on the events that had occurred, but on the type of person they had occurred to. The Chief Justice emphasized Fikes's character, limited mentality, and background, with particular emphasis on the evidence of his insanity. He summarized in these words the situation as he saw it:

> Here the prisoner was an uneducated Negro, certainly of low mentality, if not mentally ill. He was first arrested by civilians, lodged in jail, and then removed to a state prison far from his home. We do not criticize the decision to remove the prisoner before any possibility of violence might mature, but petitioner's [Fikes's] location and the conditions of his incarceration are facts to be weighed in connection with the issue before us. For a period of a week, he was kept in isolation, except for sessions of questioning. He saw no friend or relative. Both his father and a lawyer were barred in attempts to see him. The protections to be afforded to a prisoner upon preliminary hearing were denied him, contrary to the law of Alabama. . . . He was questioned for several hours at a time over the course of five days preceding the first confession, and again interrogated at length before the written confession was secured.
>
> There is no evidence of physical brutality, and particular elements that were present in other cases in which this Court ruled that a confession was coerced do not appear here. On the other hand, some of the elements in this case were not present in all of the prior cases. . . . The totality of the circumstances that preceded the confessions in this case goes beyond the allowable limits. The

use of the confessions secured in this setting was a denial of due process.

. . . We hold that the circumstances of pressure applied against the power of resistance of this petitioner, who cannot be deemed other than weak of will or mind, deprived him of due process of law.

Thus, for a majority of the Court, no one fact was determinative of the result, as would have been the case if the police had struck Fikes with a rubber hose. Rather, the entire course of conduct by the police made the confessions "involuntary" as a matter of law. The long period of detention, the incommunicado nature of that detention, the leading and suggestive questions, the weak mentality of the prisoner, the failure to take him before a magistrate—all these and other facts added up to a situation so basically unfair as to shock the conscience. Although the opinion asserted that the facts themselves rendered the confessions void, there undoubtedly was a feeling among the Justices that the circumstances involved here lent themselves too easily to the possibility of abuse. There was simply no way of telling what had happened during that long, isolated period of detention, and it probably was this possibility of abuse that tipped the scales.

Perhaps feeling, as he often did, that Warren's opinion did not adequately suggest the difficulties of the case, Justice Frankfurter added a brief opinion of his own, concurred in by the new Justice, Brennan. Said Frankfurter:

A case like this is not easy for one who believes very strongly that adequate power should accompany the responsibility of the States for the enforcement of their criminal law. But the Due Process Clause of the Fourteenth Amendment has placed limitations upon the discretion, unbridled for all practical purposes, that belonged to the States prior to its adoption, and, more particularly, confines their freedom of action in devising criminal procedure. It is, I assume, common ground that if this record had disclosed an admission by the police of one truncheon blow on the head of petitioner [Fikes] a confession following such a blow would be inadmissible because of the Due Process Clause. For myself, I cannot see the difference, with respect to the "voluntariness" of a confession, between the subversion of freedom of the will through physical punishment and the sapping of the will appropriately to be inferred from the circumstances of this case. . . . No single one of these circumstances alone would in my opinion justify a reversal. I cannot escape the conclusion, however, that in combination they bring the result below the Plimsoll line of "due process."

This last line inspired Richard H. Field, a Harvard professor, to whimsy in the sedate *Harvard Law Review.* Field's long poem, indicating that the Justice may have been wide of the mark in his metaphor, was also read at the next dinner that the Frankfurter law clerks gave annually for the Justice. Sam Plimsoll, it develops, was responsible for pushing through Parliament a statute requiring ships to paint a line—"the Plimsoll line"—around their hulls to indicate the safety mark in loading, and forbidding them to set sail unless the line was showing. Since the Plimsoll line was quite precise and discernible, and since Frankfurter regarded due process as unsettled, ill-defined, and shadowy, Field charged that:

Words are the skin of living thought,
But here's an overstuffed one.
This time the mark you overshot;
Indeed, you simply muffed one,
Unless perchance we find the key
In some sly Freudian twist:
A yearning for the certainty
You say cannot exist. . . .
But Burbank is not brought to book
For one imperfect calyx;
So we're prepared to overlook
One metaphor infelix.

The three dissenters in the Fikes case were Harlan, Reed, and Burton, with Harlan writing for the group. Harlan could not bring himself to rule, on the basis of this record, that the state had gone too far. "The setting aside of this conviction, in my opinion, oversteps the boundary between this Court's function under the Fourteenth Amendment and that of the state courts in the administration of state criminal justice."

He then demonstrated why the business of judging is such a fascinating business. Taking the same record and the same facts that the majority of the Court had found shocking, he came to an opposite conclusion. "Concededly, there was no brutality or physical coercion. And psychological coercion is by no means manifest. While the total period of interrogation was substantial, the questioning was intermittent; it never exceeded two or three hours at a time, and all of it took place during normal hours; 'relay' tactics . . . were not employed. True, petitioner's mental equilibrium appears to have been less than normal, but these facts were before the trial judge and the jury."

He went on to explain to his own satisfaction each of the facts relied upon by Greenberg. But at the end, he put his finger on the real point of departure between the majority and the minority of the Court: "I find nothing here beyond a state of facts upon which reasonable men might differ in their conclusions as to whether the confessions had been coerced. In the absence of anything in the conduct of the state authorities which 'shocks the conscience' or does 'more than offend some fastidious squeamishness or private sentimentalism about combatting crime too energetically,' . . . I think that due regard for the division between state and federal functions in the administration of criminal justice requires that we let Alabama's judgment stand."

In other words, in a close case, where there was little of substance that Harlan could point to and say, "Look, this is obviously, shockingly wrong," he was not willing to assume that the state had transgressed permissible limits. Warren, on the other hand, was not willing to take a chance in a death case that a man who confessed during ten days of detention, much of which was incommunicado, had done so voluntarily. For

Harlan, the state started with a presumption in its favor which Fikes had not overcome by anything approaching real proof. For Warren, the benefit of the doubt lay with the man who could not have proven coercion if it had been used, and who was now scheduled to die. The basic facts were the same for both men. But the viewpoint was totally different.

In some respects, the lineup of the Justices was along clearly established patterns—Justices Black and Douglas joining with the Chief Justice in reversing, and Justices Burton and Reed joining Harlan in dissent. The two most interesting votes were those of Clark and Brennan. Clark was often looked upon as a "swing man" in this type of case in the sense that he approached each situation afresh and could not be counted on by either camp until his vote was irrevocably cast. He probably had a good deal of trouble with the Fikes decision. His votes in other cases would indicate that Alabama's failure to arraign Fikes, and its refusal to let him see his family and counsel, did not bother Clark as much as the long period of secret questioning and Fikes's weak mentality. Clark had been a part of the government's prosecuting arm long enough to know that when interrogations take place in secret, the police sometimes use legally unacceptable methods of coercion, short of brutality, that can have a shattering effect on the untutored mind. It was typical of Clark, however, that even though he may have felt much concern over this case, he refused to join Frankfurter's opinion expressing that concern. Where possible, Clark avoided concurring opinions.

The interest in Brennan's position lies not in his vote to reverse but rather in his joining with Frankfurter. Brennan was new on the Court—and still to be confirmed by the Senate. For a long while, each junior Justice on the Supreme Court finds himself with doubts and qualms that do not plague him in his later years. He is constantly impressed by the closeness, the vagueness, the seriousness of the questions that confront the Court—by the strong arguments that can be made for diametrically opposed positions. He feels a need to express this concern, to say to the bar: "I voted, but I want you to know it was not easy. I'm still not certain I was right." Within a year, Brennan would be voting to reverse criminal convictions not only without the compulsion to express his doubts, but without many of the doubts themselves.

An unknown factor in the case was the part played by Fikes's sentence. Did it make any difference that Fikes was under penalty of death? An argument can be made that since a coerced confession is never admissible, and since Fikes's confessions were coerced or not without regard to the sentence he ultimately received, his sentence was immaterial to the case and to the result. But the plain fact of the matter is that his sentence probably had much to do with the Court's decision, and may even have been decisive. The Court itself has intimated on several occasions that a capital case involves special consideration and that the ordinary rules do not necessarily apply. The Court's reasoning, though never explicitly spelled out, seems to be that when a government takes life, it bears an added burden to show that the condemned man has received every protection the law affords, because a mistake cannot be remedied. In Fikes's case, it is not unreasonable to assume that Warren would have lost two essential votes—those of Frankfurter and Clark—if the death sentence had not been involved.

The reversal of Fikes's conviction for first degree burglary presented the Alabama authorities with a difficult decision. If the Supreme Court had reversed on either of the two other points raised by Greenberg—the failure to allow Fikes to testify about his confessions, or the discriminatory selection of the grand jury—Alabama undoubtedly would have tried Fikes again for the same offense, or proceeded against him on the next indictment. The grand jury would then have been more carefully selected, and Fikes would have been allowed to testify. But the Supreme Court had ruled that Fikes's confessions were invalid, which meant that those confessions could not be used at any future trial. Reviewing the record, the circuit solicitor concluded that Fikes could not be convicted of the attack on Mrs. Rockwell without the confessions. The only evidence linking Fikes to this particular attack was his blood type, which Judge Callen had not even allowed to be introduced in evidence; and Mrs. Rockwell's identification. But the identification simply would not stand up, absent other proof. Fikes had worn a towel over his head, and even if a jury were to believe that Mrs. Rockwell could positively identify her assailant by a glimpse of one eye, a reviewing court would not. She had not been sufficiently definite at the trial. The circuit solicitor reluctantly decided that he would have to be content with the life sentence which Fikes was serving for the rape of Mrs. Stenson.

But if the decision reached by the circuit solicitor was difficult, the one confronting Fikes's attorneys was downright appalling.

One of the confessions in the Rockwell case which the Supreme Court had held unconstitutional had been obtained on the same day and by the same methods as the confession used against Fikes in the Stenson case. All of the legal infirmities of the Rockwell confession were applicable to the Stenson confession; and it was clear that Fikes had been convicted in the Stenson case as unconstitutionally as the Supreme Court had now held he had been convicted in the Rockwell case. Thus, assuming that the point could be raised properly in the Alabama courts, Fikes's attorneys were certain that they could obtain a reversal of the Stenson conviction.

But did they want to? Did they dare to? Mrs. Stenson, unlike Mrs. Rockwell, had been quite certain that Fikes was the man who attacked her, and she had remained unshaken on cross-examination. If the Stenson conviction were reversed, the state almost certainly would try Fikes again, ignoring his confession and relying instead on Mrs. Stenson's identification, with evidence of other crimes as a type of corroboration. Everyone knew that Fikes had escaped the death penalty at his first trial solely because one juror had not believed in the death penalty. Would Fikes be as fortunate a second time? His attorneys thought not. They simply could not gamble his life on such odds.

And so the decision was made to do nothing at all about Fikes's conviction for the rape of Mrs. Stenson, even though a reversal would have been virtually assured.

In one sense, Fikes is a very fortunate man. He had been indicted for seven separate offenses—every one of which involved an attack by a Negro on a white person in the State of Alabama, and every one of which carried a possible death sentence—and he had been convicted twice. Yet he still lives today, peacefully serving out a life sentence.

In another sense, Fikes is the victim of unfortunate circumstances. For he is serving a life sentence almost certainly based upon an unconstitutional conviction. And, without jeopardizing his life, there is not a thing anyone can do about it—not his family, not his attorneys, not even the Supreme Court of the United States.

The town of Selma was soon back to normal. The housebreakings stopped on the night of Fikes's arrest, and soon the bars were taken off windows, and the police returned to their regular schedule. Roland Harris and Mr. and Mrs. Youngblood divided the thirteen-hundred-dollar reward money.

William's father and mother and the brother who never got into trouble still live in Marion. They have a warm, comfortably overstuffed house. In the living room, which is painted pink, the poor fit of the wood logs that run from floor to ceiling is hardly noticeable, nor is the sap that long ago oozed from the knotholes and dried over the pink paint. Every other Sunday, Mr. and Mrs. Fikes pack their car and drive one hundred and forty miles to Atmore Prison, north of Mobile, where William was moved from Kilby. On the way, they talk about the day when their son might come home, though they both know very well he never will. When they arrive at the prison, they stay as long as they can with William, telling him the news they have stored up for two weeks, and when they go, they leave him a large basket of food.

Every other Sunday, it is the same story. As soon as they reach the outside of the prison, Mr. Fikes asks his wife, "How do you think Baby looks?"

And Mrs. Fikes replies, "I think Baby looks just fine."

2

Green—with Envy

Everett Green had never been a gambler. He didn't like the horses, and he couldn't roll the dice. But you can't gamble more than your own life, and Everett Green decided he would rather go to the chair than spend another day in jail. . . .

Monday morning, May 25, 1953, arrived gray and close in Washington, D. C., wholly unlike the bright days the city had come to expect of May. The weather uniquely fitted the mood of Alva Cornelius as he started out on the unpleasant business for which he was paid. Cornelius was a deputy United States marshal, and he carried a court order of eviction for the occupants of 1115 Massachusetts Avenue Northwest. If necessary, it was his duty to throw the occupants out on the street, furniture and all.

Although Massachusetts Avenue is perhaps Washington's loveliest street—the street of embassies and churches and grand apartment houses—the particular section in which Cornelius found himself was middle-income and of a neuter gender, neither attractive nor run-down. Number 1115 was a three-story row house of heavy stone, sandwiched in between another home and an apartment building. Unlike its companions, it stood from head to toe in a red hue, the color of old pottery. Across the street was a small park that boasted several metal benches and an innocuous statue of Edmund Burke. Eight blocks to the southwest sat the White House, and equidistant to the southeast stood the Federal Bureau of Investigation.

Cornelius made his way up a concrete walk adjoining a brief

lawn, less than thirty feet across. He was met at the front door by a man whom Cornelius recognized as Everett Green by vital statistics supplied in advance—white, heavy-set, early sixties, blue eyes. Cornelius explained his mission. He had orders to evict Green because of nonpayment of rent. Cornelius explained that he must wait for the owner of the premises; the law requires the owner to be present when tenants are evicted.

The two men stood chatting until it became obvious that the owner would not appear. Cornelius then asked if he could call his office for instructions. Green led him into his home and down a narrow hallway to the telephone. As he followed Green, Cornelius passed a bedroom on his left and caught a glimpse of an elderly white-haired lady sitting in an old-fashioned rocker.

Cornelius learned from his office that the owner could not appear until the following day. Green said that by then he hoped to have raised enough money to pay the rent, and he added as Cornelius left that if "they" put him out of his house, "they would be sorry."

At noon on the same day, Miss Elsie Shannon, who lived about four blocks away, received a telephone call from Green. She had known him for over twenty-five years. Green suggested that since she had not stopped by for some time, she might come visiting that evening.

She did, arriving about eight o'clock. As was her custom, she immediately went in to see Miss Bettie Brown, who lived with Green. Miss Brown was eighty-three years old, a kindly white-haired lady whose poor health showed in her alabaster white skin. Elsie Shannon and Bettie Brown chatted for almost three hours. Green was in and out of the room several times during the visit, and once he carried in ice cream and cake for all three of them. When Elsie Shannon finally left, Green walked her home.

They talked easily, as old friends will. Green seemed relaxed. As they reached her house, he said casually that he wanted to "fix up" his house but did not have the money. Could she lend him several hundred dollars? She was very sorry, but she didn't have it. He seemed disappointed, but not upset.

By the next morning, the weather had cleared. Shortly after seven thirty, Private John Leacock of the Metropolitan Police Department was walking his beat along Massachusetts Avenue when he suddenly noticed smoke spiraling out from under the eaves of the roof of Green's house. There was no mistaking it—this was a big blaze. The smoke was thick and ugly. Leacock bounded up the front steps and rapped on the door with his night stick. There was no answer. A passer-by yelled that he didn't think anyone lived there. Leacock ran down Massachusetts Avenue to the nearest police call box and phoned in the alarm.

He ran back to the house and tried the cellar door, but it would not budge. He scampered up to the front porch and found that door locked too, so he broke the glass with his night stick, put his hand through the hole and turned the latch from the inside. He could see smoke clouds billowing along the narrow hallway. Just as he opened the door, firemen arrived and brushed past him into the house.

Several companies of firemen had driven up at the same time, and they began attacking the house with admirable abandon. Three men hoisted a ladder from an aerial truck and climbed to the second and third floors, breaking windows as they went. One of them reached the roof and broke two skylights. The fire captain ran to the rear of the house, helped lay a hose along the alley, and tried to force the kitchen door. When he found it locked, he kicked it in. He went in through the kitchen and encountered several firemen who had entered from the front. Finding the situation on the first floor under control, the captain relaxed a little and loped back into the alley with the easy gait of an old fire horse. The basement door and an adjoining window were locked; he kicked in the door and broke the window.

In the meantime, firemen in the front of the house were wrenching open a first-floor window with a claw tool—a metal bar with a pryer at one end and a hook at the other. One fireman stepped through the window into hot, thick, blinding smoke. He found himself in a bedroom, but he could see very little except the outline of a sliding door which led into the first-floor hallway. As he felt his way around, he came to a bed and was startled to detect someone—he could not tell whether male or female—under the covers. The body showed no signs of life. He picked it up and, with another fireman who had followed him through the window, carried it outside and placed it on a stretcher on the lawn. The body was that of an elderly lady dressed only in a nightgown and an undershirt, neither of which, surprisingly, were burned at all. Her thin face, cracked with jutting wrinkles, was pale as death. A team from the rescue squad began working on her with a resuscitator, quickly and with expert precision.

As his fellow firemen had been entering the first-floor window, John Malinak of Number Three Truck Company was treading his way into the areaway under the front porch, where he tried in vain to force open a basement door. Finally, he pounded on it with his claw tool until it gave way. Smoke forced him back, and he put on his mask. Taking the nozzle of a small hose, he worked his way into the basement. About ten feet inside the door he found a fire built against a wall on his right, and he played water on it until he had killed the flames. Before he had gone another twenty feet, he encountered a second fire burning beside the same wall, and he put that one out too.

Hoping to force some ventilation into the basement, Malinak opened the first door he could find, directly across from the fire he had just extinguished. Hampered by the mask, which narrowed his view, and by the thick smoke that hung heavy at every level of the basement, Malinak could barely make out the rough outline of objects around him. But he could tell that the door he had opened led into a small bathroom, with toilet, basin, and bathtub. He stepped quickly into the room and stopped. He sensed that someone was in the room with him.

He adjusted his mask and looked down. In the bathtub, lying motionless and face down in two inches of blood-red water, was Everett Green. He wore shoes, socks, suit pants, and an undershirt.

Malinak grabbed Green's head, pulled it roughly out of the water, and called for help. Word was passed along to the front yard, where the rescue team was still working frantically on Bettie Brown. Several of them rushed into the basement and helped lift Green out of the bathtub. The entire front of his undershirt was covered with blood, pulsing out from small holes in his stomach and chest and from a cut on his neck. He seemed to be unconscious. They carried him straight through the basement and out into the yard, where they laid him on the grass near Bettie Brown.

Malinak returned to the basement and opened the window in the bathroom. It was unlocked and slid up easily. Moving back and forth, still finding it difficult because of the dense smoke to make out objects very clearly, Malinak suddenly stopped and listened. He thought he heard a hiss—a low, steady sound that disturbed his practiced ear. Following the direction of the sound, he came upon a pipe leading into the gas meter. Someone had removed the plug from the pipe, and gas was steadily escaping into the smoke-filled basement. Malinak spotted the plug on top of the meter and replaced it, cutting off the escaping gas.

Now came the investigators—stealthy, quiet, sometimes efficient men who followed along like tired but conscientious bloodhounds after the chase has passed over the hill. Sniffing and scenting, probing and poking, they trod their way through the havoc created by others.

Fire Marshal Raymond Roberts entered the house by way of the basement. He noted the remains of the two separate fires that had already been extinguished. On the floor in the bathroom, he discovered an old ice pick. And, against the woodwork directly outside of the bathroom door, he found a Stillson wrench. For identification purposes, he made scratch marks on both instruments with a key he had in his pocket, but he made no attempt to preserve fingerprints. He proceeded up the inside steps to the first floor. Here he found the smoldering remains of three more fires—one in the narrow hallway and two in the room immediately adjoining Bettie Brown's. He continued his search on the second and third floors and then returned to the basement.

Inspector Warren Kelly of the Fire Department, charged with determining the origin of fires and the extent of their damage, detected an odor of turpentine on the first floor. In the kitchen he found a quart bottle that smelled of turpentine but was empty except for a slight dampness at the bottom, and on the kitchen table a box of stationery, a pencil, and a pair of reading glasses. Tracing his way back to the first-floor fires, Inspector Kelly sorted through miscellaneous scrap lumber and trash that had been piled on one fire and examined deep cracks in the floor, which indicated to him that an inflammable liquid had been used to spur on the flames. More scrap, including a box-spring frame, a lawn mower, a coil of rubber garden hose, and double pieces of lumber had been piled on the fires in the basement. Evidence of this scrap, the inflammable liquid, and the fact that each fire was separate from the other, left no doubt but that the fires had been set intentionally. The inspector also concluded that the fires on the first floor had been set first, since they apparently had burned longer than the others.

Out in the yard, rescue workers had now given up all hope of saving Bettie Brown. They removed the resuscitator from her face and stood talking and sweating in a small group on the lawn. The old lady, her long white hair hanging over the end of the stretcher, looked pathetic in death. Her body was soon removed to the morgue, where an autopsy was performed early that same afternoon.

Green, on the other hand, was alive, if bloody, and an ambulance rushed him to Emergency Hospital, where he was treated for smoke inhalation and stab wounds in the chest.

He had been at the hospital only half an hour when he received a visitor, Police Sergeant Lionel Couture of the Homicide Squad, who had already been filled in briefly by firemen at the scene. Green was lying quietly on a cot, the wounds in his chest still exposed. Couture asked him what had happened at his home. Green explained in some detail how he had smelled smoke in his second-floor bedroom, come down to the basement to investigate, and encountered a strange Negro, who attacked him with a dagger.

Couture remained with the patient only about ten minutes and then returned to Green's house, where his partner, Sergeant Alfred Clarke, had been busy in his absence. Clarke had received from the fire investigators the wrench, the ice pick, and the near-empty bottle that smelled of turpentine. Experimenting with the wrench, he found that it exactly fitted the plug leading to the gas pipe. In the kitchen, he noticed the same box of writing paper, pencil, and pair of eyeglasses that Fire Inspector Kelly had seen. In addition, Clarke noted a box partly filled with paper matches, and a pile of loose paper matches on the gas stove. On the second floor of the building, he observed that the covers on the bed in Green's bedroom had been laid back, but that the bed apparently had not been slept in.

Clarke and Couture discussed all of this information with each other and decided to return to the hospital. Green was still lying where Couture had left him. He looked the same, except that his chest wounds had been temporarily patched up. He recited to Clarke and Couture virtually the same story he had given Couture earlier. When asked about the wrench and ice pick, he said he owned several wrenches and ice picks and could not be sure whether these particular ones were his. He denied opening the gas plug, and he denied using the pencil and stationery to write any letters prior to the fire.

Following this conversation, Couture called the police station and asked that a patrolman be sent to the hospital to guard the patient. Green was now formally under arrest for the murder of Bettie Brown. He was transferred that same afternoon to the locked ward of the District of Columbia General Hospital, next to the District of Columbia Jail.

Two days later, he was visited again, this time by Sergeant Couture, Sergeant Clarke and Fire Inspector Kelly. They questioned him about various matters, including the fact that they had found a box of forty-five caliber cartridges in a dresser drawer in his second-floor bedroom. They asked him to explain this. As Couture later related Green's reply: "He said that before he would let those people get the house, he would blow the so-and-so place up and then blow his brains out; he would get a gun to fit the shells. He said he did not have a gun, but he would buy a gun to fit the shells and blow up this place and then blow his brains out."

That same day, May 28, Green was released from the hospital and transferred to the jail, and five weeks later he was indicted by a grand jury on two counts: arson and murder in the first degree.

He sat in jail for eight months, awaiting trial. It must have seemed to him, as it does to most defendants during this pre-skirmish period, that he had been totally forgotten and was destined to live out his days awaiting an event consigned to oblivion by everyone but himself. Actually, gears were meshing. His attorney, Eugene Bryan, and the assistant United States attorney assigned to prosecute the case, Thomas Flannery, were both going their separate but parallel ways, interviewing witnesses, preparing motions, and catching up on the latest legal developments in cases involving arson and first degree murder. Flannery, in his mid-thirties, was tall, dark, and just short of handsome. He was reputed to be fair, bright, quick, and very tough. Bryan was fifteen years older than his antagonist. He was a nice-looking man, ruddy of complexion and gray-haired. He spoke quickly and sometimes sharply.

Artistically, the selection of a judge to try the case was perfect; Federal District Judge Charles F. McLaughlin resembled Green in the basic attributes of white hair, heavy frame, and square, pale face.

The two-and-a-half-day trial opened with a parade of witnesses on behalf of the prosecution, passing like sheep before the jury of ten men and two women. They described the happenings of May 26, 1953—the fire, the locked doors and windows, the escaping gas, the wrench, the ice pick, the writing paper, and all the rest. A doctor from the District of Columbia General Hospital testified that Green, when examined just after the fire, had "multiple small stab wounds on the front of his chest" and "two small wounds" on either side of the front of his neck. The wounds were "superficial," in that they had not penetrated any vital organs.

Dr. Richard Rosenberg, the deputy coroner who had performed an autopsy on Bettie Brown, testified that in his opinion Miss Brown had died of "pulmonary edema"—that is, an accumulation of fluid in the lungs due to acute tracheal bronchitis. The diagnosis was greeted by twelve unanimously blank expressions from the jury box. In the human body, the coroner explained, various tubes lead from the mouth to the lungs. Miss Brown's tubes were inflamed as a result of inhaling hot, irritating gases. And her blood, he said, contained fourteen per cent carbon monoxide, according to a test performed by someone else.

On cross-examination, the coroner admitted that Miss Brown had suffered from a variety of disorders, including advanced heart disease, degeneration of the liver and kidneys, and hardening of the arteries. He insisted, however, that the primary cause of her death was the inhalation of hot gases.

Then Tom Flannery, the prosecutor, called to the stand what is known in the trade as "the crusher"—his ace of trumps.

Her name was Mrs. Enid Kelly Anthony. She was in her sixties, a plump, respectable-looking lady who spoke with confidence but who viewed her involvement in this matter with obvious distaste. She reminded the spectators of a schoolteacher unhappily reporting to a distressed parent.

She said she lived in Washington and had known the defendant Green for about thirty-five years, but had seen him only three or four times in the last fifteen years. On May 27, the day after the fire, she found a letter in her box upon her return from work. The letter was from Green, and was postmarked Washington, D. C., May 26, 1953, 12:30 P.M. It was passed among the jurors. It was written in pencil. "Tuesday, a.m." appeared in the upper right-hand corner, and the body of the letter read:

> Please notify W. T. Thompson, Fredericksburg, Virginia, of Miss Bettie Brown's death, a fine and good lady and a true friend to me. We both want it this way. Good-bye, my friend, Everett. Please have my ashes thrown on the Chesapeake Bay.

At the bottom of the page was the word "over." Then on the reverse side of the sheet: "The enclosed is for flowers for her."

Enclosed in the letter were two twenty-dollar bills.

There was an uneasy silence in the courtroom as the letter passed from hand to hand. Each juror, as he finished reading, looked speculatively at Green. Flannery roamed the area in front of the jury box, in no hurry to break the spell. Bryan chatted briefly and unconcernedly with his client. Each act of each participant, though seemingly casual, was as deliberate as an actor's. When the letter finally was passed back to Flannery, he closed the case for the prosecution.

The principal witness for the defense was Green himself.

He took the witness chair slowly and deliberately, and repeated the oath in a tremulous voice. He was a short but stocky man. His most outstanding characteristic was mildness. Everything about him bespoke a tame and temperate nature. It showed in the moderate hue of his light-blue eyes, behind gray-rimmed glasses, and in his slightly florid complexion. His hair was white, with the trace of a wave on top—whiter than his almost unnoticeable eyebrows. His lips were pale and thin, the lower lip jutting out beyond the upper, not in dogged decisiveness but merely as the result of crooked, perhaps false, teeth. One lower front tooth was missing. There was a small bump under the skin right in the middle of his forehead, a permanent stigmata. He wore a gentle, quizzical expression, and his shoulders hunched forward a bit.

He identified himself, and the sound of his own low, grave voice seemed to bring his nerves to the surface. Bryan asked him to speak up and to explain in detail the events of the day before the fire.

Green told how, in the early afternoon, he had bought a large supply of groceries. "I cooked two of the chicken legs that night for supper. We had supper, and after the dishes were cleaned up, the table was set for the next morning."

His voice had begun to quaver and to drop in tone. He was quite pale.

Judge McLaughlin interrupted: "Just a moment, Mr. Green. Just calm yourself."

Mr. Green: "I will try, Judge."

Judge McLaughlin: "The marshal will bring you a glass of

water. Take your time now before you start testifying again." The water was brought, and Green sipped at it. "Are you able now to go on?"

Mr. Green, a little uncertainly: "I will try to."

Judge McLaughlin: "Very well. . . ."

Mr. Green: "Well, we went in the front room and turned on the radio, and I guess supper was over about 6:30, and I turned on the radio and listened to that.

"Approximately around 8:00 o'clock or a little after, Miss Shannon came in and paid us a visit, and we all sat there and talked, and I imagine it was about 10:30 when I went out to get some ice cream and cake. . . .

"Approximately around 11 o'clock . . . I had to walk home with [Miss Shannon], about four or five blocks. I guess I was gone about 20 minutes. That would put me back to my home at 20 minutes to 12.

"Well, when Miss Brown was undressed and sitting on the side of the bed ready to get in, I helped her to get in bed." As soon as he had mentioned Miss Brown's name, Green broke down. Tears welled up in his eyes, and his thin lips quivered. Bryan turned away until his client could regain his composure. This same reaction—a kind of emotional catalysis—was triggered each time Green thereafter mentioned the name of his former friend.

"I noticed that she was very weak, appeared very weak. Usually she is able to get into bed herself but that night I helped her. She was lying slightly diagonal across the bed." Once again, his voice faded, and several jurors sat forward trying to catch his words.

Mr. Bryan: "Just a moment. I can't understand you."

Mr. Green: "I will try to speak louder."

Mr. Bryan: "Take your time. If you feel you are getting too upset, stop for a minute. It is very important that the jury and counsel and the Court understand everything that you are trying to convey."

Mr. Green: "Well, as I said, I helped her in bed and put the covers over her.

"She seemed very weak.

"Of course, she has been, more or less, more than a semi-invalid, and I noticed that when she said she was all right.

"Then I went upstairs and I got in bed and stayed there for a while, maybe 20 minutes to half an hour, and I thought I didn't like her being in that weak condition, and so I slipped on my pants and shoes and went back on down, and I opened the door and went in there.

"I didn't hear any sounds at all coming from her, and I walked over closer and I felt her and lifted her arm up, and it dropped, and I then put my ear to her nose to see if she was breathing, and she wasn't breathing.

"Then I felt her pulse and there was no pulse at all, and I knew then she was dead. That was approximately 12:30 midnight, at least, a.m., May the 26th.

"Now, the reason that I can't speak without breaking down, I have known her for 39 years, and I would say we have lived together with two different houses, renting rooms, for approximately 20 years or longer, and she has been square in every way, shape and form. . . .

"After I found out she was dead, I went out to the kitchen and I put on that light, and the writing paper was on the side there, and I got that out and wrote that letter and put in those two $20 bills."

Green said he then went out and mailed the letter to Mrs. Anthony, went to bed, dozed for an hour or so, and finally, about quarter of seven in the morning got up. "In and around the house there, I wear an old pair of loafing shoes, and I put them on and socks and just an undershirt, and I went downstairs, down the back stairs, the way I nearly always go, and when I got down—well, before I started to go down to the first floor, there was a faint smell of smoke, which is nothing unusual in that neighborhood because the houses up there, they burn wood quite often. If there is a heavy atmosphere that odor, a very slight odor, penetrates to my house.

". . . I thought to myself that I still had something to live for, and I made up my mind that I was going to call Mrs.– I know her as well as I know myself, as far as that goes–Mrs. Anthony, because I have known her for about 35 years, between 30 and 35 years, and tell her not to pay any attention to [the letter] because I would take care of things during the day.

"Well, then, I came back to the kitchen, and I attempted to call her, but I had the wrong number, what I thought was her number, and I never got any answer. . . .

"Then I went to the kitchen and I noticed the basement door was standing open, the door that has a key in it and it is always locked, which is checked every night before I go to bed, the same as the downstairs first floor windows.

"That door was open and the light in the basement was on, and I went down the steps there and the smoke was a little bit stronger, but not dense at that time, just hazy, and it wasn't a fire in front of the bathroom door, as these people referred to, that I saw, but the fire I referred to at the coroner's inquest was about so high. . . ." He gestured just below his knees.

"That is the fire I saw, and then through that little haze, coming up through this passageway there from the front . . . this man came up.

"He had now what I know to be that Stillson wrench, that has been shown here, in his hand, and I said to him, I said: What in the hell are you doing in here?

"And he never opened his mouth. He was probably, when I said that, he was 6 feet away from me coming towards me, and he hit me across my head, right here.

"Well, I fell, I would say, about two-thirds of the way in the bathroom. It may have been 18 inches out of the bathroom door, on the floor, and he jumped on me and I was dazed then, and my head was spinning around.

"Well, then, he jumped on me with this thing and I passed

out, and I felt something hit me, pushing into me, and I passed out completely.

"Now, the only excuse—the homicide officer questioned me about why was it not holes were in that undershirt I had on, and he wanted to know what explanation I had about that. That is the words he used, what explanation I had about that.

"I said: I haven't any; I don't know.

"But later on it came to me that when I came partially to, I felt something pinching me right in my heart, just like a snatching at your heart, everybody has had that, and I have had it quite often, and I looked down and there was this ice pick in me, all the way up to the handle, and I caught hold of it, like that, and I had difficulty pulling it out, and I wanted to have those x-rays summoned because I think they would show that one of my ribs had been punctured when the ice pick went through because I had such difficulty getting it out, and it dropped on the floor.

"Well, I never heard or knew anything else until I heard the fire engines screaming. I was still dazed, unable to move.

"Well, about that time I got up off the floor, and it was hot there, the fire was burning outside the bathroom door, and the smoke was thick. It had lowered to the top of the bathtub and I was choking and gagging, and it was very hot there, and I turned on what should have been the cold water spigot, it was the cold water spigot, but that heat in the basement it heated up the pipes running across the ceiling so hot that that water was scalding.

"I turned it off, and there was only about two inches of water in the tub, and I got in it, and I fell in the basement tub, and the water was so hot, and this is what turned out at the hospital, my hands were red, just blood-red, but it wasn't hot enough to blister them and they were red for two or three days after, intensely red.

"The fire marshal or the homicide man questioned me why my hands were so red. They were insinuating that I had gotten them blistered or burned by being close to the fire, which I wasn't. I don't think there was a hair scorched on me, but it is as hot a place as I have ever been in my life.

"Well, I was partially to and conscious when they took me into the yard, enough to hear sounds, but not to move or say anything. My eyes were blinded. I could not see or open them. All I could do was hear sounds.

"Well, I guess they gave me four or five shots of oxygen. I could feel it hit my veins.

"Then they said: Take him to the hospital. All I knew going down in the ambulance, I could hear the siren screaming, and they carried me in there, and it seemed like a long time before they did anything for my eyes."

There was a long pause. Green took off his glasses, pulled a clean white handkerchief from his pants pocket and slowly rubbed the lenses. His mild blue eyes bore a pained expression as he recalled the anguished moments in the ambulance, when he was half dead, half alive.

With patient questioning, Bryan drew comments from his client on each piece of the government's evidence.

Green for the first time identified the wrench definitely as his own, last used several months ago and left sitting at the bottom of the basement steps. The ice pick could be his, but he was not sure; he owned several of them.

He denied telling Cornelius, the marshal, that "they would be sorry" if they forced him out of his home. "My words were these: That if they rob me of my home, the party that did it, I was going to take my gun and blow their damn brains out. They are my words, and I will admit them anywhere."

He explained that certain persons had been working "underhand" to drive him out of his home because he had complained to the Morals Squad about boisterous, offensive parties in the apartment house next door.

The locked doors and windows of his home on the morning of the fire he explained by the fact that a prowler had been operating in the neighborhood a dozen times during the last year.

He emphatically denied that he had set any fires or killed Bettie Brown.

On cross-examination, Flannery approached Green in a kindly manner belied by the persistence of his questions. He asked why Green had not told Sergeants Clarke and Couture about Bettie Brown having died in the middle of the night, hours before the fire. Green replied that he was dazed during his interviews with these gentlemen, weak from shock and loss of blood, and, besides, he could see that they had stacked the deck against him and that he had better save the true story for his trial.

He explained the letter to Mrs. Anthony by asserting that at the time he wrote it, "I did have some intention of bumping myself off." But, he added, he had definitely changed his mind by the next morning.

When Green had concluded his testimony, Bryan introduced several pictures into evidence. The pictures were of Bettie Brown's room, taken immediately after the fire. Similar pictures introduced by the government had been dark, with what purported to be smeared and discolored walls. Bryan's pictures were lighter and showed no evidence of the fire.

Bryan recalled Mrs. Anthony to the stand as his final witness. She admitted she had left home at her regular time, 6:35, on the morning of the fire, so that if Green had called her at 6:45, as he said he had, she would not have been there to answer.

Flannery's summation to the jury was brief and temperate. Here was a man, he said, who had decided in advance that he would never give up his home. Now his hopes of saving it were gone. He could not raise or borrow any more money, and the next morning the deputy marshal would put him and Bettie Brown out on the street. Rather than lose the only home he had, he decided to take his own life and destroy the building. But what about Bettie Brown? Green had cared for her off and on for over twenty years, and who would care for her now? She would be shunted off to an institution, separated forever from her best friend, her home, the only life she could cope with. And so, theorized Flannery, Green decided to kill her rather than leave her alone. Methodically and deliberately, Green spent that May night roaming about the house preparing for the fire. He built five separate blazes where they would have the most effect—three near Bettie Brown's room and two in the basement where he intended to kill himself. After lighting each fire in the morning, he turned on the gas in the basement, climbed into the bathtub and stabbed himself in the chest and neck with the ice pick. Flannery laid particular stress on the carbon monoxide found in Bettie Brown's blood. He reasoned that Miss Brown could only have absorbed the carbon monoxide by breathing it, which ruled out any possibility that she had died hours before the fires were lit, as Green contended.

But Flannery did not ask the jury to convict Green of first degree murder, which carried the death penalty. He conceded that "this is a sad case, it is a pitiful case," and he said he was content to allow the jury to decide whether to convict on first degree murder, or on the lesser offense of second degree murder.

Bryan, in his argument, principally attacked gaps in the government's case. Where, he asked, are the three most important doctors involved in this case—the one who examined Miss Brown on the lawn as soon as she was removed from the building, the one who had actually performed the blood test on her (Dr. Rosenberg had merely reported the findings of someone else), and the one who had treated the defendant at Emergency Hospital immediately after the fire? Why were these doctors not called as witnesses by the government?

Affirmatively, Bryan relied on Green's version of Miss Brown's death, emphasizing that the firemen had found the window in the basement bathroom unlocked, so that a prowler could easily have entered by that route and attacked Green.

Then came the instructions to the jury—instructions which were objected to by neither the defense nor the prosecution, but which were to develop into the focal point of the entire case.

"You are instructed," Judge McLaughlin told the jury, "that you may find the defendant guilty of an offense the commission of which is necessarily included in that with which he is charged. . . ." In other words, even though the indictment charged only arson and first degree murder, the jury could find the defendant guilty of arson and *second* degree murder, if the evidence warranted such a finding.

"Murder in the second degree may be committed without a purpose or intent to kill, or it may be committed with a purpose or intent to kill but without premeditation and deliberation. An accidental or unintentional killing constitutes murder in the second degree if it is accompanied by malice."

The jury was out for two hours and a half.

Its verdict was announced by the foreman:

"We, the jury, find the defendant Everett D. Green guilty of arson on count one.

"We find the defendant guilty of second degree murder on the second count."

Green had escaped the death penalty. Judge McLaughlin sentenced him to two prison terms—from one to three years on count one, and from five to twenty years on count two, the two sentences to run concurrently.

Green himself wrote a letter to the Court of Appeals, which the court interpreted as an appeal of the conviction. In such cases, when defendants cannot afford to hire counsel, the Court of Appeals appoints attorneys to represent them. These attorneys serve without compensation. And so here, the Court of Appeals appointed as Green's counsel a young attorney less than one year out of the University of Virginia Law School.

George Blow was tall and thin, with a shock of slightly curly hair above a high forehead. He was not handsome, but a wide grin surrounded prominent white teeth, and the effect was good. He delayed his laugh; it came a fraction after it was expected. But its arrival was punctuated by loud staccato sounds that amply compensated for the delay. His job with Washington's largest law firm had not, to date, included any trial work or any criminal work.

Blow obtained a copy of the transcript of the trial and studied it in great detail. Carefully he went over, time and again, every aspect of the proceedings. He spent hours reviewing the opinions in criminal cases in the District of Columbia. On several occasions, he interviewed Green at the jail.

Finally, he returned to Green with very sober news. There was, he felt, an error in the record, but presenting that error to the Court of Appeals would place Green's life in danger.

Judge McLaughlin had allowed the jury to consider both first and second degree murder. The only evidence at the trial as to the cause of Bettie Brown's death was rendered by Dr. Rosenberg, and he had concluded that she died as the result of the fire. The jury had decided, by its finding of arson under count one, that Green had set the fire. Therefore, explained Blow, if Green had caused the death, he necessarily did it in the course of committing arson, a felony.

The District of Columbia has a "felony murder" statute. This law provides that if anyone causes the death of another while committing a felony, he shall be guilty of first degree murder, even if he did not intend to kill. Thus, reasoned Blow, if Green had caused Bettie Brown's death while committing the felony of arson, he *must* be guilty of first degree murder; there was no evidence whatever to support a verdict of second degree murder, and Judge McLaughlin had been in error in even instructing the jury on second degree murder.

With great care and precision, Blow explained to Green the possible consequences of an appeal on this point. If the Court of Appeals reversed the second degree murder conviction, it would return the case for a new trial, and at a second trial the jury would be instructed only on first degree murder. If the verdict was guilty, Green would have to be sentenced to death, because the death penalty is mandatory for first degree murder in the District of Columbia.

It is true, said Blow, that he had devised a theory by which he hoped to avoid a second trial. But he had no guarantee whatever of its validity, or of its ultimate success.

Green was given time to think over his desperate situation. Shouldn't he, after all, be content with a jail sentence? Isn't confined life far better than the risk of no life at all? How could this mild, almost timid, man gamble with stakes that were so high and with odds so poor? And for *any* man, was the chance of freedom worth the agony of another trial, of standing once more while a nameless foreman stated the short, pungent, expressionless words which told you whether you would walk out free or walk to your death?

But it was not a searing decision for Green. He said he fully understood the consequences, but he would rather go to the chair than spend the rest of his life in jail. In fact, he added, he would rather die than spend another day in jail. He adamantly instructed Blow to file the appeal.

And so George Blow wrote a lengthy brief setting forth his contentions, and he argued the case orally before a three-judge panel of the Court of Appeals.

Two months after the argument, the court rendered its decision. By a vote of two to one, the court agreed with Blow and reversed the conviction. After quoting at length from Dr. Rosenberg's testimony, the court concluded that "all the testimony as to what occurred in the burning house pointed to murder in the first degree and nothing else. . . . In seeking a new trial at which—if the evidence is substantially as before—the jury will have no choice except to find him guilty of first degree murder or to acquit him, Green is manifestly taking a desperate chance. He may suffer the death penalty. At oral argument we inquired of his counsel [Blow] whether Green clearly understood the possible consequences of success on this appeal, and were told the appellant, who is 64 years of age, says he prefers death to spending the rest of his life in prison. He is entitled to a new trial."

The dissenting judge thought that even if there had been error in instructing the jury on second degree murder, the error should be disregarded, because it was favorable to the defendant—the defendant benefited from the error rather than being prejudiced by it.

And so, four months later, Green prepared for his second trial in Federal District Court. Since he had not appealed from his conviction of arson, that issue was no longer involved. And the Court of Appeals had now held that no instruction could be given on second degree murder. The sole issue was whether Green was guilty of first degree murder. If so, the judge was required by statute to condemn him to death.

The United States Attorney's Office was not enthusiastic about this turn of events. As Flannery had said, this was a pathetic case rather than a brutal one, and the thought of asking a jury to send Green to his death was not pleasing. After a number of consultations within the United States Attorney's Office, word was sent to George Blow that a plea of guilty to manslaughter would be acceptable to the prosecution.

Once again, Blow returned to the jail. Once again he explained patiently and with great care the alternatives open to Green. A plea to manslaughter would involve a relatively short jail sentence. A new trial, on the other hand, would mean the chance of an adverse verdict, and of death in the electric chair. Blow urged his client, with all the persuasive force he could marshal, to accept the prosecution's offer.

Green said no. He said he would not plead guilty to anything because he was not guilty of anything. He had faith in the future and in his own destiny, and he would take his chances with a new trial. George Blow, feeling solemn and old beyond his years, left the jail and turned his thoughts to the preparation of his first trial.

Fortunately for Blow's peace of mind, the courts assign two attorneys to the trial of all first degree cases. Appointed to work with Blow in this case was Charles Ford, perhaps Washington's outstanding criminal lawyer. Charley was not a bookworm. He shunned libraries, advance sheets, and overly long opinions, and the law he expounded came principally off the top of his head and from under his hat. But if you allowed Charley within sniffing distance of a jury, his adrenal glands began pumping, his corpuscles expanded, his liver contracted, and he became a quivering mass of animal magnetism. In fact, it was said around town that a sure-fire dinner party would include Charley and twelve other guests, because as soon as he sensed the magic number present, all of his visceral reactions would set in, and a first-class show would ensue. Big, energetic, mercurial Charley Ford had never let a client go to the chair.

The judge at the second trial was F. Dickinson Letts. Just turned eighty, Judge Letts was a man of long experience on the bench, having served for over twelve years on an Iowa court and for twenty-four years on the District Court in Washington. His eyesight and hearing were not of the very best, but his rulings were clear, decisive, and not subject to change.

Tom Flannery, being thoroughly familiar with the facts, was again assigned to prosecute Green.

Prior to trial, Green's attorneys presented a motion to dismiss the indictment. This was the move which Blow had outlined to Green, a desperate effort to kill the first degree murder charge.

Their argument was this. The jury in the first trial not only had found Green guilty of second degree murder but had, in effect, found him *not* guilty of first degree murder. Or, to put it another way, Green had once been in jeopardy of a first degree murder conviction, and the jury had failed to convict. Therefore, argued Green's attorneys, he no longer could be tried for first degree murder; to do so would put him twice in jeopardy for the same offense in violation of the Fifth Amendment to the Constitution.

Judge Letts rejected their argument and proceeded to trial. It lasted one day longer than the first trial and included twenty-five witnesses compared with the nineteen who had appeared previously. For example, the chemist who had actually tested Bettie Brown's blood testified to the fourteen per cent carbon monoxide he had found. And two character witnesses appeared for Green, testifying as to his good reputation in the community.

But essentially, the second trial followed the form, if not the precise content, of the first. Green gave the same account of the fire; in addition, he recounted a bit of his background. He was a native Washingtonian, his father having been an interior decorator with a downtown shop. Green's first job was with the Bureau of Engraving and Printing. He served briefly in World War I and then married in 1920. Divorced ten years later because of "in-law" trouble, he moved to the 1500 block of Ninth Street Northwest, just two doors from Miss Bettie Brown, an old friend. One evening in 1930, he visited Miss Brown during a snow storm. When it came time for him to go, he complained of feeling ill, and she insisted that he was too sick to leave. So he stayed a month, laid up with pneumonia and the flu.

At the end of the month, when Green returned to his old room, the owners had moved. So he returned to Miss Brown and rented a room from her. They lived quietly at this address for some twenty-two years until finally, in June, 1952, they moved to 1115 Massachusetts Avenue, where the fire occurred.

Miss Brown had never married. She supported herself by teaching music and renting rooms. But in her later years she became sickly, and Green often had to wait on her, making her meals and giving her medicine (a fact attested to by their joint friend, Elsie Shannon).

Green's attorneys in the second trial tried to introduce police records showing that during the two-week period of May 1 to 25, 1953, reports of housebreakings, rapes, and robberies in Green's neighborhood were made to the police. This evidence, they said, tended to corroborate Green's story of the Negro prowler. But Judge Letts ruled the evidence too remote and excluded it.

Flannery bore in on Green during cross-examination. If you loved Bettie Brown so much, he asked, how could you climb the stairs after finding her dead and go soundly to sleep, as you said you did? Objection. Objection sustained. If you went to bed, why did Sergeant Couture testify that the bed hadn't been slept in? Objection. Objection sustained.

But no objections were sustained when Flannery questioned Green as to each phrase, one by one, specifically and pointedly, in the letter to Mrs. Anthony. And Flannery finally came to the most damaging sentence of all.

"And you say this, Mr. Green, and I want you to explain this to the jury; you said: 'We both want it this way.' Now what did you mean by that?"

Mr. Green: "That was one thing there, when it was first read at the Coroner's Inquest, I didn't exactly remember putting it on there, but it was my intentions—"

Judge Letts interrupted: "Wait. Answer his question."

Green turned to Flannery. "What is your question?"

Mr. Flannery: "What did you mean by, 'We both want it this way'?"

Green looked uncomfortable. "Well, as I said before, I thought I had erased that and changed it."

Mr. Flannery: "My question is, what did you mean by 'We both want it this way'?" Do you understand that question?"

Mr. Green: "Sure, I do."

Mr. Flannery: "Well, what did you mean by it?"

Mr. Green: "At the time, I was considering committing suicide myself."

Mr. Flannery: "How were you going to commit suicide?"

Mr. Green: "That is an easy matter. There are hundreds of ways."

Ford became impatient. He told his client: "Just answer the question, will you?"

Mr. Flannery: "How were you going to do it?"

Mr. Green: "I hadn't even figured out any way."

Mr. Flannery: "Were you contemplating suicide?"

Mr. Green: "Yes, I grant you that, but I hadn't determined on any method of it."

Mr. Flannery: "Yes, but my question now is, why did you say 'We both,' 'We both want it this way'?"

Mr. Green: "Well, that is a little—it is a sort of a misquote there. That was not my thought exactly."

Mr. Flannery: "You wrote it?"

Mr. Green: "I know I wrote it."

Mr. Flannery: "What did you mean by it?"

Mr. Green: "I didn't mean that."

Mr. Flannery: "What did you mean?"

Mr. Green: "She has made the remark lots of times—"

Mr. Flannery: "No. My question is—you just take your time and answer my question. If you don't understand it, tell me you don't understand it. What did you mean by 'We both want it this way'?"

Mr. Green: "Well, I was putting my own feelings along the same line that she has expressed herself along that line. She said that she would rather be dead than go in a public institution."

Mr. Flannery: "Didn't you then mean when you wrote this letter that you were not only at that time going to destroy yourself, but her also?"

Mr. Green: "No, no."

And so the trial ground to its climax.

In his closing argument, Flannery repeated the same points he had made at the first trial, though in more detail and with greater emphasis on the letter to Mrs. Anthony. Both Ford and Blow spoke for the defense. Blow was brief, matter-of-fact, scrupulously methodical, while his older compatriot appealed to the emotions and fears and sensitivities of each juror. If you decide he is guilty, warned Ford, "he goes to the electric chair, and nothing will stop it. It is mandatory." So it behooves each of us, he said, "to take great care and caution on the facts in this case lest we make a mistake that we cannot take back. We must think of that. It is here. It is real. It is human."

Where are Miss Brown's bedsheets and pillowcase, Ford wanted to know. Why were they not brought in here for the jury to see? Was it because they showed no signs at all of smoke and fire? For that matter, where is her clothing, and where are the window curtains? Here was a woman, after all, who was suffering from all kinds of illnesses at eighty-three years of age. Where is all of this relevant evidence to help you decide how she really died?

Pointing at Green, he leaned close to the front-row jurors and concluded in a hoarse whisper: "How can anyone say that he is a first degree murderer when he followed the precepts of God: feed the hungry, clothe the naked, give aid to the sick? He did those things!"

Carefully, Judge Letts instructed the jury. The alleged crime, he explained, had four elements, each of which the government must prove beyond a reasonable doubt. The government must prove that Green burned or attempted to burn the building, that the building belonged to someone else, that in attempting to burn the building, Green acted with malice, and, finally, that Bettie Brown's death was caused by and was the direct result of Green's act of burning or attempting to burn the building.

The jury of eight men and four women filed out of the room. It was 4:10 in the afternoon.

When a jury retires to consider its verdict, an ominous silence descends on a courtroom. It is not the relaxed silence of a schoolroom at the end of the day, or of a barracks in a deserted camp. There is a tense, uneasy quality to this silence, and neither the banter of the court reporter with the clerk, nor the sudden appearance of newspapers in the hands of spectators can dissipate it.

In a close case, the defense is grateful for each moment that the jury is out. The more time that passes, the more trouble the jury must be having. And the more trouble they are having, the more likely it is that some recalcitrant individualist—some hardy soul who too seldom is allowed to assert himself at home—will refuse to bend and instead will force the others to bring in a verdict of not guilty.

The defendant, back in his cell, thinks of those twelve strangers, thinks hard, and tries to force his will, telepathically, upon them. He mulls his fate, and how he got where he is. It is an almost unbearably depressing recess from the tense, diverting histrionics of the courtroom.

And finally, there is a knock on the jury-room door. The marshal moves it ajar and receives word that the jury is ready. The word spreads. The judge is notified in his chambers. The lawyers are called, and the defendant is led back to his seat, past the pathetically reassuring smiles of his attorneys. The jurors file in, most of them looking down self-consciously, perhaps one or two glancing shyly at the defendant. They carry a secret which he does not know whether he wants to hear or not.

The Green jurors at this second trial deliberated for six hours and twenty minutes. At 10:30 P.M., they notified the marshal that they were ready. The courthouse was completely dark except for the one room into which they filed. They formed a long line, facing Green. The clerk asked the foreman, "What say you as to the defendant Everett D. Green on Count 2?"

The reply came firmly: "Guilty as charged."

Green took the verdict with stoicism. Blow, who had realized from the beginning the frightful risk they were taking, and Ford, who had always been able to avoid a verdict of death, seemed more shaken than the defendant. They turned to him with reassurances, as if trying to reassure themselves.

All too soon, it seemed to Green, Judge Letts was holding a hearing for pronouncement of the sentence. Asked if he had anything to say before sentence was imposed, Green replied that he did—he had "a lot to say." His hands trembling, the white-haired man asserted that "This is supposed to be a court of justice, but I want to see where the justice is. I've been persecuted. But if I was on the outside I could prove this case. . . . I got 80 witnesses. . . . Those who lied want to see smoke in the chair. . . . I thought the world of her, Miss Brown. I never would have harmed a hair on her head. I respect the grave where she lies today."

Judge Letts heard him through and then proceeded on to what surely must be the most distasteful duty that rests on a judge. "Everett D. Green, you have been found guilty . . . and . . . you are hereby sentenced to the punishment of death by electrocution. . . ."

The marshal turned to lead Green away. But the elderly defendant, looking squarely at Judge Letts, had the last word. "I can only thank God we have got a Court of Appeals and we have a Supreme Court," he said.

Back to the Court of Appeals went his attorneys. As they had argued to Judge Letts, they now argued to the appellate court that this conviction was void because in violation of the Constitution. Green had been twice tried for the same offense.

On February 9, 1956, the three-judge panel unanimously affirmed the conviction. They ruled that there had been no violation of Green's constitutional rights.

Green's attorneys returned to the same court with a petition for rehearing, asking that all nine judges hear the case. The Court of Appeals, though it numbers nine judges, normally hears cases in panels of three. In extraordinary cases, however, all nine judges may sit on the same case. That is what Green requested, and that is what he got. In a beautifully paneled courtroom of the United States Courthouse, separated from the Supreme Court Building by the rolling lawns of the Capitol, the nine Court of Appeals judges gathered to hear George Blow reargue the case. Assisting Blow was a young associate in his office, George Rublee; Charley Ford, who appeared on the brief, did not take part in any further oral arguments.

Blow and Rublee presented a number of points to the court, but the three principal ones were these. First, Green's conviction violated the Fifth Amendment to the Constitution, in that he had been twice tried for the same offense, first degree murder. Second, the statements which Green gave to Couture and Clarke in the hospital should not have been admitted in evidence, because he had not yet been arraigned and warned of his rights. Third, Tom Flannery had made prejudicial statements during his closing argument to the effect that it was up to the courts rather than the jury to decide Green's ultimate fate.

The court seemed particularly interested in the double jeopardy argument. After all, the entire double jeopardy clause of the Constitution is stated in only twenty words: "nor shall any person be subject for the same offence to be twice put in jeopardy of life or limb." Over the years, the courts have had to establish certain ground rules by which these ambiguous words are applied.

For example, under the Fifth Amendment when a jury finds a defendant not guilty, the government cannot appeal the verdict, regardless of how many errors were made during the trial. And "a defendant is placed in jeopardy once he is put to trial before a jury so that if the jury is discharged without his consent he cannot be tried again." However, if a jury cannot agree on *any* verdict, a new trial can be ordered. Finally, if a defendant appeals and wins a reversal, he can be tried again for the *same* offense with which he was originally charged; by appealing, he "waives" his right to claim double jeopardy.

But what about Green's situation? He had appealed and won a reversal of his conviction for second degree murder, but the government had not prosecuted him again for second degree murder. It had prosecuted him the second time for *first* degree murder. Green's attorneys claimed that Green, by appealing the *second* degree murder conviction, did not waive his rights in regard to the *first* degree acquittal.

Questions from the nine Court of Appeals judges soon made it clear that the focal point of the entire case was to be a decision handed down by the Supreme Court in 1905, *Trono v. United States*.

In the Trono case, three defendants were acquitted in the Philippine Islands of first degree murder and convicted instead of the lesser crime of assault. They appealed to the Supreme Court of the Philippines which, under a peculiar Spanish procedure, could in effect try the whole case over again, and the Philippines court reached the conclusion that the defendants were really guilty of second degree murder. The defendants appealed to the Supreme Court of the United States, claiming that for the Philippine court to convict them of second degree murder after they had already, in effect, been acquitted of second degree murder, was a violation of the applicable statute (which was worded much like the double jeopardy provision of the Constitution). The Supreme Court affirmed the convictions. Four Justices—David Brewer, Henry Brown, Rufus Peckham, and William Day—joined in an opinion which stated in part that when a defendant appeals, and the court reverses, the entire controversy is opened up, so that a new trial can be held on any of the original charges. At the end of the opinion appeared the brief statement that "Mr. Justice [Oliver Wendell] Holmes concurs in the result"—that is, he agreed that the convictions should be affirmed, but he gave no reasons for his vote. And then came the four dissenters—Melville Fuller (the Chief Justice), John Marshall Harlan (the grandfather of the present Mr. Justice Harlan), Edward White, and Joseph McKenna.

This, then, was the Trono decision which Blow, Rublee, and Ford somehow had to distinguish from Green's situation. Their reasoning was ingenious.

The Trono case, they said, was entirely different because the Philippine appellate court, unlike our own Court of Appeals, had power to try the entire case itself. Also, the Supreme Court in the Trono case had been interpreting a statute rather than the Constitution. And finally, the so-called "opinion of the Court" was not really an opinion of a *majority* of the Court at all, since Mr. Justice Holmes had not joined in it, and therefore the decision was not binding authority that had to be followed by the Court of Appeals.

As ingenious as their argument was, Green's attorneys failed to convince the Court of Appeals.

The nine judges splintered off in four different directions. A majority of five held that the conviction was valid—the Trono case controlled, and there had been no error at the trial. One judge concurred in that result, saying that he could see no way around the Trono case. Three judges dissented on the ground that Green had unconstitutionally been put twice in jeopardy for the same offense. And two of the three dissenters objected on the additional ground that the incriminating statements taken from Green in the hospital were inadmissible in evidence.

Time was running out for Green. All the ponds had dried up but one.

And so his attorneys turned to the highest court in the land—the Supreme Court of the United States. The final arbiter.

The feeling of arriving at Olympus affects not only lawyers and litigants but the Justices themselves. They are made constantly aware, in each move they make, that someone, somewhere, has come to the end of the line, and that his fortunes —whether life, liberty, or worldly goods—are in their hands. As great as are the responsibilities of a judge on a court of appeals, he at least is fortified by the assurance that a mistake, if made, can be remedied elsewhere. But after the Supreme Court, there is nowhere else to appeal. It is a sobering rather than a heady thought. Each Justice becomes a bigger man under its impact than he was before the President appointed him.

The Court decides only a small percentage of the cases it is asked to decide. Of the more than two thousand suits which are filed each term, the Court chooses those of sufficient importance and leaves the others alone. Thus, the first task of any litigant is to file a "Petition for a Writ of Certiorari," a stylized way of requesting that a superior court direct a lower court to send up for consideration some pending case.

Green's petition was filed at the end of July, 1956, some three years after Bettie Brown's death. Important changes were taking place on the Court. During that same summer, Mr. Justice Sherman Minton of Indiana resigned, and Mr. Justice William J. Brennan, Jr., of New Jersey was appointed by President Eisenhower to succeed him. Brennan had taken his seat, though he had not yet been confirmed by the Senate, when the Court voted to grant Green's petition and hear argument on his case. But before oral argument, Mr. Justice Stanley F. Reed of Kentucky also resigned from the Court, and Mr. Justice Charles E. Whittaker of Missouri was appointed in his place. Both of the new Justices were confirmed and took their seats just one month before the Green argument.

Minton and Reed had been known quantities. Minton with his bulldog face and sparkling wit, his great love of sports and his impatience with legalistic, overly technical arguments, and

Reed, the well-named: a thin reed of a man with bald head, a low, inquisitive voice, and a penchant for long, involved opinions. These two conservatives had been on the Court long enough so that old hands could categorize and pinpoint and forecast them with a high percentage of hits. But the new fellows, despite prior judicial experience, were largely question marks insofar as the highly specialized work of the Court was concerned.

It soon developed that a clue to Brennan might be forthcoming. The Justice had accepted an invitation to participate in a "moot court" panel at Harvard Law School. The fictional case to be argued by the students was an exact duplicate of the Green case. Blow contacted a friend at the law school and asked him to sit in on the argument. The friend reported back Brennan's every question and comment. But as good as the report was, it did not reveal which way the Justice was likely to vote.

On April 25, 1957, a very nervous George Blow walked up the blindingly white marble steps of the Supreme Court Building, between the towering marble columns, and along the wide marble hall that leads undeviatingly to the courtroom. Has anyone ever entered that chamber without a feeling of awe? It is a heavy, boxlike room, its ceiling high and ornate and its borders partitioned by gold gates. At each of its four sides are marble columns backed by dark maroon drapes. All eyes automatically center on the Honduras mahogany bench running almost the width of the room, and on the nine chairs of assorted shapes and sizes ranged behind it.

Sharply at the appointed hour, the clerk bangs a gavel and the drapes part. Everyone rises. The nine Justices, each in a flowing robe, step through as the clerk intones, "The Honorable, the Chief Justice and the Associate Justices of the Supreme Court of the United States." And then, when the Justices have lined up behind their chairs: "Oyez, Oyez, Oyez—all persons having business before the Honorable, the Supreme

Court of the United States, are admonished to draw near and give their attention, for the Court is now sitting." A pause. Then solemnly: "God save the United States and this Honorable Court."

The Justices, lawyers, and audience are seated, and the Chief Justice proceeds immediately to welcome the new members of the bar of the Court. Not every attorney can argue before the Supreme Court; unless given special permission, each must meet certain qualifications, pay a fee, and be formally admitted, as George Blow had been only six months before. The ceremony of admittance is brief, as the Chief Justice says a few words and the attorneys are sworn in by the clerk at the left of the bench. It is then time for oral argument.

The work done during the previous weeks by Blow and his gifted associate, Rublee, now came to fruition in one brief hour. The days and nights spent poring over opinions, treatises, law reviews and statutes all receded; what remained was a reservoir of knowledge waiting to be tapped for the key question that might make the difference between success and failure.

The Green case was called, and Blow stepped up to the large podium, directly in front of Chief Justice Warren. Not many years before, the Justices on either end of the bench would have had difficulty hearing him—or even each other. The acoustics in the chamber are notoriously poor. But an amplifying system had been installed, so that Blow's low, nervous voice was picked up, carried along the bench, and buffeted back to the audience.

As these things go, the Green argument evoked relatively few questions. But there was wrapt attention. Whittaker and Harlan, the sparrow and the hawk, sat near the edge of their seats, alert and completely absorbed; the ruggedly handsome Harlan, tall and lean, peered alternately over his spectacles at Blow and through them at the briefs in front of him. Douglas, still young-looking after eighteen years on the Court, repeatedly yanked off his reading glasses and in quick, nervous gestures rubbed first his forehead and then the side of his nose. Occasionally, he motioned to a page boy, whispered, and in a moment received a law book which he read in haste and handed back. Black, the Alabama liberal, and Clark, the Texas middle-of-the-roader, reclined in their seats, relaxed but observant. The quiet, dignified Burton sat like a stone, staring attentively at the rostrum. At the center of the bench, like a large eye at the center of a hurricane, sat Chief Justice Warren, his gaze never leaving that of the speaker. He was bigger than his pictures hinted, and an impression of physical strength emanated from him. Brennan, though a freshman, asked occasional questions and, with his Harvard moot court experience behind him, displayed a close familiarity with the pattern of the argument.

The only agitation along the bench centered about Frankfurter. He snapped out questions, swiveled to the right and to the left, wrote notes, and generally expended his energies through action and temper. He engaged Blow in an extended argument on the common law derivations of double jeopardy.

Leonard Sand, representing the government, followed Blow to the rostrum. The Justices questioned him closely but courteously. He was almost through his presentation when the Chief Justice picked up a copy of the record and began reading from Flannery's closing remarks to the jury. The Chief Justice wanted to know if Mr. Sand felt that these remarks constituted fair comment or whether they were flagrantly prejudicial to Green. Blow and Rublee looked at each other in surprise. They had not even had time to reach this part of their argument, and yet the Chief Justice's tone indicated that he was seriously disturbed by Flannery's remarks.

Sand told Warren he thought Flannery's remarks were quite fair when compared with the statements in Ford's summation which had provoked them. Flushed with anger, the Chief Justice then entered into a discourse which led Sand ten minutes over his time period. The Chief Justice read each of Flannery's remarks which he considered prejudicial and asked Sand to point to each of Ford's statements which supposedly prompted it. Sand handled the matter as best he could, and the oral argument ended on this note.

The next day, the Washington *Daily News* headlined, "Green Case Goes to High Court—Gambler for Life Asks Re-Shuffle." The story summed up the situation: "Everett D. Green, an old man who bet his life in the courts and lost, yesterday asked the Supreme Court to let him out of the bargain."

On each succeeding Monday for two months, Blow took a cab to the Court, sat in a front-row seat at noon, and awaited an announcement of the decision in his case. On June 24, the last day of the Court's session before the summer recess, a long list of opinions was rendered, winding up the current term. Blow was confident that an opinion would at last be forthcoming on this particular Monday, because the Supreme Court normally disposes of virtually all of the cases on its docket by the end of each "term" of court. He was amazed, therefore, when the Court issued a brief order stating that the Green case was "restored to the calendar." In other words, the Court had been unable to reach agreement and wanted to hear argument for a second time in the fall.

And so the arduous, time-consuming task of preparing for oral argument began all over again. Blow and Rublee batted questions back and forth, worked through the trial record once again to make certain of their facts, and brought their precedents up to date. Everything they did, every thought they had, was geared to the split on the Court. Which Justice was unable to make up his mind? What particular issue was the crucial one? What telling point might tip the balance? All in all, it was an uncomfortable summer.

On October 15, 1957, only a week after the Court had returned from its summer recess, Blow was back at the rostrum, threading his way once more through the legal intricacies of his argument. But now the atmosphere had changed. The Court was obviously deeply divided into two camps. The Justices were serious, intent, short-tempered, and brusque. They argued not so much with counsel as with each other. Their questions seemed designed more to enlighten their brethren than to settle their own doubts. Tongues were sharp. Comments were acid.

An almost unbecoming contest developed between the Chief Justice and Mr. Justice Frankfurter. On several occasions, Frankfurter either interrupted Warren's interrogation or attempted to rephrase Warren's questions. Finally, the Chief Justice reached the end of his patience, turned on Frankfurter, and said that he would appreciate it if the Justice would be quiet; he, Warren, would ask his own questions, and then Frankfurter could ask his.

Outbursts of this kind are infrequent, though frequent enough to startle unsuspecting attorneys and spectators. But after all, they are symptomatic of strong personalities deeply interested in and clashing over important and involved constitutional questions. A lawyer would much rather face this kind of a Court than an apathetic one; he would rather be caught in a dogfight than argue to the bored and insensitive expressions of mentally supine judges. This is not to say that on occasion some Justices do not carry their enthusiasm too far; but at least their pique is understandable.

Unlike the first argument, when the few questions which were asked had ranged over a wide field, this second argument centered almost entirely on the double jeopardy point. Several Justices made their positions quite clear. Clark, for example, said he could not distinguish the Trono case from this one. Black, on the other hand, carefully designed his questions to bring out the distinguishing aspects of Trono. Frankfurter again debated the common law with Blow, citing cases, statutes, and statistics, many of which Blow disputed. Whittaker was the enigma. His questions were few, and they did not reveal his position. They did show, however, that he was worried about a reversal of the conviction. He asked Leonard Sand, who again argued for the government, whether there was not some way Green could again be tried for second degree murder or some other offense. The answer was no.

And so the arguments were completed for the second time, and the Court once again retired to consider Green's fate. Blow wrote a brief description of the argument and sent it to Green, who was still in the District of Columbia Jail and who, like all defendants in custody, had been unable to attend the Supreme Court sessions himself. Charley Ford had been present during the oral argument but had not participated. Less than two weeks later he died suddenly of a heart attack.

On Monday morning, December 16, 1957, with the Christmas season upon him, George Blow sat in the courtroom of the Supreme Court as he had sat on each of the last seven Mondays.

The very first decision announced by the Court was *Green v. United States*. The majority opinion had been written by Mr. Justice Black but was read by Mr. Justice Douglas because of Black's absence. The opinion ran thirteen and a half printed pages and was joined in by Warren, Brennan, and Whittaker.

These five Justices reversed the conviction, holding that Green had twice been put in jeopardy for the same offense in violation of the Fifth Amendment.

"The underlying idea" of the double jeopardy clause, wrote Mr. Justice Black, "is that the State with all its resources and power should not be allowed to make repeated attempts to convict an individual for an alleged offense, thereby subjecting him to embarrassment, expense and ordeal and compelling him to live in a continuing state of anxiety and insecurity, as well as enhancing the possibility that even though innocent he may be found guilty." Green, he said, was "in direct peril of being convicted and punished for first degree murder at his first trial." The jury refused to convict on that charge. Therefore, Green could not be tried on it again. To say that Green "waived" his protection against double jeopardy by appealing the second degree conviction would be to say that a man cannot appeal an erroneous conviction unless he is "willing to barter his constitutional protection."

As for the Trono decision, said Mr. Justice Black, it should not be "extended beyond its peculiar factual setting to control the present case." The Trono decision had interpreted a statutory provision and not the Constitution; it dealt with the Philippines, which had legal procedures alien to the common law, and even then, "a majority of the Court was unable to agree on any common ground." Thus Blow's unique argument—that the Trono decision was not really a decision of the Court—had prevailed.

Mr. Justice Black concluded: "The right not to be placed in jeopardy more than once for the same offense is a vital safeguard in our society, one that was dearly won and one that should continue to be highly valued. If such great constitutional protections are given a narrow, grudging application they are deprived of much of their significance. We do not feel that *Trono* or any other decision by this Court compels us to forego the conclusion that the second trial of Green for first degree murder was contrary to both the letter and spirit of the Fifth Amendment."

Mr. Justice Frankfurter's dissent outlasted the majority opinion by eight pages. He was joined by Justices Burton, Clark, and Harlan (who thus was at odds with his grandfather in the Trono case). Justice Frankfurter reviewed at length the origin and development of the double jeopardy clause. He said that Trono directly controlled Green's case, and that the majority was ignoring precedent. He pointed out that the jury in the first trial had not found Green innocent of first degree murder but had only remained silent on the subject.

He went so far as to say that the jury had been given an opportunity by Judge McLaughlin "for compromise and lenity" and, by finding Green guilty of both arson and *second* degree murder, had reached "an irrational verdict."

Thus, the Supreme Court, by a vote of five to four, reversed the conviction. Green was a free man. He had already served his sentence for arson. He could no longer be tried for second degree murder, because the Court of Appeals had ruled that there was no evidence of second degree murder—it was first degree or nothing. And now the Supreme Court had ruled that he could not be tried for first degree murder, because the jury at the first trial had already acquitted him of that offense.

From hindsight, the interesting man in the case was Justice Whittaker. The votes of Black and Douglas were in line with their often-expressed desire for a broad application of the Fifth Amendment, and the votes of Warren and Brennan now seem in keeping with their later approach to these problems. But Whittaker developed along different lines.

Born on a farm near the little town of Troy, Kansas, he had begun breathing the law before he was out of high school. He worked as an office boy for a Kansas City law firm and in the late afternoons and nights attended the Kansas City School of Law (now the University of Kansas City). At age twenty-two he was admitted to the Missouri bar and in a few years became a junior partner, and then a partner, in the firm for which he had once been office boy. He specialized in trial work for about ten years, and then for twelve years concentrated on appellate work and counseling. His career as a judge was rapid and straight up. A Republican, he was appointed by President Eisenhower to the District Court in 1954, the Court of Appeals in 1956, and the Supreme Court in 1957.

On the Supreme Court, he tended to side with Frankfurter and Harlan on those questions that involved the criminal law, and to keep strictly to proper lines of criminal procedure. It must be recalled that the Green case was one of the first on which Whittaker sat when he came to the Court, and the awful specter of death hung over the result. Who can gauge the psychological impact of arriving at Olympus and being asked to decide, as one of his first acts, whether an elderly man should be electrocuted? It is probably safe to assume that it was Whittaker, as much as any other Justice, who wanted reargument in the case so as to help him resolve his many doubts.

It is in this area—the area of what persuades the mind—that the work of the Court becomes most fascinating. Nine men are presented with identical facts and arguments. They arrive at opposite conclusions. Why? Surely there is no single reason but rather a plethora of pulls and tugs and crosscurrents, a series of reactions built on heredity, environment, experience, mentality, and judgment. Into this rumbling, bubbling pot is thrown the element of death. A man's life is at stake. An adverse decision rendered, and the man suffers inhuman agonies until he is finally strapped into a metal chair and convulsively jarred until his heart stops. There is no recanting then. No second thoughts or hindsight or better judgment. There is no bringing him back.

This is the one factor that distinguishes the death case from every other. The factor of death cannot be measured, but it is there. It wears thin the judge's nerves and makes him hate his job. And in the close case, the case in which all the elements but one seem to balance out, the fact of death can be decisive.

Green's timing was undesignedly perfect. If he had arrived at the Supreme Court a few months earlier, he would have been faced with Reed and Minton rather than Brennan and Whittaker, and his reception no doubt would have been less cordial than it was. On the other hand, if he had arrived a few months later, after Whittaker had more fully adjusted to the demands and rigors of the Court, perhaps he would have lost Whittaker's crucial vote.

George Blow, the most active of the defense counsel, had

spent over three and a half years on the case. He had argued it on five separate occasions—three times in the Court of Appeals and twice in the Supreme Court—and had participated in one of the two trials. He had written or helped write innumerable briefs, reply briefs, supplemental memoranda, motions, and other papers. As is common at the bar, where attorneys are appointed without compensation to defend indigent prisoners, Blow received nothing for his services. Nothing tangible, that is. As for Charley Ford, he posthumously revived his record of never having had a client go to the chair.

It was a happy Christmas for Green. He was free, and he was a prophet. Hadn't he told Judge Letts, "I can only thank God we have got a Court of Appeals and we have a Supreme Court"? And, of course, on top of it all, this timid man had become one of the most daring of gamblers. He had gambled his life, and won.*

*Green lived peacefully in Washington until 1961, when he died. As a veteran, he was buried in Arlington National Cemetery.

3

If at First

The cell in the jailhouse at New Iberia, Louisiana, was square, drab, and depressing. There was a putrid smell about it, the legacy of a few addicts and countless alcoholics. A pipe leading to the seatless toilet leaked, and the water angled off to find shelter where the bars fitted into the cement floor.

The boy in the cell looked older than seventeen, but seventeen was all he was. He appeared lanky, bony, and angular, with his hundred and fifty pounds stretched out over a five foot ten inch frame. His feet and hands were big, out of proportion to the rest of him. He wore his thick black hair cropped close, and a large, well-formed lower lip, set off by ears which stood out from his head, made the smile sardonic, not necessarily expressive of his nature but merely twisted into shape by the natural curve of the shy and awkward mouth.

His name was Willie Francis. He may even have been christened that. But in any case, everyone knew him as Willie.

The newspapers said he was an illiterate Negro. As a matter of fact, he could read and write, and he thought clearly, if not entirely in an organized manner. But he suffered from one defect which caused him untold agony. He stuttered.

It was May 2, 1946. A Thursday night. Outside, the townfolks were thinking ahead to the weekend and listening to the radio news of Mr. Justice Jackson's cross-examination of the Nazi war criminals in Nuremberg. Willie was thinking ahead to the weekend too, but he wasn't interested in news from abroad. His was a tight little world—no longer, no broader, no higher than his cell. This will be a mighty short weekend, he thought.

Gilbert Ozeene padded up to the cell and looked through, but Willie, standing at the barred window, hardly noticed. Ozeene was sheriff of Iberia Parish, an oddly shaped Louisiana "county" fronting on Vermillion Bay, just off the Gulf of Mexico.

"Would you like anything to eat or drink, Willie?"

Willie looked away from the window and nodded. He said he wanted something good to eat.

The sheriff went out and bought the best steak he could find and some ice cream and cake. Willie took the food gratefully and sat on the cot with the tin plate balanced on his knees. He solemnly ate every bit of the food, staring at it and thinking about it to keep his mind away from the weekend that wouldn't happen. He found he could cut his thoughts off from the following day—since he was not clear as to exactly what would take place—easier than he could from the indelible events of the last year and a half.

He remembered what a stir had been created in St. Martinville back in November, 1944, when Andrew Thomas had been found murdered. Willie was only fifteen at the time. St. Martinville, with its population of about four thousand, was eight miles due north of New Iberia and over the line in St. Martin Parish. Andrew Thomas was a popular St. Martinville druggist who lived on the main highway. He had come home from work one night and put his car away. As he stepped away from the garage, he was shot five times by someone standing in the shadows. One bullet crashed through his right eye, two more entered under his right armpit, and the last two struck the center of his back as he spun around. When the police found him stretched out in the driveway, a watch and a wallet containing four dollars were missing from his clothes.

Harold Resweber, sheriff of St. Martin Parish, working closely with the state police, searched fruitlessly for months, following up every hunch, every tip, every possible thread that might lead to the killer. A neighbor of Thomas's said the shots had wakened her, and she had seen a car parked in front of Thomas's house with its lights on, but no trace of the car could be found. Resweber's one break came when a city employee, clearing away the tall grass a short distance from Thomas's house, found a pistol which had been stolen from the car of one of Resweber's deputies a few months before.

In the meantime, an unrelated search had been going on in Port Arthur, Texas, two hundred miles southwest of St. Martinville. The chief of police of Port Arthur and several of his men were waiting at a railroad station to meet a man they suspected of carrying illegal narcotics. When the man alighted from the train, the police followed him. The man saw them, dropped his suitcase, and ran. As the police approached the suitcase, they saw a second man, a Negro, crouched under a nearby tree. Thinking the Negro might be an accomplice of the dope peddler, they picked him up and took him in for questioning.

The Negro identified himself as Willie Francis of St. Martinville, Louisiana. In his pocket was a wallet which had belonged to Andrew Thomas. After a brief interrogation, Willie stammered out a confession that he had assaulted and robbed an elderly white man in a Port Arthur apartment just a few days before. And in his confession, Willie also admitted that months ago he had killed and robbed Andrew Thomas in St. Martinville.

The Port Arthur police had heard of the Thomas murder. While Willie's confession was being reduced to paper for him to sign, the chief of police was calling Sheriff Resweber of St. Martin Parish to tell him that Thomas's killer was in custody.

Resweber immediately drove to Port Arthur with several deputies. Because of the more serious nature of the St. Martinville crime, the Port Arthur police gave up their custody of Willie, retaining only a warrant against him in case he was later released, and turned him over to Resweber. Resweber and his deputies, with Willie in tow, began the return trip to St. Martinville.

On the way back, Willie confessed again. He said he had waited two or three hours for Thomas, whom he knew slightly, and had shot him five times with a pistol that he had stolen from a deputy sheriff's car. He pointed out to Resweber the grassy area where he had thrown the pistol after the shooting. It was the same spot in which the deputy's pistol had already been found. Willie told Resweber he had taken Thomas's watch to a jewelry store in New Iberia and sold it for five dollars. Willie also gave the sheriff the names of two Negroes who he said were implicated in the crime.

Resweber began checking out the details of the story. He could find no Negroes with the names Willie had given him, and he concluded that this part of the story was fictitious. The pistol was sent to the Federal Bureau of Investigation in Washington along with a bullet recovered from Thomas's body, but the package was lost in the mails and never recovered. Resweber took Willie to the jewelry store in New Iberia where the watch had been sold, but the jeweler could not remember Willie or the watch. Several days later, however, the jeweler found among his bric-a-brac a watch case with the murdered man's initials on the back.

The deputy's pistol had been encased in a holster at the time it was stolen, and Resweber kept pressing Willie as to what he had done with the holster. Finally, a few weeks before his trial, Willie led Resweber to a railroad culvert behind Thomas's house where he said he had tossed it. Working with hoes, Resweber's men dug out all of the accumulated dirt under the culvert and discovered at last a holster with the same leafy design as that owned by the deputy. The case against Willie Francis was complete.

His trial for murder lasted three days. Since no one had witnessed the crime and the pistol had been lost in the mails, the state's evidence consisted almost entirely of Willie's two confessions—the written one signed in Texas and the oral one given to Sheriff Resweber. A dozen witnesses appeared for the prosecution to testify as to the voluntary nature of these confessions. Willie's two court-appointed attorneys called no witnesses in his behalf. The neighbor who had seen the car parked in front of Thomas's house did not testify. No transcript of the trial was taken, no request for a change of venue (site of trial) was entered, no motion for a new trial was made, and no appeal was filed. Just a week after his indictment, a jury found Willie Francis guilty of murder. The next day he was sentenced to death by electrocution, and five months later, Governor James H. Davis signed a mandatory death warrant, calling for Willie's execution on Friday, May 3, 1946, between the hours of noon and 3 P.M.

Sheriff Resweber was not taking any chances on mob rule. He transferred custody of Willie over to his friend Sheriff Ozeene for safekeeping in the New Iberia jail until the day of the execution.

And now it was already May 2, and Willie was finishing the biggest steak of his life and scooping up the last of the ice cream. That was a good meal. He had heard that a man was entitled to a last meal of his choice, and this had been a good one. Even his nervousness did not prevent him from enjoying it.

He put the tin plate on the floor and stretched out on the cot. Well, he thought, one thing for sure. Seventeen was pretty young to die.

Sheriff Ozeene came by to say good night, and the two men chatted briefly on either side of the bars. Willie ended the conversation by saying he guessed he was ready to die. Ozeene left, and Willie lay down on the hard cot. He slept fitfully. Before he realized it, a grey shadow replaced the inky black of the cell. Ozeene brought him breakfast, but this time Willie was not very hungry.

Soon the sheriff and several of his deputies came to Willie's cell and told him it was time to go back to St. Martinville for the electrocution. As they left, Sheriff Ozeene noticed for the first time some writing laboriously etched on the wall of the cell. It read: "I kill Andrew Thomas and today he is lying in a grave and I am not a killer but I wonder where I am going to be lying and in what kind of grave I don't know."

The men drove mostly in silence during the eight-mile trip to the St. Martin Parish jail in St. Martinville. Willie, handcuffed in the back seat of the sedan, looked out the windows at the familiar sights but said very little. He and his brothers had been raised in this area. Willie had left school early to work at odd jobs—in a food products plant, in a garage, and at various places around town. He had been in a few scrapes during his early teens, but nothing serious until the Thomas affair. He had liked St. Martinville. Now he looked at the approaching town without really seeing it, and as the sedan swung around the courthouse square, where Willie had often played as a child, and pulled up in front of the town's main building, which served the parish as both courthouse and jail, Willie seemed hardly conscious of his surroundings. He was ushered inside, where Sheriff Resweber took charge and led him into a small cell, indistinguishable from the one he had occupied in New Iberia for the last seven months.

Unlike some states, Louisiana executes its citizens "on the spot," so to speak. Instead of transporting condemned criminals to a central prison where a permanent death cell is maintained, Louisiana sends its equipment about the state, executing criminals in the various jails where they happen to be held. The portable, hardwood electric chair is carried from town to town in a truck operated out of the Louisiana State Penitentiary at Angola.

The truck had arrived in St. Martinville the night before and now stood parked at the side of the courthouse with the electric chair still inside. The chair had already been tested by the penitentiary's chief electrician and found in perfect working order. As was his custom, the chief electrician intended to remain at Angola and send an assistant to take charge of the actual electrocution. In this instance, the assistant would be a prison inmate, Vincent Venezia. The man actually in charge of the chair would be Captain E. Foster, a regular member of the penitentiary staff.

Normally, the warden of the penitentiary accompanied the portable electric chair on its rounds. On this occasion, however, he stayed behind to entertain Governor Davis, who happened to be calling at his home in Angola.

The inmate, Venezia, arrived at St. Martinville shortly after 8:30 A.M. He joined Captain Foster at the truck, and the two of them, assisted by courthouse personnel, began unloading the portable electric chair and a large panel of switches and wires. The chair and panel were carried into the courthouse and placed in a kind of anteroom—almost a hallway—where the execution would take place. The room was bare, with cells ranged around it and emptying into it on three sides. The chair was placed in the middle of the room and the instrument panel laid nearby. The chair was so heavy that it did not have to be screwed into the floor. Venezia began attaching the wire leading from the chair to the panel and then ran several wires from the panel out through the window and on to the lawn outside. He went outside and attached these wires to the penitentiary truck, which carried its own generator, serving electric current directly to the chair inside the courthouse.

When he had completed the rather complicated wiring procedures, Venezia set the generator voltage at 2500 and tested his ammeters, A.C. and D.C. He ran the generator for about five minutes to make certain that everything was in working order. It was 11 A.M. before he and Captain Foster were able to relax and enjoy a smoke.

Willie was being prepared for the ordeal. Another inmate shaved all of the thick hair from his head and the smoother hair from his wrists and legs. Willie did not protest. He remained quiet, his mouth hanging open a bit, his large eyes looking straight ahead.

While Willie was being prepared, his father arrived at the jail in a hearse carrying a wooden coffin. The coffin was unloaded and carried inside, where it would be ready as soon as Willie had been pronounced dead by the coroner. A man across the street from the courthouse saw the father "walk frantically and stupidly around like a drunk man." Several curious bystanders began to gather about the courthouse square.

Just before noon, the Reverend L. Maurice Rousseve, the chaplain who would officiate at the execution, arrived at the courthouse and was immediately ushered into Willie's cell. He spoke in soft tones, and Willie stuttered back a few words. The priest decided that the boy was resigned to his fate.

Precisely at noon, Sheriff Resweber and his deputies opened the cell door and told Willie it was time. Willie got shakily to his feet, looked once at the Reverend Rousseve, and walked out. The small group moved self-consciously together to the nearby anteroom which had been converted into an execution chamber. About a dozen men were present, only a few of whom Willie knew. Four of them had been appointed by Sheriff Resweber as official witnesses of the execution. Captain Foster, in charge of the chair, stood in the center to supervise the preparations, while Venezia waited outside by the truck. Sheriff Ozeene, Sheriff Resweber, a few of their deputies, and a state police captain milled about inside, seeing to last-minute details. Two Negro priests watched uncomfortably. The coroner of St. Martin Parish, the same man who had performed an autopsy on the murdered man, waited off to one side to pronounce Willie dead. Another doctor was also present, as required by law.

The condemned boy and the Reverend Rousseve entered the anteroom close together. Willie hypnotically surveyed the chair, oblivious of the curious stares of the onlookers. He was led to the chair and seated. Deputies began strapping down his arms and legs. It took a few minutes to make sure the straps were secure; they had to withstand the strain of the body when the current slammed through it.

Captain Foster placed a gauze dipped in salt water around Willie's head to help speed the electric current. The charge would dry the gauze and burn the covered area of the head. Electrodes were attached to Willie's left leg and to his head over the gauze. Wires were connected. Finally, Captain Foster walked to the window and signaled to Venezia that everything was ready to go. Venezia had the generator going, and his gauge checked out. By now, a large crowd had gathered around the truck, some drawn by the deafening roar of the generator and others by their knowledge of the event scheduled to take place inside.

In the jail, the Reverend Rousseve stepped up to the electric chair and administered the last rites of the church to Willie. He held up a cross, and Willie kissed it. The priest stepped back, and Sheriff Resweber leaned close to the boy to ask if he had anything to say. Willie remained silent, staring straight ahead.

The sheriff took a black hood and placed it over Willie's head, covering his eyes but leaving his mouth free, with a small slit at nose level to allow him to breathe.

The sheriff stepped back and nodded to Captain Foster. The captain checked the dial on his instrument panel once more—it registered at the proper level—and in a quiet voice that seemed unconscionably loud in the complete silence of the crowded room, said, "Good-by Willie."

Willie did not answer, and Captain Foster, with a quick downward motion, threw the switch.

For a fraction of a second, nothing happened. Then Willie jumped. He strained against the straps. He groaned.

But even those who were witnessing their first execution knew something was wrong. Willie's body, though arched, was obviously not at the point of death. Captain Foster, all in one motion, frantically threw the switch off and then on again. Those closest to Willie heard him strain out the words, "Let me breathe." Captain Foster yelled out the window at Venezia to give him more juice. The startled Venezia yelled back that he was giving him all he had. His gauge showed that electricity was being generated, and he could not understand what the difficulty was.

Only a few seconds had passed, and yet the horrified spectators inside the jail felt as if they had stood transfixed for minutes. As they stared at Willie, they saw his lips puff out and swell like those of a pilot undergoing the stress of supersonic speeds. His body tensed and stretched in such catatonic movements that the chair, which had not been anchored to the floor, suddenly shifted, sliding a fraction of an inch along the floor.

"Take it off. Let me breathe."

The agonizing words spewed out from between the puffed lips. They roused Sheriff Resweber into action. He signaled to Captain Foster, who by now knew that his apparatus would not kill Willie Francis. He threw the switch back into an upright position. All in all, about two minutes had now passed since the switch had been thrown, and some of those present realized they had hardly breathed during the entire period.

The hood was lifted from Willie's head, the electrodes were removed from his head and left leg, and the straps were unbuckled all around. Although obviously shaken, Willie was able to get to his feet by himself. He was taken by Sheriff

Ozeene into an adjoining room, where they were joined by the coroner.

Ozeene asked Willie if he was hurt. Willie said no, but that the electricity had "tickled" him. The coroner, listening to Willie's chest through his stethoscope, heard a fast heart beat but otherwise no unusual symptoms. He said nothing to Willie, and Willie did not speak to him.

When the coroner had gone, Ozeene asked Willie if he wanted any water, but the boy, sitting hunched over on a cot, shook his head. The Reverend Rousseve entered the room and stayed about twenty minutes.

In the meantime, Sheriff Resweber had taken Captain Foster to his office in another part of the jail, and Foster was placing a call to the warden's home in Angola. The warden answered and, as soon as he learned the nature of the call, said he would let Foster speak directly to Governor Davis. The governor listened patiently to Foster's explanation of what had happened, decided that a reprieve from an immediate second attempt at electrocution was in order, and told Foster to take Willie back to the New Iberia jail. The governor and the warden agreed that another date for the execution should be set at once, but when the governor started to fix the following Saturday, May 11, for the new attempt, the warden informed him that another execution was scheduled for Leesville on that day, and he could not handle two at one time. The governor therefore moved the date back one day to Friday, May 10, and personally wrote out a temporary reprieve and a second death warrant.

Captain Foster returned to the room where Willie was resting and told Ozeene of the governor's decision. Ozeene and his deputies took Willie out of the cell and into the hallway where Sheriff Resweber was waiting to ask how his prisoner was doing. Willie said simply, "The Lord was with me that time," and the group moved quickly out into the sunlight.

The waiting townspeople, excited by those mysterious signals from Foster to Venezia, were astonished to see the man who supposedly had just been electrocuted come striding out between two deputies. He was hustled into the sedan, which roared away, heading north from the courthouse square.

Willie was driven the eight miles back to New Iberia and placed in the same cell he had occupied the night before—the cell he had thought he would never see again. Though nervous and shaken, he ate a full lunch. Ozeene checked on him at five o'clock and again at seven o'clock that evening, but by then, the story of what had happened at St. Martinville had reached the press, and reporters were arriving to take pictures. When they left, Willie tried to sleep, but that night and for two nights thereafter he was extremely nervous, starting up in his sleep and breaking out into sudden swaths of perspiration. Then he became calmer and settled back into the routine life of the jail.

The miracle that saved Willie Francis from death caught the public's imagination. The story was featured all across the country, and letters began pouring in, commiserating with Willie and admonishing the governor not to send the boy through this experience again. Willie read all of the letters delivered to his cell and even tried to answer most of them. It was a good way to pass time.

Willie's father was a farmer who eked out the family income on poor and uncharitable land. He began asking where he could find a lawyer to help his son. A friend advised him to go see Bertrand de Blanc, a thirty-five-year-old graduate of the Louisiana State Law School who had just returned from three years in the service and had hung out his shingle next to the jail. The father went to see the lawyer and explained to him his impoverished circumstances, but de Blanc said he would do what he could. His first task, he knew, was to delay the new execution date so that he could file appropriate papers in court. He accomplished this when the state's lieutenant governor, acting during the governor's absence, issued a thirty-day stay of execution.

De Blanc now had to face up to the legal problems confronting him. Two methods of proceeding were open. He could go to the courts, or he could appeal to the governor and the State Board of Pardons.

The route through the courts was beset with difficulties. His argument against another attempt at an execution would have to be based upon some principle recognized in the law. Since there had been no appeal from the conviction, he felt he could not raise at this late stage a number of issues relating to the trial itself, but instead would have to argue that regardless of whether or not the conviction had been valid originally, the unsuccessful attempt at electrocution violated the defendant's constitutional rights and vitiated either the conviction itself or at least the sentence of death. This would require some legal tightrope walking, and he doubted whether the Louisiana courts would listen to him.

His route by way of the governor and the Board of Pardons was more inviting. The argument here could be based upon more equitable grounds. The board and the governor had discretion to commute a sentence for whatever reasons they deemed sufficient but were not required to hold either the conviction or the original sentence illegal, void, or in any way deficient. De Blanc felt that regardless of the obstacles in the way of a strict legal argument, the equities were certainly with him.

Nevertheless, he decided to proceed first through the Louisiana courts. His reasoning was that after the courts turned him down, the choice would lie squarely in the hands of the executive branch, and the board and governor could not then avoid their duty by arguing that de Blanc should first pursue other remedies. Therefore, he petitioned for a writ of habeas corpus in the same court that had convicted Willie. He argued that the state and Federal constitutions had been violated in two respects. First, Willie had once been put in jeopardy of losing his life, and to attempt to electrocute him again would constitute double jeopardy. Secondly, to put Willie back in the chair after his agonizing experience would be such cruel and unusual punishment as to violate due process of law. The trial court denied the petition.

De Blanc immediately filed papers in the Louisiana Supreme Court. Because the case was so unique, he was not certain precisely which method of appeal he should follow, so he filed four different writs (certiorari, mandamus, prohibition, and habeas corpus) just to make sure. The Louisiana Supreme Court, without a hearing, denied all four of them. The court concluded that it had no authority to act. Since the trial and the sentencing had been entirely regular, there was nothing the appellate court could do simply because something had gone wrong with the execution. The only authority to grant a pardon or commute a sentence was vested in the governor, who in turn could act only upon recommendation of the Board of Pardons.

The case was now in the posture de Blanc had anticipated. The courts had placed the responsibility squarely in the laps of the board and governor. With only a week left before the execution, de Blanc requested a special meeting of the Board of Pardons in New Orleans. At the same time, however, he looked ahead to a possible denial by the board of his plea for clemency, in which event only one course remained open—an appeal to the United States Supreme Court. Through a friend, he contacted a Washington attorney, J. Skelly Wright, and asked him to prepare appropriate papers in the event that resort to the Supreme Court became necessary.

Wright (since appointed to Federal Appeals Court) was the same age as de Blanc, thirty-five, and was also a native Louisianian, although he practiced law in the nation's capital. A graduate in philosophy and law from Loyola University in

New Orleans, he had become a member of the bar at twenty-three, had entered the United States Attorney's Office, and had begun handling all types of civil and criminal cases for the United States, including the trial of some of the Louisiana scandal cases of 1940 and the sabotage cases of 1941. He had entered the coast guard in 1942, done a tour of duty on a sub-chaser, and then been assigned to Europe for work in connection with the transportation of material to the Continent. After two and a half years in service, he had returned to the United States Attorney's Office as first assistant and had prosecuted a number of war fraud cases. He resigned in May, 1946, to enter private practice in Washington, and this is where de Blanc found him. Wright said he would be happy to prepare the necessary papers for the Supreme Court.

An extensive correspondence developed between de Blanc and Wright, as they attempted to correlate their efforts. De Blanc was informed by the lieutenant governor that if a petition were filed in the United States Supreme Court prior to the Board of Pardons hearing in New Orleans, the board would not act until the Supreme Court disposed of the case. Therefore, de Blanc requested Wright not to file his petition in the Supreme Court until the board reached its decision.

On May 31, 1946, one week before the new date of execution, the Board of Pardons met in New Orleans. Captain Foster and Venezia, the inmate, both gave their stories. They told of setting up the chair, of testing it, and of their attempts at electrocution. Although Foster was not an electrician and Venezia had not been present in the jail, both gave their opinion that no electricity could have passed through Willie's body. They pointed out that the chair had never failed to operate before or since May 3 and that in fact it had been used successfully the following day in another part of the state. Venezia said that he had carefully investigated the chair after the mishap and had discovered a loose wire running from the panel to the truck. It was his opinion that the electricity generated by the truck had run directly into the ground and had failed to reach Willie. Foster agreed. He said Willie's protruding lips could have been caused by the hood being fastened too tightly around his head, and the chair could have shifted simply as the result of Willie moving his feet.

Sheriffs Resweber and Ozeene explained briefly the history of the Andrews murder and Willie's arrest, and the coroner told of his examination of Willie after the attempted execution. The warden related the phone call which resulted in the reprieve. He also said he had received a letter from the general manager of the Texas prison system, telling of an execution that failed in Texas in 1938. On that occasion, one John Vaughn was led to the electric chair and strapped in place. The electrical system, however, totally failed to function. The governor granted two successive reprieves, and one court granted a restraining order against a further attempt, but the judge who had originally sentenced Vaughn dissolved the restraining order, and Vaughn was subsequently electrocuted.

The district attorney who had prosecuted Willie's case summed up his position before the board: "How can we expect [juries] to convict men to pay their debts to society when, afterwards, what they have done is undone by another authority of law having the power to do so." And he warned the board, "There is another side to this case. I don't want to refer to an unpleasant question, but those are facts that happen. We have repeatedly known in the past, unfortunately, of lynchings going on after crimes are committed. The only way and safest way to keep that from happening is to bring to justice and punish, according to each case, the guilty party. Society looks to us to do our duty, and I know that you gentlemen are not going to be carried away by sentiment in this case and that you are going to carry the law as far as it is possible to do so."

Several persons appeared on Willie's behalf. Perhaps the most effective was a white priest who belonged to a religious order called "The Holy Ghost Fathers" and who had prepared Willie for the execution during his seven months in the New Iberia jail. There was also a message from the boy's bishop, who wrote: "The torture of mind and body through which Willie Francis, St. Martinville negro, has already passed entitles him in my humble opinion to reprieve and commutation of sentence. It would be most unfortunate if the impression were created that there is no justice or mercy for a negro in Louisiana."

De Blanc made a detailed and eloquent statement on Willie's behalf. He presented six affidavits from witnesses who had seen Willie when the switch was thrown and who thought that electricity had swept through his body. As de Blanc summed it up, "Everything was done to electrocute this boy up to and including the pulling of the switch and the passing of electricity into his body. He died mentally; his body still exists, but through no fault of his." De Blanc said this was the first time in Louisiana history that a boy as young as fifteen had committed a homicide for which he had been given the death penalty. And he added: "The main point which I wish to stress, gentlemen, is that no man should go to the chair twice. No man should suffer impending death twice. The voice of humanity and justice cries out against such an outrage. You men who compose this Honorable Body are just and sincere and I know that you will be guided only by the hand of justice. I am not asking that this boy be set free. I am only asking that his sentence be commuted from death to life imprisonment in the State Penitentiary. Is that too much to ask for a boy who has gone through the mental and physical torture that he has?"

De Blanc then cited several unique cases of his own to support his position that justice required a commutation. The first was that of John Lee of Dorset, England, in the year 1889. Lee was placed on the scaffold three times, and each time the trap failed to operate, despite the fact that when he was removed from the scaffold, his weight in sand operated the trap perfectly. After the third try, Lee was reprieved by the Home Secretary.

The second case was that of Shadrach, Meshach, and Abednego, cast into the fiery furnace by King Nebuchadnezzar for refusing to bow down to a gold statue. When the flames failed to burn them, they were pardoned and allowed to go on their way. The third case was also from the Old Testament. Daniel, refusing to obey King Darius's edict against petitioning anyone but the king, was cast into the den of lions, and the den was sealed with the king's ring. The next day Daniel was found alive and unharmed. This was considered divine intervention, and he was pardoned.

Then there was the strange case of Will Purvis, sentenced by the State of Mississippi to be hanged on February 7, 1894. Something went wrong, Purvis was not killed, and when the sheriff immediately attempted to hang him again, the crowd witnessing the event opposed it, and the condemned man was returned to jail. The governor refused to commute the sentence, and three appeals to the courts failed. A mob then rescued Purvis from jail, and he lived for some time with relatives and friends. A new governor agreed to commute his sentence to life imprisonment if he surrendered, and two years later he was pardoned altogether when the state's star witness said he could have been mistaken in his identification of Purvis. Years afterward, another man confessed to the crime, and the Mississippi legislature voted Purvis five thousand dollars as indemnity for the agony of his earlier years.

Finally, de Blanc cited the peculiar circumstances surrounding the case of Lonnie Eaton, another Louisiana Negro, who was convicted of killing a white man in December, 1917, and sentenced to be hanged. Some time after the date of the hanging, the sheriff wrote the governor that he had been "so rushed with work" that he had forgotten to hang Eaton. The governor promptly signed a commutation of Eaton's sentence from death to life imprisonment.

De Blanc paused in his recitation and surveyed the impassive faces before him. In a gentler tone, he reminded them of Willie's fine prison record, and he ventured, "I'd stake my reputation that he would make a model convict at the State Penitentiary." He pointed out that Willie's conviction rested almost entirely on his confessions, and he argued the unreliability of such confessions, citing a number of instances in which persons had confessed to crimes they had not in fact committed.

Suddenly, in the midst of this argument, de Blanc reached into his briefcase, took out a picture, and held it up before the board. It showed Willie strapped in the electric chair. Where it had come from was something of a mystery, since no one specifically remembered it having been taken during the excitement and confusion of the attempted execution. Some thought the Reverend Rousseve must have snapped it and others a police photographer, but in any case, there it was, and it served as a grim reminder of what had occurred and of the serious business before the board. Pointing to the picture and waving it before the members, de Blanc admonished them: "Look at him strapped to the chair of death, the chair that had already claimed twenty-three victims, the chair that was later to claim another victim. What chance did he think he had of surviving? Look at him, gentlemen, a beaten animal; do you think there was any hope within that brain? Here you see the picture of a human being facing death, a boy on the threshold of eternity, a picture that speaks a thousand words. Here is a boy who, were it not for a quirk of fate, was about to plunge headlong into the dark abyss of death. What thoughts ran through his mind? Is there any belligerency in that bowed head? Is there anything but humility in those dark features? Is this not a picture of total resignation?"

Then de Blanc pointed his finger at each of the three board members in turn and asked sternly: "What assurance, gentlemen, does this boy have that he will go to his death in a humane manner, quickly and painlessly? Supposing that the chair doesn't work a second time? Suppose it doesn't work the third time? That could happen; it's happened once and it could happen again. What is this going to be? An experiment in electricity? An experiment in modern forms of torture? An experiment in cruelty? Is the State of Louisiana trying to outdo the Caesars, the Hitlers, the Tojos, the Nazis, the Gestapo in torture? How long does the State of Louisiana take to kill a man? If we want to make it cruel, let's do it right; let's boil him in oil. Why not burn him at the stake, or put him on the rack? Then we would be sure that by sundown he would be dead.

"Gentlemen, the whole system of capital punishment which is the policy of this State is in jeopardy because of the inhuman method in which it is being inflicted in this case. I say, without equivocation, that unless this Board sees fit to say that this boy will not suffer the torture of death again, the critics of our method of execution shall have ample ground to condemn as a whole our system of punishment.

"Gentlemen, I have traveled throughout southern Louisiana since the attempted electrocution on May 3rd, and I can say with certainty that public opinion is against this boy being electrocuted again. If this boy goes back to the chair, they will say that the one and only reason is to satisfy the bestial lust for blood, to satisfy this cry for revenge. If he goes back to the chair they will say that it is nothing short of murder.

"People all over America have written to me expressing their sincere belief that it was the hand of God that stopped the electrocution. They have expressed their horror and disgust at a second attempt. I say in all sincerity that I believe that Willie Francis was not killed because it was not meant that he should be killed, that there was some reason, perhaps not explainable, but still there was a reason in the design of Fate that this boy should live. Fate acts in strange ways. I, for one, would want no part in his re-execution. When I meet my God face to face, I would not want the stain of his blood on my hands."

Then, in ringing tones, he concluded: "You, gentlemen, are the heart and soul of the State of Louisiana in this case. Men and women everywhere are asking: What will Louisiana do in this case? Will they return this boy to the chair? Will Louisiana be fair to this Negro? A boy's life is in your hands. I have done my duty. All remedies have been exhausted—the case is in your hands."

The board, to a man, was unmoved by the plea. Three days after the hearing, de Blanc wired Wright in Washington: "Board refused to commute sentence. File petition and wire me." Wright was prepared with his petition asking the Supreme Court to hear the case, and he filed it the next day. In view of the fact that Willie was due to be electrocuted in three days, the Court immediately issued a stay of execution until it could decide whether to hear the case. At the same time, Governor Davis was also issuing a reprieve "until further order" so that Willie would have time to take his case to the high court.

The following Monday, June 10, the Court handed down a brief order. Wright was immediately notified by phone. Sadly, he wired de Blanc: "Supreme Court denied writ Francis case today." And he wrote de Blanc the same day that he was "consoled by the fact that we did everything in our power to be of assistance." De Blanc told Willie's parents that the Supreme Court had refused to hear the case and then visited Willie in jail to explain that all avenues had been covered, that there seemed to be no further hope, that there was nowhere else to turn. Willie was badly shaken, as was de Blanc. For a long while, the youngster sat quietly with his attorney, his mind now filled not with the unknown, as before, but rather with a vivid awareness of the horrible experience he had already undergone and would have to undergo again. After a while, he rallied and told de Blanc he would see the reporters who were clamoring to obtain a statement from him. He told them: "I'm praying harder than ever. Got myself a new prayer book. All I can do is wait." The governor, in the meantime, prepared to set a new date for the execution.

The next day, Tuesday the 11th, there came to light an occurrence virtually unparalleled in Supreme Court history. A horrified clerk at the Supreme Court discovered that a terrible error had been made, that due to a clerical mistake the Willie Francis case had been designated "denied" instead of "granted." The Court had in fact decided to hear Willie's case, and Mr. Justice Black had even ordered that "execution and enforcement of the sentence of death imposed upon petitioner, Willie Francis . . . be, and the same is hereby, stayed pending further order of this Court."

As soon as he had discovered his mistake and had discussed it with the Chief Justice, the clerk phoned Wright and Governor Davis and notified reporters. Wright immediately called de Blanc, even as the news services were sending the story out over the wires. By the time de Blanc reached the jail with candy, cigarettes, and magazines for his client, reporters were already converging on the scene, and they were soon allowed to talk to Willie. They found him sitting on the cot of his cell, chewing a nickel candy bar. Asked for his reaction to the news, Willie said, "That's funny, sort of. I was expecting good news yesterday, and I got bad. And now when I'm expecting bad news, it's good." He smiled. "I feel pretty good."

Willie said he guessed his father, who had visited him the day before, would be glad. When the reporters asked what his father had said during the visit, Willie stammered, "I don't rightly know. I got an awful short memory. I forgets quick." The reporters pressed him as to whether he would be content with life imprisonment if he were lucky enough to have the death sentence commuted. On this point, Willie was neither reticent nor forgetful, but adamant. "A life in prison would be a lot better than that chair."

De Blanc was jubilant. He told reporters he was "tickled to death"—a macabre though unintentional pun on Willie's plight. "I told Willie that he must pray hard, that his case was before the highest court, and Willie said he had a new prayer book and would do so. I think there is something of Divine Providence in this case."

The Supreme Court had acted at the very end of its term, so that oral argument in the case of *Louisiana ex rel. Francis v. Resweber* could not be heard until the following fall. In the spiraling, undulating Louisiana heat of that summer, Willie Francis waited. The public furor over his predicament died down; his mail lessened to a few miscellaneous notes. A magazine, *The World's Messenger*, had established a "Willie Francis Defense Fund" which still drew a little money, from ten cents to five dollars from each of dozens of contributors around the country, but on the whole the public lost interest.

One interesting letter, however, arrived at the Supreme Court addressed simply "To the Attorney for the man who was saved from the electric chair by a faulty electrode, c/o Clerk of the Supreme Court of the U. S., Washington, D. C." It was duly forwarded to Wright. The letter, from a man in Williamsburg, Virginia, began:

> Do you remember these lines from *Robinson Crusoe* which may be of some help to you in your case? "I was now landed, and safe on shore, and began to look up and thank God that my life was saved, in a case wherein there was some minutes before scarce any room to hope. I believe it is impossible to express, to the life, what the ecstasies and transports of the soul are when it is so saved, as I may say, out of the very grave; and I do not wonder now at that custom, when a malefactor, who has the halter about his neck, is tied up, and just going to be turned off, and has a reprieve brought to him—I say, I do not wonder that they bring a surgeon with it, to let him bleed that very moment they tell him of it, that the

surprise may not drive the animal spirits from the heart, and overwhelm him, 'For sudden joys, like griefs, confound at first.'

De Blanc and Wright finished their brief and filed it with the Court. In addition to the arguments already advanced by de Blanc, Wright added two additional ones so that every possible avenue of escape would be probed. He argued that Willie had been denied equal protection of the law—that is, he had been treated differently by the state from its other citizens—because Willie was not put to death mercifully but instead had to face two electrocutions. Wright also argued that Willie's trial had been such "a farce and a travesty" that even though there had been no appeal, the Supreme Court could now recognize a denial of due process. But his chief argument remained the one based upon the Eighth Amendment, which provides succinctly: "Excessive bail shall not be required, nor excessive fines imposed, nor cruel and unusual punishments inflicted." What are "cruel and unusual punishments"? Only a few times in its history had the Supreme Court attempted to deal with this provision, which originated in an Act of Parliament of 1688. The Court had clearly established that an electrocution properly carried out was not in itself such a cruel and unusual punishment as to violate the Constitution, but beyond that, little had been decided which aided Wright in his argument. He could only reason from logic that for the State of Louisiana to put a defendant through the agonies of electrocution not once, but twice, was so cruel, so unusual, that the Constitution prohibited it.

Right up until the time of the argument, the two lawyers were thinking of new ideas and reviewing old ones. At one point, de Blanc wired Wright: "To counteract any possible suppositions on the part of the Court that it is impossible to survive electrocution it has been suggested to me that the citation of actual certified hospital cases on file of workmen on high powered lines who have been electrocuted and have survived might prove important." And Wright, for his part, was obtaining historical materials from such sources as the New York State Library and asking friends at law schools to look into background documents dating back to Magna Carta dealing with the "double jeopardy" and "cruel and unusual punishment" clauses.

The day of the argument was a chill, bone-crackling November 18, 1946. De Blanc flew to Washington to sit at the counsel table, but Wright made the oral presentation. He looked short, standing at the large lectern, though his heavy build lent conviction and strength to his appearance. He had curly, dark brown hair and regular features—a handsome Irish type.

He was confronted by legal difficulties which the laymen present could not very well appreciate. The so-called "double jeopardy" clause of the Fifth Amendment and the "cruel and unusual punishment" clause of the Eighth Amendment had been held not to be prohibitions directly against the states. Through a long process of interpretation in the Bill of Rights, though not directly binding on the states, they are part of that "due process of law" which every state as well as the Federal Government must provide its citizens. Therefore, Wright's job was to convince the Court not only that a second electrocution would constitute double jeopardy and cruel and unusual punishment but that these prohibitions were a part of the limitations of due process.

He realized that even if he had little precedent to go on, the factual situation was to his advantage. And so he drilled home the facts of the case—the long ordeal of preparing for death, the final hours, the horror of being put into the chair, the hood and straps and electrodes and wires, the final rites, and then the moment of truth itself. Yet when he began to show from the affidavits of eyewitnesses that some electricity must have reached the condemned man's body, Chief Justice Fred M. Vinson stopped him. Those affidavits, he said, were not officially part of the record and could not be relied upon. Wright tried to explain that since no hearing had been ordered in the state courts, he had been given no opportunity to create a record, and he was forced to rely on the affidavits whether officially admitted into evidence or not. Moreover, if there was any question about the facts as recited in the affidavits, the Court should at least send the case back for a factual hearing into just what did occur at the execution.

Several of the Justices asked Wright what would happen if they reversed the case. They were concerned because of the statement in the Louisiana attorney general's brief that utter confusion would result, since state officials lacked authority to impose another sentence. Francis might be held in jail indefinitely simply because the legislature had never dealt with this situation. But Wright told the Court that the solution to the problem of imposing a sentence less than death could be left to the discretion of the state; he was sure the officials could find a way once the Court ruled that the death penalty in this case was unconstitutional.

The state's case was presented by L. O. Pecot, the man who had prosecuted Willie in the trial court, and Michael E. Culligan, an assistant attorney general of the state. They argued that the Supreme Court had no jurisdiction in the case. The Louisiana courts had ruled that as a matter of state law, they could do nothing; the Supreme Court could not now rule that they must act. Sending the case back would be a futile gesture, since sole discretion to commute a sentence lay with the Board of Pardons and the governor, whom the Supreme Court could not direct to act.

It was a quiet though dramatic argument on both sides. The Justices seemed unusually subdued, perhaps under the impact of the terrible events which had already befallen Willie and the possibility that those events would be repeated if the Court failed to intervene. The spirit of the Court was almost sullen, and the Justices, straight-backed or bent forward, looked like brooding Rodin figures, black-robed and black of mood, almost resentful that this insoluble problem had been put before them.

Each "decision" Monday after the argument, Wright checked with the clerk of the Court as to whether the Justices had reached a result. And each Monday, he wired de Blanc, who waited in his office until he had received the news that as yet nothing had come down.

The opinions in the Willie Francis case were rendered on January 13, 1947, just two months after the oral argument and over two years after the murder of Andrew Thomas. There was no "opinion of the Court"—that is, a majority of the Court could not agree on any single opinion. Instead, Chief Justice Vinson and Justices Black and Jackson (who had returned from Nuremberg only a few months before the argument) joined in an opinion by Mr. Justice Reed holding that there was no constitutional bar to another attempt at executing Willie. Justices Douglas, Frank Murphy, and Wiley Rutledge joined an opinion by Mr. Justice Burton arguing that because of the cruel and unusual punishment involved in a second attempt at execution, the case should be sent back to the Louisiana courts for a factual determination of whether an electric current had passed through Willie's body. The ninth and deciding vote was cast by Mr. Justice Frankfurter, who joined in neither of the other opinions but wrote one of his own. Reluctantly, he concluded that no constitutional violation was involved.

Thus, by a vote of five to four, the Supreme Court turned down Willie's plea.

Reed's opinion acknowledged not only that this was a "unique situation" but that "So far as we are aware, this case is without precedent in any court." For purposes of the decision, he assumed, without deciding, that violation of the double jeopardy and the cruel and unusual punishment clauses would violate due process. Thus, so far as these four judges were concerned, Wright had successfully leaped his first hurdle. However, Reed then gave short shrift to the double jeopardy argument. "Our minds rebel," he said, "against permitting the same sovereignty to punish an accused twice for the same offense." But under previously decided cases, a state can obtain a new trial after conviction due to errors and try the defendant again without violating due process, and Reed could see no distinction between that situation and the one in which a state attempts a second execution after a failure of equipment.

The argument based on cruel and unusual punishment gave him considerable difficulty. "The traditional humanity of modern Anglo-American law forbids the infliction of unnecessary pain in the execution of the death sentence," he wrote, and he cited as examples such barbarisms as burning at the stake, crucifixion, breaking on the wheel, and the like. Punishments are cruel when they involve torture or a lingering death, but not simply because they involve death itself. "The fact that an unforeseeable accident prevented the prompt consummation of the sentence cannot, it seems to us, add an element of cruelty to a subsequent execution. There is no purpose to inflict unnecessary pain nor any unnecessary pain involved in the proposed execution. The situation of the unfortunate victim of this accident is just as though he had suffered the identical amount of mental anguish and physical pain in any other occurrence, such as, for example, a fire in the cell block. We cannot agree that the hardship imposed upon the petitioner rises to that level of hardship denounced as denial of due process because of cruelty."

Reed rejected the equal protection argument on the ground that Louisiana had not singled out Willie for unequal treatment; he had simply been the victim of an accident. And as to the suggestion that Willie had been inadequately represented at trial, Reed said that the record before the Supreme Court was too sparse to support any such contention.

To the surprise of many, Mr. Justice Black joined in this opinion. Black is often described as a "liberal" and a "leading member of the civil rights bloc." His vote in this case shows how misleading labels can be when it comes to judging judges. Black is not a humanitarian in the sense often pressed by liberals. He does not decide cases on the basis of a visceral reaction. He is not moved by an argument that a state's action is an outrage against humanity, or that it shocks the conscience of civilized man. He considers himself, in fact, a strict interpreter of the Constitution, and this is what so confuses the casual observer of the Court's business. The reason he has so often been in league with Justices like Douglas, Murphy, and Rutledge and Chief Justice Warren is that he comes to their result by interpreting the language of the Bill of Rights almost literally. To oversimplify for purposes of example, a ban against restraints on free speech means to Mr. Justice Black that all speech is free—not some speech under some circumstances, but all speech under all circumstances. And so here, the difficulty for Black must have been that Willie Francis was asking him to rule, not on the basis of a precisely prescribed prohibition in the Constitution, but rather on the basis of a shocked conscience and vague, undefined principles of liberty and justice. Finding nothing in the Constitution which specifically prohibited what had occurred, he probably could not bring himself to vote with the dissenters.

If it was surprising to find Black voting with Reed, it was just as unusual to discover Mr. Justice Burton writing for Douglas, Murphy, and Rutledge. Burton, a quiet, sensitive but utterly detached judge, was normally identified with the more "conservative" element of the Court. A former mayor of Cleveland and United States senator, he was precise and undramatic but sometimes extraordinarily effective. His ten-page dissent in the Willie Francis case persuasively built fact upon fact and premise upon premise until the whole piece conveyed a strange and exciting depth of conviction. Calling the case "unique in judicial history," he admonished his brethren that "Where life is to be taken, there must be no avoidable error of law or uncertainty of fact." He said that taking life by unnecessarily cruel methods "shocks the most fundamental instincts of civilized man," as evidenced by the fact that some states have eliminated capital punishment altogether. Certainly no state could authorize capital punishment by repeated applications of electricity over a period of time until death finally resulted. The only thing that makes electrocution constitutional at all is that it is instantaneous and not "death by installments."

Thus, to Burton, the all-important consideration in determining the constitutionality of an execution is whether it is "so instantaneous and substantially painless that the punishment shall be reduced, as nearly as possible, to no more than that of death itself." He wrote: "If the state officials deliberately and intentionally had placed the relator [Francis] in the electric chair five times and, each time, had applied electric current to his body in a manner not sufficient, until the final time, to kill him, such a form of torture would rival that of burning at the stake. Although the failure of the first attempt, in the present case, was unintended, the reapplication of the electric current will be intentional. How many deliberate and intentional reapplications of electric current does it take to produce a cruel, unusual and unconstitutional punishment? While five applications would be more cruel and unusual than one, the uniqueness of the present case demonstrates that, today, two separated applications are sufficiently 'cruel and unusual' to be prohibited. If five attempts would be 'cruel and unusual,' it would be difficult to draw the line between two, three, four and five." It is interesting to note the similarity between some of this language and de Blanc's argument before the Louisiana Board of Pardons.

Burton conceded that Louisiana's highest court had ruled that the issue was an executive rather than a judicial one and that the state courts were without authority in the matter. But he said that in this respect the Louisiana court was in error; the defendant had properly pleaded facts which, if true, made a second attempt at electrocution unconstitutional. That is, he had alleged that electricity actually passed through his body. There had as yet been no court hearing to determine whether the alleged facts were true, and therefore the case should be sent back for just such a hearing. As support for his thesis, he quoted in his opinion the very affidavits which Chief Justice Vinson had chastised Wright for citing during oral argument.

It was Mr. Justice Frankfurter's opinion, joined by no other Justice and yet decisive in the result, which must have been torn from the soul. For Frankfurter was an avowed opponent of capital punishment. He opposed it not only on intellectual grounds but on grounds of conscience and morality and personal revulsion. He abhorred the sensationalism accompanying a death case, the subjection of human beings to the agonies involved in preparing for death, and the taking of life itself. And so his opinion stands as a personal monument to judgment over feeling.

For five pages he argued that the "double jeopardy" and "cruel and unusual punishment" clauses were not, *per se*, binding on the states. Only if what occurred so violently offended justice that it overreached due process could it be prohibited to the states. Frankfurter was here expressing his answer to Mr. Justice Black's view that the prohibitions against the states are specific and enumerated. Although quick to point out that he might rule differently if there were a series of abortive attempts at electrocution, Frankfurter nevertheless concluded, in the sometimes concise and sometimes lumbering style for which he is noted:

I cannot bring myself to believe that for Louisiana to leave to executive clemency, rather than to require, mitigation of a sentence of death duly pronounced upon conviction for murder because a first attempt to carry it out was an innocent misadventure, offends a principle of justice "rooted in the traditions and conscience of our people." . . . Short of the compulsion of such a principle, this Court must abstain from interference with State action no matter how strong one's personal feeling of revulsion against a State's insistence on its pound of flesh. One must be on guard against finding in personal disapproval a reflection of more or less prevailing condemnation. Strongly drawn as I am to some of the sentiments expressed by my brother BURTON, I cannot rid myself of the conviction that were I to hold that Louisiana would transgress the Due Process Clause if the State were allowed, in the precise circumstances before us, to carry out the death sentence, I would be enforcing my private view rather than that consensus of society's opinion which, for purposes of due process, is the standard enjoined by the Constitution.

The vagaries of fate which had plagued Willie and his lawyers from the beginning were still operative. When Wright called the Supreme Court on the day these decisions came down, he was told that the Louisiana court had been "reversed." Fortunately, he checked back before spreading the news and found that once again, someone had made a mistake. The Louisiana court was in fact affirmed, and Wright had lost the case. The mistake, however, led Wright to a more careful reading of the Justices' texts, and he came to the conclusion that what Burton had written had at one point been a majority opinion. He pointed out to the press that certain language in the Burton opinion sounded very much like a majority order. It said, for example, "We believe that the unusual facts before us require that the judgment of the Supreme Court of Louisiana be vacated and that this cause be remanded for further proceedings not inconsistent with this opinion," and, later, "We believe also that the Supreme Court of Louisiana should provide for the determination of the facts and then proceed in a manner not inconsistent with this opinion." To lawyers, this was strange language for a dissent. It was Wright's idea that perhaps Mr. Justice Jackson had changed his vote—and the result—at the last minute. While this is pure conjecture, it is not incompatible with the completely independent nature of the highly likable Jackson. That independence was instilled from childhood.

Jackson grew up a Democrat in a Republican county of New York. He clerked in a law office while still in high school despite his father's hearty disapproval of law as a career. He never went to college, and began the actual practice of law after one year of law school and while only twenty-one years of age. He was a quick success at the bar. He had a flair for it, a feeling for it, a natural bent that made him think like a lawyer and act instinctively like one. If a client had to be told he could not proceed in a certain way, Jackson was quick to suggest other courses that accomplished the same result with less possibility of censure. After many years of practice, his acquaintanceship with Franklin Roosevelt ripened into friendship and finally into government posts. He was perhaps the finest Solicitor General the country has had. He moved from there to the Attorney Generalship and then to the Supreme Court. Less than a year before the decision in the Francis case, he had been engaged in the now famous feud with Mr. Justice Black.

Jackson constantly worried about the Court's habit of telling the states how to conduct their criminal procedures, and in his beautiful prose style—pungent, witty, and incisive—he did not hesitate to communicate his fears to his brethren. Even a practical awareness that police and local officials were often overzealous did not dissuade him from a dislike of what he once called "interferences with states' rights under the vague and ambiguous mandate of the Fourteenth Amendment." It would not have been unlike Jackson to vote originally against a second electrocution and then, when the opinions were in cold print, to change his vote in favor of leaving Louisiana to its own devices. If Jackson had not yet returned from Nuremberg, and the votes of the other Justices had remained the same, the decision would still have gone against Willie, but by a different method. The Louisiana court would have been affirmed by an equally divided Supreme Court, but no opinions would have been written.

Sheriff Ozeene brought Willie the news of the Supreme Court's decision and found the boy standing at the window of his cell, looking out at the bleak winter scene. Willie listened and then sat down hard on the cot, got up again, and walked up and down the cell. "It's the same thing again," he stammered. "It's the same thing all over again. I got to start worrying again, and, boss, I thought I'd get out of it. But I guess a man's got to die some time. And I reckon my time has come."

The sheriff offered to take the news to Willie's relatives, but Willie declined. "No thanks. If I need you, I'll let you know. I got four bucks and some funny books and the Good Lord's Bible, and I still got the breath in my chest. No thanks."

Once again the reporters descended on New Iberia to interview the jail's most celebrated inmate. They were ushered in and found Willie singularly cool and composed. He told them he was "right interested to find out if I can die like the man I thought I was." He leaned back against the damp wall of the cell. "I always sort of wondered if I was a brave man. Now I guess I'm gonna find out. And I'm going to find out the hard way, boss, so there won't be no doubt in my mind when I leave. A lot of men never find out. A lot of men die still wondering if they was the men they thought they was."

The reporters told Willie that Governor Davis had just announced he would sign a new death warrant as soon as the mandate from the Supreme Court arrived. Willie smiled.

"Death and me is old neighbors," he said, stuttering on the word "neighbors." "But remember this, I'm a closer neighbor of the Lord."

De Blanc told the reporters that Willie "is a lot calmer than he was last May when he walked away from the chair." The attorney shook his head. "He's amazing. And he's still got a chance, since the Supreme Court ruling against him was only five to four. We're filing for another hearing as soon as possible."

Willie was not so sure. He prophesied: "This time it'll be different. That electric chair is going to work."

In Washington, Wright was filing a petition for rehearing in the Supreme Court. In it, he pointed out an interesting fact that had escaped notice up until this time. Prior to Willie's attempted execution, Louisiana law laid down no specific qualifications for the operator of an electric chair. Two months after Willie's experience, however, the Louisiana legislature changed the statute to require that the operator of the electric chair be "a competent electrician who shall not have been previously convicted of a felony." This was an admission by the State of Louisiana, argued Wright, that the attempt to electrocute Willie had been carried out in an incompetent manner. This was particularly important in view of the fact that Mr. Justice Reed's opinion had assumed "that the state officials carried out their duties under the death warrant in a careful and humane manner."

The Supreme Court, however, denied Wright's petition for rehearing and his supplemental petition for rehearing and vacated the stay of execution which it had previously entered. Almost immediately, de Blanc requested a second hearing before the Board of Pardons in Louisiana. For the first time in any pleading, he alleged that "at least one" of those who acted as officials in conducting the electrocution "was thoroughly intoxicated." De Blanc hoped that the close vote in the Supreme Court, the expression of personal distaste by the Justices, the nationwide attention focused on the case, and his new allegation in regard to intoxication, would all combine to sway the Board of Pardons. He was greatly disappointed when the board once again unanimously rejected his pleas.

Time was now a critical factor, with the end of April approaching and a new execution date set for Friday, May 9, 1947. At one point, Sheriff Resweber later told reporters, Willie threatened to kill himself with a razor smuggled into his cell in a Bible. In the meantime, de Blanc persisted in his efforts. He filed, instead of habeas corpus in a Federal court, a motion for a new trial and a motion in arrest of judgment in the trial court of the state. By the time the trial court and the Louisiana Supreme Court had denied his motions, it was May 7, with only two days to go.

De Blanc flew to Washington. He and Wright filed in the Supreme Court not only a petition for a writ of certiorari, the traditional method of requesting the Court to hear a case, but also an original petition for a writ of habeas corpus. This is the writ issued by a judge directing a jailer to produce the prisoner and state the reason for his being held; it is the traditional method of testing the legality of someone's detention. Normally, habeas corpus is filed first in a Federal District Court and then appealed up to the Supreme Court, but there was no longer time for any such procedure. The ground for their petitions was that they had discovered new evidence. The "newly discovered evidence" was an affidavit signed by a former city judge of New Iberia. On the basis of this affidavit, Willie's lawyers alleged that "on the day so appointed for [Francis's] execution, [Francis] was placed in an electric chair, that at the time, the executioner and other persons connected with carrying out the execution were so drunk that it was impossible for them to have known what they were doing, that the scene was a disgraceful and inhuman exhibition, that as soon as the switch controlling the current was taken off, the drunken executioner cursed Willie Francis and told him that he would be back to finish electrocuting him and if the electricity did not kill him, he would kill him with a rock. [Francis] also alleges upon information and belief that the executioner was actuated by sadistic impulses and either willfully, deliberately and intentionally applied less than a minimal lethal current, for the purpose of torturing [Francis], or acted with such wanton, reckless and inhuman indifference to the probability of inflicting excruciating and unnecessary pain upon [Francis] that in fact less than a minimal lethal current of electricity passed through the body of [Francis]; and that as a consequence of the premises, [Francis] was cruelly, inhumanly, and excruciatingly tortured. The punishment thus inflicted upon [Francis] was cruel, unusual, and due to the conscious cruelty or wanton indifference of the executioner."

These petitions were filed in the Supreme Court on the day before the new date for execution, and the Chief Justice immediately called a special session of the Court to consider them. The allegations were obviously serious. It is one thing to fail to execute a man because of a simple mistake; it is quite another to subject him to this experience because of intoxication on the part of the executioner. While the torture to the condemned man may be as great regardless of why the execution failed, the culpability of the state is clear in one case and not in the other. The difficulty for the Justices, however, was that in the Hawk case, decided three years before, they had ruled that habeas corpus must first be filed in the Federal District Court rather than in the Supreme Court. Hearing Willie's case would mean overruling Hawk.

On that same afternoon, May 8, while de Blanc was still in Washington, the Supreme Court handed down a brief order: The petition of Willie Francis "for leave to file an original petition for writ of habeas corpus is denied for reasons set forth in *Ex Parte Hawk*, 321 U.S. 114. In view of the grave nature of the new allegation set forth in this petition, the denial is expressly without prejudice to application to proper tribunals."

This rather pointed language might be roughly translated: "We are powerless to help you in view of our previous decision. But you've got a good point, and there's nothing to stop you from filing the same petition in the Federal District Court." Mr. Justice Murphy thought the petition should be granted; Mr. Justice Rutledge thought the petition should be treated as a petition for rehearing and granted and the case sent back to Louisiana for a factual hearing; and Mr. Justice Douglas took no part in the decision.

De Blanc flew back to Louisiana and immediately went to see Willie in the New Iberia jail. They had a long and serious conference. When he left the jail, de Blanc wired Wright that Willie had requested him not to initiate any further proceedings. Willie was ready to die.

The next morning, Willie Francis was taken back to St. Martinville over the same eight miles as before, past the familiar sights, around the square and up to the front of the courthouse. The only difference was that this time the day was warmer and the hour earlier–Sheriff Resweber was taking no chances on letting Willie come through the crowd that would be gathering a little later in the day. He was put in the same cell as before. The same truck and the same heavy, portable, wooden electric chair arrived from Angola, although a new electrician accompanied it. The chair was carried to the same anteroom as before, and the wires run through the window to the truck. The generator was warmed up to its deafening pitch. Willie was shaved in the appropriate places. When the time came, shortly after noon, just as before, he was taken to the anteroom and strapped into the chair. The dozen witnesses milled about, nervous, uncomfortable, embarrassed, and a few of them not feeling very well. Willie was given the last rites and asked if he had anything to say. He didn't.

One year and six days after the first try, the switch was thrown again.

It was all the same, except that this time the chair worked. The gauze on Willie's head dried up, and the burns appeared where they should have. This time the coffin could be used, and the crowd was not disappointed.

As the hearse drove away, with Willie's father up front, bent over with grief, Sheriff Ozeene stood on the courthouse steps. He might have been recalling the garbled epitaph of a boy old beyond his years. "I kill Andrew Thomas and today he is lying in a grave and I am not a killer but I wonder where I am going to be lying and in what kind of grave I don't know."

4

Wondrous Ways

Baxter Griffin lay on the couch in his three-room apartment, waiting for supper. It was five o'clock, February 8, 1947, and his wife was cooking his favorite meal of black-eyed peas, spareribs, and apple pie.

Baxter overflowed the couch. He was six feet one inch, and he weighed over two hundred pounds. The couch groaned and expanded under him as he shifted around to get a better look at what was on the stove.

He had been raised in North Carolina but had come to Washington, D.C., in time to meet and marry his wife in December, 1939. They had had no children. Aside from a conviction for simple assault in Virginia in 1941, Griffin had stayed out of trouble. He loved his work—operating a bulldozer for a contractor in nearby Anacostia, Virginia—and he loved to play cards. No one knew which he loved more.

Whenever cards were mentioned, the middle part of Baxter's face spread into an impish grin, and his tiny mustache, never conspicuous on the broad expanse above his mouth, folded into the smile and became almost lost from view. His normally puffy eyes scrunched up in delighted anticipation, and his light-brown, almost reddish, complexion became mottled from the strain of the merriment.

But he liked to work the bulldozer too. It gave him a peculiar sense of power to operate that machine. He would slam the gears into place and lurch over the landscape, taking everything with him as he went, like an All-American back stampeding a light line.

Dinner was almost ready when the thought occurred to Baxter that this would be a fine night for cards. He was feeling particularly restless, and a game might simmer him down. But then Baxter eyed the stove, and he was not so sure.

This was a hard choice—between cards on the one hand and black-eyed peas, spareribs, and pie on the other—and Baxter chose wrongly. He told his wife he was going to play cards.

He picked up two friends, Charles Cornwell, an employee of the Government Printing Office, and Charles's date, Fannie Pickett. The three of them walked to the apartment of Lurline Bost at 1718 Ninth Street, just a block from where Baxter lived and directly across the street from the New Bethel Baptist Church—"organized 1902."

Unlike Griffin's apartment house, with its smart brick exterior and tidy rooms, the building in which Lurline lived was completely without pretense. Not much wider than the average room, it huddled sulkingly between an alley and an apartment house. The only exception to its white and green exterior was the fading red with which it faced the alley. The windows on the first floor were only two feet across but fortunately, as it later developed, were large enough to jump through.

The three adventurers arrived and pushed hard on the front door; it was off its hinges, with one end resting comfortably on the sidewalk. The entrance led by way of a landing to Lurline Bost's apartment. Further stairs led to the second floor, where Lurline's brother, Lee Hunter, lived with his common-law wife, Esther Taylor, and their child.

Two of Lurline's friends, Daisy McClullough and Henry Harritt, were already in Lurline's apartment, and soon Lurline herself arrived. The party expanded with the arrival of Lee Hunter and his wife from upstairs.

In the meantime, Baxter's wife had eaten her way from the spareribs through the pie and had gone visiting. On her return, she noticed a large crowd gathering on the sidewalk about a block from her apartment. Police were arriving, windows were opening, and small children were running about and yelling. She stopped for a moment but could make nothing of it, so she returned home. Her husband was still out. Half angry, she left to visit a girl friend on the other side of town. By the time they were through chatting, it was too late for her to go home alone, so she spent the night.

The next morning, Mrs. Griffin arrived back at her apartment to find the lock on the door broken. No one was inside. She was standing in the hallway, wary and frightened, when a first-floor neighbor called up to her.

"Don't you know what's happened?"

"No."

"Baxter's done gone and shot a man, and they've come gotten him."

Mrs. Griffin remembered the crowd and confusion she had seen the night before and wished she had investigated. Now it was too late. Her husband was being held at the jail, charged with first degree murder in the death of Lee Hunter. He had already made a statement to the police, and at his request the police had called a lawyer to represent him.

Certainly no one in Washington could have appreciated what Griffin was going through better than the lawyer they called, Robert I. Miller. Only three years before, Miller himself had been charged with this same offense: first degree murder.

The legal community recognized Miller as one of its most colorful personalities. His face was a mass of white, intersticed by a full-grown white mustache and topped by a shock of white hair, the whole impression tapering off to a large and mobile double chin. He wore a broad-brimmed hat and often a pair of pince-nez attached to his coat with a wide black ribbon. His manner was courtly, and he addressed juries in a flowing prose style reminiscent of William Jennings Bryan.

Even the most insignificant cases received the full brunt of his long, impassioned pleas and magnificent gestures. He carried "lucky money," a gift from gypsy clients, and wore a watch fob imprinted with a masonic emblem on one side and a green shamrock on the other. Quite often, in full view of the jury, Bob Miller would wipe his pince-nez with a thousand-dollar bill. At one time his coterie of friends had included Vice-President Charles Curtis, and the two of them would be seen driving in style behind a police escort to the Maryland race tracks. In fact, Miller, a former stable boy himself, now owned several horses in his own right, the best known of which was dubbed Not Guilty. A graduate of National University Law School, Miller had spent thirty years at the bar and averaged almost a case a day, most of them in the police court.

On February 21, 1944, three years before Baxter Griffin was arrested, Miller watched his wife walk out of the Woodward & Lothrop department store at one of downtown Washington's busiest corners and approach a coupé stopped at the curb. The driver of the car was Dr. John E. Lind, fifty-seven-year-old senior medical officer at St. Elizabeths Hospital and one of the city's most prominent psychiatrists. Miller followed his wife to the car, yanked the door open, and leaned inside. Hundreds of passers-by came to a standstill as two shots rang out. Dr. Lind slumped over the wheel, with blood running from his left temple and his chest. A crowd converged, and a patrolman rushed up. Miller handed him a .38-caliber Smith & Wesson, stating quietly that he had shot in self-defense. The patrolman found a second pistol in a bloodstained white envelope on the seat beside Dr. Lind's body. Ironically, Miller was taken to the same police precinct where he had once worked as a janitor.

Miller's trial for first degree murder was a *cause célèbre* in a city jaded by politics. The chief witness for the prosecution was a Negro porter employed by Woodward & Lothrop, who swore that he had seen Miller toss a white object—presumably the envelope containing the pistol—on the seat of the car immediately after the shooting. The effect of this evidence was largely dissipated, however, when a surprise witness for the defense testified that on three previous occasions he had seen in Dr. Lind's possession a Manila envelope containing a pistol. Mrs. Miller tearfully took the stand. She told of an illicit relationship between herself and Dr. Lind and how Dr. Lind had repeatedly obtained money from her on threat of revealing their relationship to her husband. Miller, testifying in his own behalf, said he had followed his wife to the car on the critical day for the sole purpose of pleading with her not to join the doctor. He admitted firing the fatal shots but claimed that he did so in self-defense after Dr. Lind reached to the seat beside him and threatened to blow out Miller's brains. Three psychiatrists testified that Miller was insane and two that he was sane.

The jurors were out an hour and four minutes. (One of them said later they would have come in earlier, but they were afraid it might not look seemly.) The foreman announced in a loud, clear voice their finding of "Not guilty," and two days later Miller was back in court at his regular practice, defending a woman on a larceny charge.

This, then, was Robert Miller, something of a legend in court circles, who agreed to defend Baxter Griffin against a charge of first degree murder. Griffin, who lived only five blocks from Miller on Eighth Street, could hardly have found a more sympathetic ear.

A coroner's inquest was held at the morgue only two days after the shooting to determine officially the cause of Hunter's death and whether anyone should be held for the grand jury. The morgue was a small brick building at the edge of the grounds encompassing the jail and the District of Columbia General Hospital. Its entrance led to a courtroom where the inquests were held and then to a smaller room where the bodies were stored in large metal drawers not unlike, in outward appearance, suitcase lockers in railroad stations. The morgue drawers rolled out and revealed the wrapped bodies lying flat inside. One large cabinet, its door much like the front of a new refrigerator, provided storage space for the bodies of babies, neatly piled one on top of the other, until they could be identified and disposed of.

A staircase led to the autopsy room, pervaded by an acrid odor of formaldehyde, blood, alcohol, and strong soap. In the center of the room were two metal tables, their tops raisable at one end so as to allow drainage. The autopsy of Lee Hunter was performed on one of these, and the conclusions noted carefully in a notebook. In an adjoining room were rows upon rows of bottles, each containing a brain, a liver, a muscle, or some other segment of the anatomy, all identified and classified so as to be quickly available if needed for dissection or as evidence.

Inquests are dreary affairs, and the jurors, six in number, go about their task with little relish. The only drama is an occasional shattering scream from the adjoining room as someone identifies the body of a recently deceased friend or relative.

But inquests do give attorneys on both sides a chance to sound out witnesses, to prod them on details, and to discover new facts, without the danger of some unexpected and damaging piece of evidence being trotted out in full view of the petit jurors who will actually decide the accused's fate at trial. For example, Miller wanted to know whether he could claim at trial that the witnesses to the shooting were so drunk they could not have known what actually occurred. When his associate questioned Daisy McClullough along this line, she produced a bit of Americana reminiscent of the 1920's.

Q. "Now, how many drinks of liquor did you have out of the bottle?"

A. "I only got one drink."

Q. "Was it a small or a large drink?"

A. "It was a small glass."

Q. "Were you drinking out of an ordinary little whisky glass or out of a water glass?"

A. "No, it wasn't a water glass."

Q. "Just a whisky glass?"

A. "It wasn't a whisky glass. It was a coffee—you know what I mean."

Q. "One of those little demijohns?"

A. "No, I'll tell you. It was a coffee cup."

Q. "A coffee cup?"

A. "Yes. What you drink coffee out of."

And so it went. Some of the witnesses would be surprised months later, at trial, when their casual testimony at the inquest was quoted back to them and they were asked to square it with what they were then saying.

The coroner's jury, not surprisingly, found that Lee Hunter came to his death as the result of a gunshot wound of the head, and further that he was shot with a gun "held in the hand or hands of Baxter Griffin."

Within three weeks Griffin was indicted, and within six weeks he was on trial for his life. He was an arresting sight beside his attorney, a study in contrasting colors. Restrained brown beside vivid whiteness. And as if to complete the contrast, pitted against both of them was a lady, Mrs. Grace Stiles, who bore the unladylike title of assistant United States attorney.

Mrs. Stiles, married in the 1920's, had entered the Washington College of Law after her daughter reached junior high school. For five years Mrs. Stiles practiced law with a private firm and then—perhaps feeling a need for additional excitement—entered the United States Attorney's Office. She represented the government first in civil and then in criminal cases and by the time of the Griffin case in 1947 had prosecuted virtually every type of offense from robbery to rape. Attractive and vivacious, she exuded a feminine confidence that disconcerted her male adversaries. On the bench at the Baxter

Griffin trial, however, was a man not lightly swayed. The maverick of the District Court, Alexander Holtzoff was a small, peppery, caustic but brilliant judge, the scourge of incompetent or unprepared counsel. His love was the law, and he gave it his whole heart.

Seven persons had witnessed the shooting of Lee Hunter, in addition to Hunter himself and Griffin. Two of them, Henry Harritt and a laundry boy, could not be located by the police. The remaining five all testified against Griffin and, despite some minor discrepancies, gave remarkably similar stories. In fact, never was the prosecution blessed with such consistent testimony. Mrs. Stiles could hardly believe her luck.

The sole witness for the defense was Griffin himself. He agreed with the five prosecution witnesses on one point: he had shot Hunter. But on every other important facet of the incident, his version differed wildly from theirs. It was as if Griffin were talking about some entirely different occasion.

The composite picture of Hunter's shooting, as painted by the five prosecution witnesses, was this:

Lurline's room was very small, twelve feet across and only slightly longer from end to end. The windows were all at the southern corner facing Ninth Street. The entrance from the hallway stood directly across the room from an oil stove and a dresser. A divan, an armchair, and two smaller chairs all seemed heavy and slightly grotesque, compressed as they were into the little dark room with the floral design wallpaper, the dirty window shades, and the fetid odor. That nine people could have lounged there in apparent comfort was a mute tribute to Lurline's hospitality.

Griffin suggested a game of whist. This game went out with high-button shoes, but all five witnesses swore under oath it was whist they were playing. A card table was set up in front of the divan, and the game began. Shortly, Griffin suggested that they send out for a pint. No one was sure who went, but soon the group was enjoying a bottle of whisky and either two, three, or four bottles of beer (recollections varied on this point). Lurline cooked a little something, and the group ate. About six thirty, Lee Hunter went upstairs and came down with his baby. Lee, a dark, slim lad of twenty-three, was five foot nine and weighed less than a hundred and forty pounds; he had dark features and short black hair, and the child looked like him. He was proud of the baby and obviously wanted to show him off. His wife, however, saw that the child was sleepy and took it back upstairs. But very soon the baby began to cry, so Esther again climbed the stairs, got the baby and brought it down to the party.

By the end of an hour, the group at the table had completed two rounds of whist. They gave it up and sat about the room talking. Griffin, on the divan, took the baby on his lap. Casually, he began pulling the baby's arm. Griffin had been drinking more than the others, and Lee Hunter became worried. He told Griffin to put the baby down. Griffin said, "If you don't want me to play with your baby, I will take your wife and baby around to my house."

Lee Hunter replied, "If you don't stop pulling on my baby's arm, I'll kick your teeth down your throat."

Griffin stopped pulling on the baby's arm. Everyone in the room had heard the threat, "I'll kick your teeth down your throat," and it put a crimp in the conversation. But in a few moments, someone picked up the thread, and the chatter resumed.

Five minutes later, Griffin rose from the divan, put on his overcoat, and said he was going to get a Pepsi-Cola. He told Charles Cornwell and Fannie Pickett, who had come as his guests, that they could stay if they wanted to, but he was leaving. Lurline Bost, who had rejoined the party after washing her clothes, let him out.

The rest of the visitors stayed, but after about ten minutes a few began making moves as if to get their coats. A laundry boy arrived, and he and Charles Cornwell stood by the windows chatting. Daisy McClullough and Henry Harritt sat on the divan. Esther Taylor held the baby on her lap in the arm-chair, and Fannie Pickett and Lurline Bost stood talking near the card table. Lee Hunter stood between the oil stove and the dresser.

There was a knock on the door.

Lurline went to the door and unbolted it. She opened it and glanced out at Baxter Griffin. Recognizing him, she pulled the door open and stepped aside, turning her back as she went.

A shot rang out.

The room came to an absolute standstill. Moving figures became a tableau, petrified and immobile. Baxter Griffin stood erect in the doorway while Lee Hunter, directly opposite, slid slowly to the floor, down beside the oil stove, and slumped over on his back. In the split second of silence after the shot, Griffin's voice could be heard:

"I don't allow nobody to say they are going to kick my teeth out."

Then he swung to his left and looked at Henry Harritt sitting on the divan.

"You too," he said, and fired. The shot missed Harritt, and then all hell broke loose.

Lurline Bost fell to the floor and put her hands over her head.

Esther Taylor, holding the baby, cried, "Let me out of the room with the baby." She started to get up from her chair, but Griffin fired a shot between her legs and into the floor.

Henry Harritt and Daisy McClullough leaped off the couch, and Henry pushed Daisy toward the door. Daisy in turn pushed Esther, now on her feet with the baby, and Esther almost fell past Griffin into the hall. Henry, who had fallen to his knees on the floor, pushed the door shut in Griffin's face. Quickly, Henry reached up and rammed the bolt into place.

The sight of the closed door brought a welcome but short-lived moment of relief to the embattled occupants of the room.

Two shots came ripping through the door, leaving jagged and splintered holes behind them.

Those who were still standing needed no more encouragement. They dove for the windows. They fell through in a tumble, landing on the pavement six feet below, and hobbled off in haphazard directions.

It was all over. As Esther Taylor stood in the hallway holding her now fatherless child, Baxter Griffin walked away.

That was one story of what had happened. Miller cross-examined the five witnesses, but their versions remained basically consistent and unchanged. They were corroborated in one respect by the police sergeant who investigated the crime: he had found five bullet holes—two in the wall across from the door, two through the door, and one in the floor. The police never recovered the murder weapon.

Baxter Griffin chose to testify in his own behalf, and his story of the shooting was entirely different. In almost all respects, his version differed from those of the five witnesses for the prosecution. This is how he told it:

Mr. Miller: "Do you remember this unfortunate affair, the night it happened? You went up to the place with a couple of people?"

Mr. Griffin: "That is right."

Mr. Miller: "Will you start right from there and talk slowly so that these folks can hear you. What happened?" . . .

Mr. Griffin: "We goes around to the house on Ninth Street, to Lurline Bost's. I and Fannie Pickett and Charles Cornwell and Lurline Bost, we started playing—"

Mr. Miller: "Playing what?"

Mr. Griffin: "Blackjack." He said it emphatically, as if to dramatize the fact that blackjack was a far cry from whist.

Mr. Miller: "Will you tell me what blackjack is. What is blackjack?"

Griffin looked baffled. "It is a game, is all I know."

Mr. Miller: "What?"

Mr. Griffin: "It is a game."

Mr. Miller: "Do you play with cards?"

Mr. Griffin: "Yes; you play with cards."

Mr. Miller: "Tell me how you work it. Is it like throwing three cards down? How do you work it?"

Mr. Griffin: "No; you hit, you see; 21 is the game."

Mr. Miller: "You keep dealing cards until you get 21? Is that the way it works?"

Mr. Griffin: "That is right. You hit yourself. If you begin with a six or eight or nine or ten, you hit yourself until you get up to 21."

Mr. Miller: "You were playing blackjack at this place, until this fellow got shot. Is that right?"

Mr. Griffin: "That is right."

Mr. Miller: "What happened while you were playing, and how much were you playing for?"

Mr. Griffin: "Fannie asked for a dollar, and Charles said two, and this other boy said, 'Give me a dollar's worth.' And he hit blackjack."

Mr. Miller: "He hit blackjack?"

Mr. Griffin: "Yes."

Mr. Miller: "And after he hit blackjack, what happened?"

Mr. Griffin: "He said, 'I call the whole bank.' I had eight dollars in the bank, and he said, 'I call the whole bank.' I said, 'You can't call the whole bank because Fannie and Charles done hit.' So the argument started like that, and he snatched my money."

Mr. Miller: "Yes."

Mr. Griffin: "And he jumped up and started around the table, with his hand in his pocket, and told me he would kick my teeth out of my head. And that is when the shooting took place."

Mr. Miller: "Do you remember what hand he had in his pocket?"

Mr. Griffin: "He had his right hand in his pocket."

Mr. Miller: "And when he had his right hand in his pocket, did he come toward you?"

Mr. Griffin: "Yes, he did."

Mr. Miller: "And he said he would kick your teeth out of your head?"

Mr. Griffin: "That is right."

Mr. Miller: "And that is when you shot him?"

Mr. Griffin: "That is right."

Mr. Miller: "How did you come to shoot two or three other times? Do you know?"

Mr. Griffin: "I don't know. I must have got nervous."

Mr. Miller: "After that, you did leave there, didn't you?"

Mr. Griffin: "After the shooting occurred; yes."

Griffin said he caught a cab and gave the driver his brother's address in Virginia. As the cab was crossing the Fourteenth Street Bridge, Griffin threw his pistol into the Potomac River. Then he changed his mind about going to his brother's, got out of the cab on the Virginia side of the river, and took a bus back into Washington. He went to the home of his boss—the man for whom he operated the bulldozer—and received a bit of advice: to give himself up. Griffin went to his own apartment on Eighth Street, where two policemen were waiting for him.

Miller sat down, reluctantly leaving his client to the mercy of Mrs. Stiles. She rose with an almost frightening geniality. Did Griffin remember, she wanted to know, that he had fired more than one shot—five, in fact? No, he remembered firing only one shot. Did he remember saying that no one was going to kick his teeth in and get away with it? No, he didn't remember that. Was it his testimony that he had never left the apartment at all from the time he first entered it until the shot was fired? That's right.

Mrs. Stiles asked innocently, "If you say you shot the man

because he was coming at you with his hand in his pocket, why didn't you go straight to the police and tell them you had shot this man in self-defense?"

Mr. Griffin: "Well, it was just through a passion. I didn't know exactly what to do, to tell you the truth. Otherwise I didn't know what I was doing, because I got nervous, see."

Mrs. Stiles: "Did you think you had a right to shoot this man if he was going to do something to you?"

Mr. Griffin: "To defend myself, sure. He said he was going to kill me."

Mrs. Stiles: "He said he was going to kill you?"

Mr. Griffin: "Yes; he did."

Mrs. Stiles: "I thought you said he didn't say anything; he just came at you with his hand in his pocket."

Miller was on his feet objecting. "No; he didn't say that."

Griffin, racking his memory: "I said I didn't say anything to him."

Judge Holtzoff took over. He addressed Griffin: "Before, you said he threatened to kick your teeth out."

Mr. Griffin: "He did."

Judge Holtzoff: "You didn't say he threatened to kill you, did you?"

Mr. Griffin: "After he said he would kick my teeth out, he said he would kill me."

Judge Holtzoff: "Why didn't you walk out of the apartment, then?"

Mr. Griffin: "He was coming toward me, and it was a close, little apartment there, and I couldn't get out."

Miller asked to come to the bench, and the attorneys gathered in a semicircle around the judge. The last question had obviously bothered Miller. He told the judge, "Your Honor, I would like to ask you to strike your own question, when you said to the defendant, 'Why didn't you walk out of the apartment?' I most respectfully submit, I think that is prejudicial."

Judge Holtzoff shook his head. "I think it is a permissible question."

Miller argued that Griffin had a perfect right not to retreat if his life was being threatened.

The judge stood his ground. "That might be different. The Court of Appeals has held this, that a person doesn't have to retreat unless he can thereby avoid an affray. Maybe he could have avoided an affray by retreating in this case. He gave a very satisfactory answer. He said they were so close together, he didn't have a chance to get out. . . . I am going to deny the motion."

Mr. Miller: "Well, that is all right. It is just for the sake of the record."

Judge Holtzoff, in a friendly fashion: "I understand. When you are trying a capital case, you have to protect your record."

The lawyers made their final pleas to the jury, and Judge Holtzoff read his instructions. Included was this rule of law: "A person claiming the right of self-defense is not required to retreat if he is in a place where he has a right to be, unless by doing so an affray may be clearly avoided. If he is honestly and reasonably in fear of death or grave bodily harm, he may stand his ground, to the extent even of taking his assailant's life, if it is necessary."

At 10:45 A.M. on the second day of the trial, the jurors retired. By 12:25 P.M., they were back in their seats.

The clerk asked, "What say you as to the defendant, Baxter Griffin?"

The foreman answered, "Guilty in [the] first degree."

Within three weeks Griffin stood before Judge Holtzoff and received the mandatory sentence of death in the electric chair, to be carried out between the hours of 10 A.M. and 2 P.M. on July 11, 1947, three months hence.

Baxter Griffin stood numb. Three months, twelve weeks, to live. Eighty-four days in which to die.

Miller appealed to the Court of Appeals on one point only. He argued that Judge Holtzoff, by injecting himself into the cross-examination of Griffin and asking why the defendant had not walked out of the apartment, had unduly prejudiced the jury against Griffin's claim of self-defense. A judge, argued Miller, must carefully avoid the appearance of becoming an advocate for either side and in the absence of extraordinary circumstances should refrain from interrupting an examination by competent counsel.

A three-judge panel of the Court of Appeals rejected Miller's argument in an opinion by Bennett Champ Clark. Judge Clark was a positive and conservative member of the bench, qualities which made him virtually indistinguishable from his famous father, Champ Clark, one-time Speaker of the House of Representatives and the man almost nominated for President in 1912. His son, first a senator and now a judge, was as resolute, aggressive, and outspoken as his father.

He called Baxter Griffin's crime a "cold blooded murder proved by overwhelming evidence," and he held that it was not only the right but the duty of a Federal judge to participate directly in the trial and to propound questions of witnesses when such questions are essential to a proper development of the facts. In Griffin's case, wrote Clark, Judge Holtzoff's questions were beneficial to the defendant rather than prejudicial, because they allowed Griffin to make a logical explanation of why he did not retreat, an answer entirely consistent with his theory of self-defense.

Miller was hardly satisfied with this opinion. His associate filed a petition asking the Supreme Court of the United States to hear the case. In the petition, he raised the same question he had presented to the Court of Appeals, hoping that the fact of imminent death would compel the Court to hear the case. But on March 15, 1948, the regular list of orders issued by the Supreme Court contained a brief notice that certiorari was denied in the Griffin case. The Supreme Court would not hear the appeal. Despite the death sentence, the issue of law was not sufficiently important to garner the four votes necessary to grant certiorari. Griffin's execution, which had been delayed four times to allow Miller to take the case to the Court of Appeals and to the Supreme Court, was now set for April 30, again between the hours of 10 A.M. and 2 P.M. The news was sent to Griffin and to his wife. Barring the unlikely intercession of the President by means of executive clemency, Griffin had six weeks to live.

Life, as precious as it is, often hangs by threads so fine, so interwoven, as to be indiscernible even to those most intimately involved. Griffin, writing to his wife, mentioned numerous incidents and bits of gossip but not the single most important experience he was undergoing in jail. He did not mention it because he did not recognize its significance. A prisoner meets many of his fellows, who appear like ghosts and pass like ghosts into the gray limbo of prison routine. One of Griffin's chance acquaintances was an attorney named John M. Holzworth. Unfortunately, Holzworth was not at the jail visiting a client but rather was himself an unwilling and captive guest of that institution.

The fifty-nine-year-old attorney from White Plains, New York, looked like a professional tackle. Over six feet tall, well-built, and dynamic, he exuded confidence and charm, though he was somewhat erratic in behavior. His confidence sprang in part from his experience as a former assistant United States attorney in New York. But his prosecuting days were now over, and he found himself indicted on four counts for causing falsely made checks of small denominations to be transported from the District of Columbia to California, with intent to defraud. At his trial, after the first count of the indictment had been dismissed and after days of testimony on the remaining counts, the jury was unable to agree on a verdict and had to be discharged. Holzworth was now in jail awaiting a new trial.

He and Griffin—both large, both likable—took to each other at once and spent hours discussing their manifold problems. The Griffin case intrigued the attorney, and he said he would like to help his fellow prisoner as soon as he was free. But this, after all, was a common enough platitude, like an invitation to a summer acquaintance.

Soon after this friendship had ripened, Holzworth was allowed to file his personal bond and was released from jail to await his second trial. During January, February, March, and April, Holzworth made inquiries into the Griffin case. But a new date, May 14, had been set for Griffin's execution, and at the end of April, Holzworth began to receive tips that spurred him into feverish activity. He interviewed all the police officers who had arrived on the scene after Lee Hunter was shot, and as a result of what they told him, he finally went to the home of one Joe Small.

Joe was the attendant at the morgue who had been sent to bring in Hunter's body. He was in his sixties, a mild, gray fellow who walked with a limp. He performed various duties at the morgue. Sometimes he sat at the outer desk, answering the phone, supervising the arrival of witnesses at inquests, and filling out forms and records. Often he was called to the scene of an accident or a crime to take charge of a body and return it to the morgue, where he would wrap and store it pending identification. Whether or not this gentle man enjoyed his bizarre and morbid work, no one knew but Joe, and Joe was basically uncommunicative.

The two men sat in Joe's unpretentious house, the large, zealous Holzworth almost overpowering his quiet host. Holzworth asked whether Small remembered the Hunter killing. Small scratched his head. Yes, he remembered it—young fellow killed next to a stove. Holzworth said he had heard rumors that Small had found some items in the dead man's pocket. Small seemed surprised that Holzworth would even be interested.

Why, yes, he had found some items. As a matter of fact, the principal thing he found was an open penknife.

Holzworth leaned forward. Did the police know about this? Sure, said Small, he had turned the knife over to them.

The two men sat talking for a long while. When Holzworth finally left, he knew what he had to do.

He promptly filed on Griffin's behalf a "motion for a new trial." In that motion, Holzworth claimed the discovery of new evidence which he said warranted a second trial for Griffin. The motion alleged three newly discovered facts. First, playing cards had been found scattered on the floor next to the body of Lee Hunter, thus tending to show that a game had been in progress at the time of the shooting; second, an open knife had been found in the dead man's hand; and finally, the prosecution had known of these facts prior to Griffin's trial and had failed to disclose them.

The motion resulted in still another stay of execution. As soon as that had been arranged, the District Court held hearings to determine whether there was anything to Holzworth's allegations. Were they true, and, if so, were they of such a character as to raise a reasonable doubt as to Griffin's guilt? These were the questions the judge had to answer before he could decide whether Griffin was entitled to a new trial. Since Holzworth was not a member of the local bar, the court appointed a distinguished Negro attorney, George E. C. Hayes, to represent Griffin, allowing Holzworth only to sit at counsel table and advise Hayes.

Of course, the prize witness was Joe Small. He testified that he had indeed found a knife in Hunter's pocket, but not in his hand, as Holzworth had alleged. He explained that when he found the body, Hunter's right hand was in his pocket. Small removed the hand, which held a number of playing cards (he did not know how many), and as he did so, several of the cards fell to the floor. He then reached into the pocket and pulled out an open penknife with one broken blade. A dollar and a pocket book completed the contents of the dead man's pockets, and Small turned all of these items over to the Homicide Squad.

So here was the newly discovered evidence. Ordinary playing cards clutched in the dead man's right hand, and an open knife that had been concealed in the pocket of the deceased and apparently had not even been seen by Griffin. Of what significance was this new evidence?

A great deal, contended Hayes. The prosecution witnesses had all testified at the trial, he said, that the game of whist had been over for some time, that an argument over Hunter's baby had developed, that Griffin had left the apartment for some five or ten minutes, and that he had then returned and begun shooting. Griffin, on the other hand, had testified that the shooting occurred during the middle of a game of blackjack. Now, if the jurors had known that Hunter carried a few cards in his pocket at the time of the killing—and there was a dispute, after all, as to how many cards he carried—they might have believed Griffin's story and disbelieved the prosecution witnesses. Why would Hunter still be holding a few cards in his pocket if the game had been concluded some time before? Would not all of the cards have been placed back in their container at the conclusion of the game?

As to the knife, argued Hayes, if there had been evidence at the trial that Hunter's hand was in a pocket which held an open knife, the jury might well have accepted Griffin's version of the crime. What was Hunter doing with an open knife in his pocket if the guests were peacefully enjoying themselves, unaware of impending trouble? It made no sense at all.

For these reasons, concluded Hayes, Griffin was entitled to a new trial at which *all* of the relevant facts would be presented to the jury.

Mrs. Stiles admitted to the court that she had known prior to the trial of the open knife in the pocket of the deceased. But she said that since Griffin had never seen the knife, she considered this evidence inadmissible, and therefore she had felt no duty to reveal the facts to the defense. In other words, it was her view that the prosecution owed no duty to turn over information which the defense could not introduce into evidence. Certainly, she said, her failure to disclose the open knife "was with no intention of suppressing any evidence which I felt was admissible."

The District Court denied the motion for a new trial, ruling that:

The Court is unable to perceive that the presence of an open pocket knife in the pocket of the deceased has any bearing on the issues of this case.

The question is whether the Defendant shot in self-defense. All that he knew was that deceased made to the Defendant what seemed to be a menacing suggestion; namely, that the deceased put his hand in his right-hand trousers pocket. Moreover, it appears affirmatively that the deceased did not grab the knife but had a number of playing cards in his pocket. The knife was lying in his pocket, loose.

The question whether a person is justified in attacking an assailant in self-defense must be determined by the facts which were presented to the person who pleads self-defense. [Griffin] did not know, it appears, that the deceased had an open knife in his pocket, and therefore its existence is irrelevant.

The second basis for the motion is additional testimony tending to show that a number of playing cards were strewn on the floor of the room in which the shooting took place. . . . The fact that a card game had taken place is not disputed. Whether it was still in progress or whether it had ceased is not very important, so far as the Court views the issues of this case. Moreover, the fact that there were cards on the floor would not necessarily establish that the game was still in progress.

The Court realizes the importance of the issue presented to it but verdicts of juries must not be lightly set aside. The Court feels that it would be acting improvidently if it granted a new trial on the basis of the facts here presented.

Following the court's decision, Hayes withdrew from the case. But Holzworth continued his efforts with a determination just short of heroic. He filed in the Court of Appeals an appeal from the denial of a new trial. The government lawyers, however, argued that no new evidence of any substance had been brought forward and that Holzworth's appeal was so frivolous that it ought to be dismissed out of hand. The Court of Appeals, without oral argument and without any opinion, dismissed Holzworth's appeal.

In the meantime Holzworth had typed out a "Petition for Executive Clemency" addressed to President Truman and signed by Griffin. In it, Holzworth related all of the facts and included an affidavit signed by the president of a local union. The affidavit stated that "Baxter Griffin has been a member of International Union of Oper. Engineers Local #77-A.F. of L. for a period of 5 years. . . . He has always performed his work in a sober, diligent, efficient and careful manner. We have never known him to be engaged in any dispute with either his employers or any of the workmen with whom he may have been associated with. We respectfully request that a stay of his execution be granted. . . ."

President Truman promptly turned down the petition.

Holzworth, undaunted, filed in the District Court a petition for a writ of habeas corpus, repeating all of the facts but adding for the first time that the testimony of the prosecution's five witnesses at the trial had been false, that the government had known it was false, and that the government had deliberately suppressed the true evidence. For some unknown reason, he stated again in this petition that an open knife had been found in Hunter's *hand*, whereas actually it had been found loose in the dead man's pocket. Holzworth also argued for the first time that Miller had given Griffin incompetent representation at trial—a charge often made against attorneys but seldom borne out by the facts. All of this, alleged Holzworth, amounted to a violation of due process of law under the Fifth Amendment to the Constitution. The petition was denied the day after it was filed, and Holzworth immediately filed an appeal in the Court of Appeals, which stayed the execution until July 9 to give the court a chance to review the matter further. The government promptly moved to dismiss the appeal as frivolous. In the meantime, before the Court of Appeals even acted, Holzworth filed a second petition for habeas corpus in the District Court, alleging in almost identical language the same charges he had made in the first one, and the District Court predictably denied it.

June slackened to an end. Washington was hot and humid, and tempers flared on the sweltering downtown streets as motorists rebelled in the late afternoon against their earlier hours in crowded, often airless, government buildings. President Truman was preparing to be renominated, and the city was buffeted with talk of Dewey's certain election. At the Supreme Court, the current term ended in a flurry of opinions, and most of the Justices quickly left for vacations in widely scattered parts of the globe. They would have rested easier if the case load had stopped with the end of the term, but as usual, lawyers continued to file their petitions at a rate of from ten to thirty-five a week, asking the Court to consider how terribly they had been treated in the lower tribunals. The law clerks would work through the summer on these petitions, and the Justices would review a few at a time during July and August or return from their vacations early in September to go over the accumulated pile. The Court would not announce until October which of the three-hundred-odd summer cases it would review and which it would have nothing further to do with.

On July 7, two days before Griffin's execution, the Court of Appeals heard argument on the denial of Holzworth's first habeas corpus petition. The questioning was sharp and pointed, particularly when the judges wanted to know why Holzworth had alleged that the open knife had been held in Hunter's hand. Holzworth tried to explain that this allegation was based on his interview with Joe Small rather than upon Small's sworn testimony. The court was not impressed and, although it took the case under review, hinted that there might not be a further stay of execution.

July 8 arrived. With only one day left, Mrs. Griffin went to the jail to say good-by to her husband. Looking at him through the glass panel, she hardly recognized the drawn and pale face as that of her usually cheery husband. He had little to say. It was as if his last day had come and gone, so that all effort was wasted.

That same morning, the secretary of an attorney who had associated himself with Holzworth in the case wrote her employer a note: "I called Mr. Holzworth and he said that Griffin was going to die as far as he knew, but that he was trying everything possible to postpone it. He wants you to wait here until he gets in touch with you because he may want you to go see [Judge] Holtzoff with him. Told him you would be here around 6:00."

But Holzworth did not go see Judge Holtzoff. Instead, on this last day before the execution, he took a petition to the Supreme Court, asking for a stay of execution and promising that as soon as possible the Supreme Court would be asked to review the case. In the meantime, he said, if a stay was not granted Griffin would go to his death before anything further could be done in his behalf.

A stay of execution can be granted by a single Justice of the Court, and the judge assigned to the District of Columbia Circuit was Chief Justice Fred M. Vinson.

The Chief Justice was not a pretty man. His face was lumpy and craggy, his nose bulbous, his chins fleshy and loose. But his eyes were kindly. A tendency to slump in his seat made him look like a weatherbeaten but wise Humpty Dumpty.

The office he held was a peculiar one. In most ways, the Chief Justice is no more than one of nine. He enjoys but one vote, and his influence over the other Justices, if any, derives from those intangibles of personality and legal acumen which mark the man and not the office; it rises to no greater heights simply because he is Chief Justice. There is a perennial silly story, whenever a new Chief Justice comes to office, that because of his position and some inner gift of sweetness and light, he will calm the Court's troubled waters, halt the feuds, heal the wounds of many years' standing, and, best of all, diminish the number of divided decisions. This nonsense appeared in the newspapers when Taft and Hughes and Stone and Vinson and Warren each was appointed, and "observers" of the Court seemed genuinely surprised when the personality conflicts continued and the dissenting votes poured forth at their usual rate. Actually, of course, each Justice is autonomous; he counts on the Chief Justice only to carry out the administrative duties of the Court, to lead, channel and synthesize the discussion at conferences, and to "set the tone" of the attorneys' oral argument by his dignified and judicial demeanor. The Chief's one power of consequence is the right to name the author of an opinion when he himself is among the majority. But in most respects, the Chief Justice, as a judge, is no more and no less than his brethren, and if he is "followed" at all, it is because of qualities which would have made him a leader even as an Associate Justice. If the chief justiceship adds anything to the man, it is the opportunity to *reveal* these qualities more quickly and effectively than would otherwise be the case.

On this particular day in July, the Chief Justice sat alone, slumped over a large desk near the entrance to his office—an office which in size and splendor was outclassed by scores of others in Washington. His secretary announced that the clerk of the Court wanted to see him on an urgent matter. The clerk brought in Holzworth's petition, explained the emergency nature of the request, and left the document with the Chief Justice.

Vinson read it. The chances—if these can be gauged—were against his granting it. On the regular appeal of the case, the Court of Appeals had ruled against Griffin, and the Supreme

Court had refused to hear arguments. When the motion for a new trial had been made, and Holzworth had introduced evidence of the cards and knife, the District Court had denied the motion, and the Court of Appeals—the same court on which Vinson himself had once sat—had dismissed the appeal without even writing an opinion. The District Court had also denied a petition for a writ of habeas corpus, and the Court of Appeals, while it had not yet written an opinion, clearly was about to uphold the denial. To top it all, Vinson was one of the Supreme Court's more conservative members in criminal cases. The circumstances hardly looked auspicious for Griffin.

No one knows what went through the Chief Justice's mind—what particular point impressed him, what phrase caught his attention, what question was raised which he could not answer to his own satisfaction. Perhaps even his mood at the moment played a part, so that this same man, presented with this same petition on another day, might have denied it out of hand. But one thing is certain: the fact of death, circling like a scavenger, waiting patiently for the last few hours of Griffin's life to fritter themselves away, was uppermost in the Chief Justice's mind. He alone stood between Baxter Griffin and the electric chair.

As jail attendants were preparing Griffin's last supper, word reached them that Chief Justice Vinson had stayed the execution until the Supreme Court could decide whether to hear the case. This was the tenth stay of execution Griffin had received; on ten separate occasions, the courts had set a date on which he was to die, and on ten separate occasions, that date had been changed at the last moment. Griffin, waiting in death row at the jail, could hardly absorb this new development. Was it a brief reprieve—a mere prolonging of the torturous waiting period—or was he being given back his life?

It will be recalled that Holzworth had filed two petitions for habeas corpus, that both of them had been denied, and that an appeal from one of the denials had been taken to the Court of Appeals. Now, with the execution delayed by the Chief Justice, the Court of Appeals came down with its opinion and dismissed the appeal. The opinion was very hard on Holzworth. It branded as "false" the statement that a knife had been found in Hunter's hand and as "scandalous" the charge that the government knew its witnesses had perjured themselves. There was "no fact that gives even colorable support" to the argument that Miller had been incompetent.

The court used this significant language in discussing the open penknife: "If the knife had been in [Hunter's] hand, as the petition says it was; or even if his hand had been empty, so that an inference might have been drawn that he was reaching for the knife; its presence would have given substantial support to [Griffin's] story that Hunter threatened him. But since Hunter was neither holding nor reaching for the knife and, on the contrary, was firmly clutching playing cards, the fact that an open knife was readily available to him is strong evidence that he had no intention or thought of making a violent attack upon [Griffin]. It therefore gives no support to [Griffin's] contention that Hunter threatened him or appeared to do so. It even tends, in some degree, to refute that contention. Plainly, therefore, the prosecutor's course in not using the evidence of the open knife, while it may have been unwise, did not detract from the fairness of [Griffin's] trial and is irrelevant in this proceeding."

This language was significant because of what is known in the law as the "doctrine of uncommunicated threats." One defense to a charge of murder, of course, is self-defense, and any evidence is admissible which tends to support the defendant's theory that the deceased was the aggressor. This would include evidence of a "communicated threat"—a threat which was communicated from the deceased to the defendant and which may have caused the defendant to protect himself by killing. But what of an "uncommunicated threat"? That is, what of a threat which was contemplated by the deceased but which he failed to communicate to the defendant? This is more difficult. One view is that since a claim of self-defense rests upon whether the defendant was acting to protect his own life, evidence of what may have been on someone else's mind is totally immaterial unless communicated to the defendant. As applied to Griffin's case, the defense would not be allowed to prove the open knife in Hunter's pocket unless Griffin knew it was there. An opposite view is that evidence of a threat is admissible whether or not communicated to the defendant because if the deceased intended to attack, that intent may have been translated into *some* action, such as a menacing look or gesture, of which the defendant was made aware. Thus in this case, the argument goes, the open knife tended to show that Hunter meant to attack, or was even attacking, and Griffin may have been made aware that he was being attacked, although he never saw the knife.

The Court of Appeals seemed to be saying that in this instance, it was immaterial whether or not evidence of an uncommunicated threat was admissible in the District of Columbia, because Hunter made no threat at all—communicated or uncommunicated. An open knife, loose in a pocket, did not constitute evidence of a threat.

Soon after this opinion was rendered, Holzworth's part in the strange case of Baxter Griffin came to an end. He had waited ten months for the government to decide whether it would retry him for transporting falsely made checks, and nothing had been done. So he left for Canada. A few months later the government formally dropped all charges against him. Still later, he wrote to a friend and explained his absence:

> I had hoped to be able to get away from here shortly for the States but a close friend of mine with whom I had been making airplane trips in a small plane was frozen to death about two weeks ago in – 70° below zero weather about 100 miles north of here in the wilderness as a result of a force [sic] landing and I have been kept very busy in cooperation with the U. S. Air Corps in re-

covering his body and having it sent to his father and mother in North Carolina. Today I got word that the body was brought in by dog sled to Beaver, one hundred miles north from here, and if the storms and cold weather subsides we will have his body here in a few days. And then shortly I shall be able to return.

But, so far as his friend could determine, Holzworth did not return—either then or since.

Thus left to his own devices, Baxter Griffin filed a petition for certiorari with the help of his friends in the jail, asking the Supreme Court to hear his case, and a month after the Supreme Court returned from its summer vacation, it agreed to hear arguments.

With Holzworth gone, help came to Griffin from an unexpected source. As a bulldozer operator, Griffin had been a member in good standing of the International Union of Operating Engineers. The Union now came forward with an offer to supply counsel for the Supreme Court argument. Chosen for the job was Francis J. Kelly, an experienced and successful attorney, although he had never argued before the high tribunal. A small, well-proportioned man with gray hair, Kelly spoke in an abrupt and nervous manner. His staccato sentences ran right to the point, and when he listened, his mouth straightened to a tight line. He perspired easily. But "all concord's born of contraries," and Kelly's soft and benevolent eyes, behind brown-rimmed glasses, made him seem more relaxed than he was.

Opposing him was Charles B. Murray, a veteran of the United States Attorney's Office and a man thoroughly familiar with criminal practice in the District of Columbia. Ironically, Murray—who looked like a stouter version of Kelly—was the same man who had unsuccessfully prosecuted Griffin's first attorney, Robert I. Miller, for first degree murder.

The argument in the Supreme Court began at 3:50 P.M. on the afternoon of December 15, 1948, shortly before the Christmas recess. Not surprisingly, Kelly pitched his case largely on the facts, with less emphasis on the law. Although Washington is Federal territory and is run by Congress, and although its judges are appointed by the President, much of its law is "local" law in the same sense that states and municipalities throughout the country operate chiefly under local statutes. The Supreme Court has recognized this over the years by deferring to Washington's own courts on matters which are peculiarly local in character, even though the Supreme Court technically has the power to decide such matters for itself. In Griffin's case, the issue was whether evidence that the deceased carried a concealed weapon was admissible and whether that evidence, discovered after trial, warranted a new trial. That issue was of the type which the Supreme Court traditionally left to the local courts to decide, and the Court of Appeals seemed to have decided it against Griffin. Therefore, Kelly, although arguing that the Supreme Court should establish a "Federal rule" applicable in the District of Columbia in regard to such evidence, recognized that he was fighting an uphill battle on this point and concentrated on the facts as they had been developed in the District Court.

When Kelly attempted to argue the seriousness of the concealed weapon, Mr. Justice Jackson, with a wry smile that betrayed his rakish sense of humor, ridiculed the idea that anyone could be frightened by a penknife carried in the pocket. "Why look," he said, "I carry one myself." And with that, he reached in his pocket, pulled out a penknife, and held it up for Kelly to see.

Dryly, Kelly countered: "I suggest that Your Honor does not carry it open."

Chief Justice Vinson leaned forward, his eyes twinkling. "I'm not so sure," he said. "I wouldn't press your luck."

Kelly did not have time to finish his argument by four thirty, the traditional hour when the Justices left the bench The next day, after a line of attorneys had been sworn in as members of the Supreme Court bar, he concluded his presentation with a plea for his client's life. The courtroom was crowded, not for Kelly but because the Japanese war criminal cases would begin as soon as the Griffin argument was concluded.

When Kelly sat down, Murray rose and addressed the Court. He wore a rented set of tails, and Kelly kidded him later because he had to pay extra rental when the argument ran over into a second day. Murray methodically checked off the points in the government's favor, and he emphasized that the Court of Appeals had decided this case against Griffin on a matter of law peculiarly within its own area of responsibility.

Four months later, on April 25, 1949, the Supreme Court rendered its decision. All nine members agreed that the case could not be affirmed. But the Court divided five to four over what should be done with it. The majority—Justices Black, Reed, Frankfurter, Jackson, and Burton—decided that the case should be sent back to the Court of Appeals with instructions to decide the proper rule as to "uncommunicated threats" in the District of Columbia. Regardless of what rule the Court of Appeals chose, the Justices said they would not disturb it. The four dissenters—the Chief Justice and Justices Douglas, Rutledge, and Murphy—thought the Court of Appeals ought to be reversed outright and the case sent back for a new trial.

The extraordinary feature of both the majority and dissenting opinions was that every Justice on the Supreme Court simply assumed, without even deciding the point, that this *was* a case involving an uncommunicated threat.

The majority opinion was written by Mr. Justice Frankfurter. He dismissed the argument about the playing cards—the argument on which attorney Hayes had placed so much reliance—with one sentence: "The allegation regarding scattered playing cards on the floor at the time of the fatal shooting was adequately met, and this ground for a new trial need not detain us."

It was the open knife which caused serious difficulty. The

entire basis of Frankfurter's opinion was that the Court of Appeals had not yet directly and unequivocally decided whether evidence of an uncommunicated threat was admissible; such a decision must be made. To *infer* that the Court of Appeals had ruled such evidence inadmissible would not do; "solicitude for life bars reliance on such an inference. . . . It seems to us more appropriate for the Court of Appeals to address itself directly to the issue of admissibility." Since the question of admissibility was "a matter of local law," the Supreme Court would not disturb the ruling, regardless of what it was; but there had to be a specific ruling. The Justice wrote at length about the "distinctive position" of the District in matters of criminal law. He included an appendix showing that over the last ten years fourteen first degree murder convictions had come to the Supreme Court from the District of Columbia, in all of which some local rule of evidence was at least partially involved, and the Supreme Court had refused to hear all but one of the fourteen. This is strong evidence, he said, that the Supreme Court defers to local courts on local questions.

Frankfurter went on to point out the difficulty which would face the Court of Appeals in deciding whether the evidence of Hunter's knife was admissible. "The problem . . . is serious and its wise solution full of difficulty." In fact, "there are few questions of admissibility in trials for murder that have occasioned a greater contrariety of views." Most jurisdictions, he said, hold that evidence of uncommunicated threats is not admissible where there is clear proof that the defendant rather than the deceased took the initiative. Some states admit the evidence even when all other witnesses oppose the defendant's version of the killing. And at least one state allows the trial judge a great deal of discretion in excluding the evidence once he decides that there was no hostility by the deceased. In any event, concluded Frankfurter, there is no "federal rule" admitting or excluding such evidence. "We must therefore remand the case to the Court of Appeals with instructions to decide, in the first instance, what rule should prevail in the District of Columbia."

Mr. Justice Murphy, writing for the dissenters, thought that evidence of the open penknife was clearly admissible. "Uncommunicated threats and designs on the defendant cannot show his motive in killing, but they may demonstrate that a design on the defendant did in fact exist. This is the rule in 'virtually all Courts.' . . . It is certainly the federal rule. . . . And it is a thoroughly desirable rule. A defendant should be entitled to present the jury with evidence lending credence to his theory of the case. *Griffin's* case is a good example of the policy behind the rule: for the open knife is the only supporting evidence of his self-defense testimony."

Murphy objected to the majority's statement that it would not strike down whatever rule the Court of Appeals chose to adopt as to uncommunicated threats. "Self-limitation of our appellate powers may be a worthy thing, but it is not attractive to me when the behest of Congress is otherwise. Congress has given this Court the ultimate power to review District of Columbia trials. No matter how the decision is phrased, the Court's power in the premises is such that it is responsible for the evidence rule it asks the Court of Appeals to expound. . . . We should declare the evidence admissible."

Thus the entire Court treated the case as one involving an uncommunicated threat. The Court of Appeals, in its habeas corpus decision, had held to the contrary on the theory that the open knife was not found in Hunter's hand. No threat, communicated or otherwise, was involved, under the Court of Appeals' view; there was no evidence that Hunter had even contemplated aggression against Griffin. But the Supreme Court, by holding that the Court of Appeals must affirmatively decide whether evidence of uncommunicated threats was admissible in the District of Columbia, by implication ruled that the loose, open knife was in fact evidence of an uncommunicated threat. Otherwise, what difference did it make whether uncommunicated threats were admissible?

We can only conjecture about what the Justices had in mind. One possibility is that they simply misread the Court of Appeals opinion. Another is that they considered the language of the Court of Appeals mere *dictum*—a discussion not directly in point—and therefore not authoritative or binding. A third possibility is that the Justices thought the open penknife clearly constituted an uncommunicated threat (the Court of Appeals to the contrary notwithstanding), but they knew that if they discussed and decided the point directly, they would be passing upon the very type of "local law" question which they said they were leaving to the Court of Appeals. Therefore, they simply assumed that an uncommunicated threat was involved and asked the Court of Appeals to take it from there.

The Supreme Court decision thus placed the Court of Appeals in an extremely embarrassing position, as soon became apparent when Kelly and Murray went back to argue against each other in that court. Here they were, vigorously discussing what the proper rule should be as to uncommunicated threats, when this very court had previously held in effect that no such question was involved. Those familiar with the case waited expectantly for the court's opinion to see just what sort of word-juggling and rationalizations would be indulged in to explain away the prior opinion. In this they were disappointed. When the case was decided, the majority stated quite frankly in a footnote: "We do not attempt to reconcile our present opinion with our [prior] opinion. . . . The Supreme Court's opinion has intervened."

The Court of Appeals split two to one. The majority held that, henceforth, evidence of uncommunicated threats would be admissible in the District of Columbia whenever there is substantial evidence (even if it is only the defendant's testimony) that the deceased was an aggressor. And since the evidence of Hunter's open knife would have been admissible at the trial, Griffin was entitled to a new trial on his "newly discovered" evidence of the knife. The court simply assumed, in view of the Supreme Court's decision, that the open knife constituted an uncommunicated threat.

The majority opinion appended a word of consolation for Mrs. Stiles: "It would be unfair not to add that we have confidence in the good faith of the prosecution. Its opinion that evidence of the concealed knife was inadmissible was a reasonable opinion, which the District Court sustained and no court has overruled until today." Nevertheless, said the court, the case demonstrates how important it is for the government to make a full disclosure of evidence that may help the defense. Quoting from a Supreme Court case, the opinion concluded: " 'The United States Attorney is the representative not of an ordinary party to a controversy, but of a sovereignty whose obligation to govern impartially is as compelling as its obligation to govern at all; and whose interest, therefore, in a criminal prosecution is not that it shall win a case, but that justice shall be done.' "

Judge Bennett Champ Clark, now the dissenter, told the majority that "so long as I remain on the Bench I will decline to follow this case as a precedent and in any similar case will devote my best efforts to overruling it." He said the majority opinion was based upon "an entire misconception of the action of the Supreme Court in this very case and an even greater misconception of the nature and extent of the so-called doctrine of 'uncommunicated threats.' " He at least credited the majority with "manly candor" in admitting that its two opinions were in conflict; in fact, said Clark, "The two opinions simply by any conceivable process of mind cannot be reconciled." Judge Clark insisted that he could find no language in the Supreme Court decision stating that Hunter's knife was an uncommunicated threat. (Literally, he was correct, since the Supreme Court avoided the issue.) To attribute any such thought to the Supreme Court, he said, "requires clairvoyant powers to which ordinary mortals cannot aspire." Therefore, he would "adhere steadfastly" to his prior view that no threat of any kind was involved.

Even if uncommunicated threats were involved, he argued, the rule announced by the majority went wide of the mark. Evidence of uncommunicated threats should be admissible only where the threat, though not communicated to the defendant, was made known to a third party prior to the crime, and there were no eyewitnesses to the crime itself. Instead of adopting that doctrine, wrote Clark, the majority was putting the case back to its original point of departure, ready to "start out on its weary way again." And, he prophesied, "It is probable indeed that Griffin will die of the infirmities of old age before he can be brought to pay the penalty which he so richly deserves. . . . Griffin is a bloody handed murderer who has too long defeated the ends of justice."

If a majority of the Court of Appeals had agreed with this dissent and had held for the second time that no threats of any kind were involved, would the Supreme Court have bowed to this interpretation of "local law"? Perhaps even the Justices themselves could not have answered this question. In any event, they never had to.

As a result of the Court of Appeals decision, the United States Attorney's Office began preparations to retry Griffin for first degree murder, and the court appointed a new attorney to defend him. Conferences ensued. It was pointed out to the government that the witness Harritt had never been located, and that evidence of the knife and the playing cards at the new trial might well jeopardize the government's case. The government was inclined to agree. At the end of the conferences, the United States attorney let it be known that he would accept a plea to second degree murder.

Griffin was delighted. Although his new evidence might have helped him, there was no avoiding the fact that five witnesses would again testify that he killed Hunter during an unprovoked attack. He had been close enough to the electric chair to know that he preferred a prison term to death.

On March 15, 1951, Griffin pleaded guilty to second degree murder, and on April 6, 1951, he was sentenced to from five to twenty-one years in prison.

Three years before, Baxter Griffin had prepared for his last dinner. Now he was safe—a convict to be sure, but free from the electric chair. After two trips to the Supreme Court and four to the Court of Appeals, he had earned at least the right to live. He had worked his way through ten attorneys—some would say that he had suffered enough by that ordeal alone—and as many stays of execution. Credit for saving his life would be difficult to apportion, though certainly Joe Small, the morgue attendant, and the Chief Justice of the United States could claim legitimate shares. But surely Griffin's erratic attorney, Holzworth, who himself had traveled the road from prosecutor to prosecuted, stands out as Griffin's personal hero. Regardless of his motives and regardless of his disappearance at a crucial stage of the case, the fact remains that if it had not been for Holzworth, Griffin would have gone to the electric chair on July 9, 1948.

Griffin was transferred to the penitentiary at Lorton, Virginia, where he seemed destined, as Judge Clark had predicted, to "die of the infirmities of old age" before his debt was fully paid. The meals were adequate, though hardly home cooking, and during recreation periods he played cards with his fellow prisoners (whether whist or blackjack remains his secret).

God's will works in wondrous ways. On May 7, 1957, ten years and three months after the killing of Lee Hunter, Griffin was operating a bulldozer on land adjacent to the penitentiary. The authorities were using him to help clear the area for a new Youth Training Center. Griffin's thoughts, however, were not on his work. In two weeks he would be a free man. Having served out his minimum sentence without mishap, he was due for release. His wife was already planning a homecoming in the same apartment they had shared ten years before on Eighth Street.

The day was warm and bright. Griffin, atop the bulldozer, came to a large felled tree. The bulldozer crunched and sputtered against one end of the tree as Griffin tried to move it. The large branches bent under the pressure, but the base of the tree remained imbedded in the ground. Griffin jammed the gears and spun forward.

Suddenly, one large branch snapped loose and shot like a bullet over the top of the bulldozer blade. It caught Griffin squarely across the top half of his body and broke his neck.

Baxter Griffin, age forty-nine, had cheated the chair, but not death. He probably died without knowing why Lee Hunter had stood in Lurline Bost's apartment with an open penknife in his pocket. Not even the Supreme Court of the United States had found the answer to that one.

5

A Little Bit of Knowledge

The setting was right out of F. Scott Fitzgerald. The elegant, brown lanai house, wonderfully alive to the prospect of visitors, looked proudly out over the fashionable Bel Air section of Los Angeles. It was a low, flat-topped affair in the modern style, close to the road but surrounded on three sides by a beautifully kept lawn. Somera Road bellied out in front of the house before curving gently up the hill to a dead end. Out back, beyond a covered patio, a children's yard, and a connecting aisle of cropped green grass, the terrain turned suddenly to rock and shale and banked away to a canyon. A single scrub tree overhung the bank. The children's yard, to the east, was protected by a slatted board fence, neatly painted, with thick California foliage twisting and climbing a carefully regulated route along its outer sides in apparent abandon.

The patio was ideal for cookouts, and when guests were present and the sun dropped off beyond the canyon, the entire back yard was bathed in a gentle, synthetic light. From front to back, the house had the touch of wealth, perhaps not as ostentatiously as Fitzgerald would have pictured it, but nevertheless with a certain aura, a smell of success, so that you knew without looking that the patio door was a sliding door, and each bathroom window was discreetly frosted on the bottom, and the drapes were heavily lined to suppress the sun. The nursery had six closets.

Not a place of violence, but a setting for gay parties shadowed by sparkling music, and for the charm and grace of lovely women.

The mistress of the house was Norma McCauley. She was petite, half an inch shy of five feet tall, and she weighed only ninety-six pounds. Yet at thirty-three she was fully and unself-consciously attractive, emboldened by short auburn hair, keen eyes, thin but sensual lips, and a light, beguiling complexion. Separated from her husband, Frank, she gaily ruled her retinue of three children—ages seven, five, and two—her new maid, and her black mongrel dog, Cinders, who was tactfully described by a family friend as "not of singular origin."

Norma was what newspaper columnists loved to call (whether disparagingly or with envy was hard to tell) a "socialite." Her evenings were filled with parties, each a spontaneous affair with about as much control and direction as a lynching. Now two more were in the offing for the successive nights of July 3 and 4, 1955, ostensibly in celebration of Independence Day. Both were being given at the home of Norma's parents, the Thompsons, and the one on July 4 was to include Norma's three children. The Thompsons' house was also in Bel Air, a mile and a half from Norma's, and looked very much like hers except that it was larger and included what in California is a nonluxury: a swimming pool.

During the evening of July 3 Norma met for the first time a professional cameraman named Melvin Rathmann, and when the party was over at 2:15 A.M., Rathmann walked Norma to her Cadillac. They stood chatting. Suddenly, Norma started, glanced around, and asked Rathmann whether he had heard something in the bushes. He said he had not. Norma said distractedly, "I thought I heard somebody." She surprised Rathmann by asking if he would follow her home.

They sat in a curved lounge at her house and sipped coffee. Norma told Rathmann that a man she had been "going with" had threatened to kill her. What was she to do? Rathmann, quite disturbed by her tone and obvious sincerity, said she should hire a bodyguard or someone to stay at the house in addition to the maid. Norma said she just didn't know; she was very perplexed. In fact, she was so afraid of this person that she hoped Rathmann would remain with her for a few hours. He said he would, and Norma dozed while still sitting at the coffee table. Occasionally, Cinders wandered about, sniffing amicably at the stranger.

Rathmann did not leave until 5:00 A.M. The sun was just showing itself, beginning to warm the wet grass, when he drove down the hill from Somera Road. A few hours later the McCauley children were up and about, excited about their own party that evening.

At three o'clock in the afternoon, Norma and the three children drove off to the Thompsons'. They took the maid, for although Laurie Dromtra had arrived only four days before, Norma enjoyed that immediate confidence with servants born of experience and training. Months ago, she had dealt similarly with a houseboy, and there had been other domestics before him.

Despite her restless night Norma was back in high spirits, her mood matched by her red cocktail-length dress emblazoned with large pink printed flowers. It was a happy, carefree afternoon. The guests included John Baird, a public relations consultant and long-time friend of Norma's; Bob Block, a radio-time salesman; Pat Gallagher, Block's date; George Fox, a technical sales representative and Block's roommate, and Jean Davis, who had known Norma about two months. The children swam while their elders sipped cocktails and began preparing the barbecue dinner. Then there were firecrackers, rollicking off in all directions. After the children ate, Norma took her smallest child and the maid home and returned to the party.

Perhaps it is indicative of the sophistication of the group that only one guest, Jean Davis, could remember later every dish served for dinner: barbecued steak, potato salad (the potatoes, she remarked inhospitably, were not thoroughly cooked), green peas, a relish dish, coffee, and cookies. Everyone had finished by eight thirty, and Pat Gallagher announced that her friends the Whiting sisters were beginning their summer replacement of "I Love Lucy" on television at nine o'clock, and she wanted to watch. Obligingly, everyone saw the show except Norma, who took advantage of the interlude to drive her two older children home. When she returned to the party, she carried over her arm a white knit stole decorated with rhinestones.

In the meantime, Laurie, the maid, bathed the children and took them to the nursery, where she noticed that one of the beds had been moved about fifteen inches toward the center of the room and away from one of the closets. She had never seen the inside of this particular closet; she only knew from family comments that it had belonged to Frank McCauley and that it now stood empty. Without looking inside, she jostled the bed back into place. She locked the house, turned back Norma's bed, and retired to her own room. Cinders, contrary to his usual custom, slept next to Laurie's bed, with the bedroom door slightly ajar.

At the party, the guests had left the television set and were dancing to records in the basement playroom. And so the fun continued, heightened by highballs and light banter, until shortly after midnight when weariness, like a reverse alchemy, overtook the group. Shyness disappeared, cordiality cooled, the amenities were dispensed with, and each guest looked at his partner with less benevolence and more insight than before. The glamour was gone, and the party broke up.

Pursuant to agreement, Pat Gallagher and Bob Block trailed Norma and John Baird to Norma's house. Jean Davis and George Fox were supposed to follow in a third car but soon became lost and repaired to Jean's apartment.

At Norma's house, Pat and Bob waited in their car while Baird parked Norma's car in the garage and walked her to the front door. Norma went to the kitchen, where she deposited plates and pans left over from the party and put her keys down on the "breakfast bar," a dividing counter between the kitchen and the dining room. The two said goodnight at the front door, and Baird left, joining Pat and Bob in their car. Cinders, apparently undisturbed by his mistress's return, slept on.

Three quarters of an hour later, Jean Davis and George Fox, still at Jean's apartment, decided they would call Norma in an effort to contact the party-goers. Jean put through the call, and Norma answered. They talked for several minutes. Norma, usually quite vivacious, sounded "very odd" to Jean—listless and cool. She spoke in a monotone.

At 2:20 in the morning, Jean decided to call Norma again. She gave the number to George Fox, who dialed. There was no answer. Thinking he might have gotten a wrong number, he dialed again and waited through a number of rings. Still no answer. He gave up and soon thereafter left Jean's apartment and drove home.

At 3:00 A.M., Laurie the maid was awakened by "fidgeting" on the part of Cinders; he was rattling his collar in a disconsolate manner, and she let him out front for about twenty minutes.

By 6:30 she was up again, quickly involved in routine chores. She noted peevishly that for the second time a bed had been moved away from the closet. She paid no more attention and began preparing breakfast. While the children were eating, the telephone rang. As Laurie picked up the extension on the "kitchen bar," she told Kirk, the five-year-old, to go wake his mother.

Laurie stopped talking to the cleaning man in midsentence. Kirk had reappeared in the kitchen doorway and was staring at her, wide-eyed, perplexed, looking for all the world like a trapped rabbit who suspects but does not fully comprehend his predicament.

He said, "Laurie, you better go in. Mommie is in a mess."

The cleaning man was left talking to himself. Laurie rushed to the bedroom but stopped in the doorway.

Enough light filtered through the drawn drapes to reveal the room in shambles. Drawers lay open, papers littered the floor, and a black purse sat lopsidedly on the bed, its contents scattered about the rug. One chair was on its side. In the whole room only the bed looked undisturbed.

Mommie was indeed in a mess.

She lay face down on a beige chaise longue, still in her red cocktail dress, with her arms crossed under her head. The white stole, its rhinestones barely visible in the half-light, was wrapped tightly around her neck and knotted on the side. One shoe was off; the other dangled precariously from her foot.

There was blood everywhere around her–soaking into the chaise longue, angling down her feet and ankles, collecting on the floor in dark, ugly pools, and even staining the wall and chairs and window drapes. Several smears appeared on the drapes three quarters of the way to the ceiling.

Laurie stared at the blood, comprehending only the stillness. She said later she thought Norma had "passed out or she had a hemorrhage" but that somehow she was still alive. Without touching anything, Laurie ran back to the kitchen telephone, hung up on the cleaning man, and dialed the Thompsons' number. No one answered. Frantically, Laurie called Norma's brother, Jack.

By the time Jack arrived, the word had spread like oozing honey, and a Los Angeles police officer, a neighbor lady, and the cleaning man were already on the scene. Jack looked briefly at his sister, wandered into the kitchen, came across Norma's key ring, and absent-mindedly put it in his pocket. He later gave the keys to the police, and this was the only set they found.

By nine o'clock, the West Los Angeles detectives had arrived and with them came all of the frantic activity that follows a murder. Men in and out of uniform scrutinized every inch of surface space, photographers dreamed up new angles for pictures already taken, and technicians dusted objects for fingerprints but dolefully came up with only smudges. After a perfunctory examination the coroner reported what was obvious from the knotted stole and the protruding tongue—that Norma had been strangled. He also discovered eleven stab wounds—three in the chest, three in the left arm, three in the right hand, one in the face, and one in the back. Some were deep and serious, others minor scratches. As soon as this report was received, all of the knives in the house were tested for blood, but the results were negative.

Working beside the coroner, sometimes in his way, were two chemists collecting burned paper matches from ash trays. They also examined but did not analyze the blood on and around the chaise longue. They clipped Norma's fingernails in the hope of finding traces of the murderer's skin tissue under them, but in this they were disappointed.

Confusion seemed to beget confusion, as policemen and newspapermen and onlookers all milled about. Questions, questions, questions. Telephone calls. Checks and rechecks. Halting, evasive answers. Ebullient, garrulous answers. Gossip. Reflections. Troubled memories of half-forgotten bits and pieces. Suspects were eliminated—first Frank McCauley, then John Baird, then others whom Norma had known and sometimes dated. And finally, out of the miasma of a young woman's troubled life, one name persisted.

At one thirty that same afternoon, two Hollywood policemen went to 5128 Marathon Street, obtained a key to Apartment 105 from the manager, and opened the door with drawn revolvers.

Standing in the middle of the room in a plaid bathrobe and flannel pajamas was Norma McCauley's former houseboy, John Russell Crooker, Jr.

As the police were soon to discover, this was no ordinary houseboy. Educated, intelligent, and handsome, he looked at age thirty-one more like a successful attorney than an errand boy for a married couple. And as a matter of fact, at this very juncture in his life he was on his way to becoming an attorney, as a student at Southwestern Law School. The events which had changed him from a quiet, withdrawn boy in a small Maine town to a murder suspect in Los Angeles formed a pathetic study in alternate successes and failures.

John's parents in Maine were "down-eastern" folks, strict, harsh, and unforgiving. From earliest childhood, John found himself surrounded by women—six sisters in addition to his mother. When he was still quite young, he became studious and developed a flair for writing and debating. After the war, which he spent as a radarman in the navy, he entered the University of Maine, but after a year broke his home ties and traveled west to California. He had hardly settled down when he met and married a girl he had formerly known in Maine, but they soon separated, and the marriage was annulled. Later in 1949 he married a girl living in Santa Ana, California, and the following year they had a son. In the meantime, John had entered the University of Southern California.

He withdrew after only three months and entered George Pepperdine College, a small school in Los Angeles. While there, he placed third in a local journalism contest and fifth in the West Point Invitational Debate Tournament. By the time he graduated with a Bachelor of Arts degree in 1953, he and his second wife had produced their second child, a girl, and had separated.

John already had decided he wanted to become an attorney and that the Law School of the University of California at Los Angeles (U.C.L.A.) would provide the necessary opportunities. The problem was money. He had never been able to save any cash out of miscellaneous odd jobs, and further schooling presented a very practical problem. That summer of 1953, as he prepared to enter law school, he began looking for part-time work. Someone suggested he could save money by working for a private family while attending classes, so he applied to the law school for suggestions. He was referred to Mr. and Mrs. Frank McCauley on Somera Road.

John came away from the interview captivated by the McCauleys and by their home high in the hills above Sunset Boulevard, surrounded by members of the movie colony and the international set. The home had been a wedding present in 1945 from Norma's father, a millionaire contractor. Frank McCauley, a former air force ace, was good-looking in a lean, rough, clean-cut way, his chiseled features accentuated by short, dark curly hair and intense eyes. He and his tiny wife, with equally dark eyes and an attractive figure, made a handsome pair.

The proposition they offered Crooker seemed ideal. In return for waiting on bar, taking care of the children, and performing miscellaneous odd jobs, he was to receive his meals, a room (the same one later given to the maid, Laurie Dromtra), and varying amounts of cash. It was a loose arrangement, but it suited John.

In the fall, as planned, John entered U.C.L.A. Law School. He almost immediately ran into trouble. Since he had a quick mind and considerable natural ability, his difficulties apparently were emotional and could be traced in part to what was happening at the McCauleys'.

He and Norma McCauley, both lonely, confused, and disconsolate, became warm friends as soon as John moved into the house. An immediate understanding, a knowing empathy, sprang up between them. They saw each other regularly over the summer, as John moved freely about the house, and by fall they had fallen in love and their relationship had become intimate. On September 20, the day before John's law school classes began, Frank McCauley moved out of the house, and a girl friend of Norma's moved in. John stayed on, and he and Norma cautiously began to date. About three or four times a month they went to the Sapphire Club in southwest Los Angeles where they knew they would not run into friends. Their feelings for each other apparently were genuine; regardless of the moralities involved, they were in love. A waitress at the Sapphire Club said later that John was "very affectionate" toward Norma, and that "The only way I can describe it, he treated her like she was a China doll." A friend of John's confirmed that they were "very affectionate and intimate towards each other."

By Thanksgiving, 1953, Norma's girl friend had moved out. For about two weeks, John and Norma remained in the house alone with the children, until it became obvious that this arrangement would not do. And so the Thompsons, who did not know of the relationship, invited John to live at their house while he worked at Norma's. John accepted. Soon he was employed full-time by the Thompsons, but he continued to date Norma.

In June, 1954, just as John was to begin his year-end examinations at U.C.L.A. Law School, Mr. Thompson discovered John's relationship with his daughter and fired him. The millionaire later told reporters he and his wife had felt sorry for John when they first hired him. "We thought he was an ambitious young man, putting himself through school. We tried to help him. Then we found out that he was annoying my daughter, so I fired him. He went away weeping, because I got pretty rough with him. We had been kind to him—and he was biting the hand that fed him. . . ."

But John and Norma remained on intimate terms. John had bought a 1951 Plymouth with about four hundred dollars Norma had given him; she had acted as a co-signer on a three-hundred-dollar loan from U.C.L.A.; and she had given him almost six hundred dollars in loans on other occasions. In addition, the Thompsons had loaned him six hundred dollars. When John moved into an apartment after leaving the Thompsons', Norma met him there. She had a key and often dropped in when he was away, leaving notes, food, and miscellaneous mementoes. She wrote him what the newspapers later called "intellectual love letters." Some of these she signed "M" because, as John explained, "I always used to call her 'Ma'am,' whenever anyone was around, and it was a joke between us." On one occasion, when Frank McCauley came to see the children, he found John in the house, "manhandled" him, and forced him to leave until Frank was gone. Norma recited this incident when, in March, 1955, she finally divorced Frank on grounds of mental cruelty. By now Crooker had flunked out of U.C.L.A. Law School and had entered a small law school in Los Angeles called Southwestern.

John and Norma suffered through the usual tiffs and outbursts that mark the mating period, making up each time with endearments and pledges and a few tears. On one such occasion, Norma wrote John:

Darling:

We have had a rough day, haven't we? Neither of us want it to be that way, but because we care we are easily hurt and angered in our present situation. Please believe that it isn't intentional that I upset you. I would rather not have you that way at any time in our lives, and I wish I knew each time that I do beforehand so that I could prevent it. . . . Let's feel warm towards each other instead of defensive at all times, and try to remember that we are in love in spite of everything, and we are so lucky to have found each other. I feel the simple words, "I love you" all over when I write them to you, because I do love you with all my heart.

M.

But then, at the very end of May, 1955, they had a lovers' quarrel which carried on for three days. Thereafter, while John continued to love her, he had "anxieties" about her love for him. In fact, he apparently grew progressively anxious about his entire relationship with her. He admitted later that he threatened "to tell her mother about our relationship and to ask her mother to intercede in what was troubling Norma."

Norma apparently became seriously frightened. Until this time, despite the fact that she and John dated and that a few people knew of their affair, their relationship had remained essentially a secret one. But suddenly she began revealing to her friends, in varying degrees of confidence, what she had been up to. Hesitantly, with some embarrassment, she told John Baird that she had gone out with Crooker "a few times," that Crooker insisted she continue to go out with him, and that she didn't want to. She said Crooker had threatened to kill her and she was very much afraid of him. But when Baird insisted that she call the police, she refused. On another night, Norma again told Baird she was afraid of Crooker and that the strain was causing her insomnia. Exhausted, she dropped off to sleep while talking, and Baird, not wishing to bother her, read and dozed until six thirty in the morning—just as Rathmann was to do a few weeks later, the night before Norma's death.

Even while Norma was confiding to several of her male friends that someone was bothering her, her best friend, a young woman with whom she talked on the phone several times a day, was totally unaware of her relationship with Crooker. Peculiarly enough, however, the two women entered into an interesting arrangement a month or two before Norma's death: if either called the other and said she would have to break an engagement when no such engagement had been made, the other was to take this as a plea for help and call the police. But Norma never used the signal, even during the few hours immediately preceding her death.

In the meantime, the situation between Norma and John was becoming increasingly tense. On June 4, John wrote her that:

> As it is, I am aware of your intentions. You made them abundantly clear to me, especially after hearing the first writing of the context of this letter. You made the fact crystal clear that you intend to attempt to purge every breath of our love from your life, and you mean to do this despite any effort or caution which I may direct toward you. So I am sending this letter to you, praying that you have the courage born of past feelings and nurtured by future hopes to give expression to the bond which exists between us. For I have not made the bond between us, nor do they have the power to break that bond. That power is far beyond our earthly means. You are sweetness, gentleness personified, and I have met you and you have given yourself to me. Never before

to any other, and never again to any other. Then if my prayers are for naught, I will then write to your dad, to your mother, and to your brother separately. I will explain our love. I will explain that I am your husband in fact. I will describe the bond which exists between us. I will tell them the moral course and that if it isn't pursued I can no longer consider myself singly responsible before God, society, or myself for the past, the present, or the future, and I will be relieved of a great burden.

Less than a week later Norma met John for lunch and gave him three hundred dollars. John claimed it was a loan, but Norma told Baird over the telephone that John had demanded the money from her to return to Maine and had refused to leave after she gave it to him.

On June 18, Norma telephoned still another friend and told him that her ex-houseboy had just called and threatened to come over and hang himself in her back yard in front of the three children. The friend advised her to call the police, which she did, so that John had no sooner arrived at the house than he was accosted by an officer. John told the officer he had come for his law school notebook which Norma was copying for him, and Norma went into the house and got it for him. The officer stayed until John left. That afternoon John sent Norma a telegram: "Have tried to contact you. Must leave for the day. Will return late. If unable to contact you by tomorrow will proceed without further consideration. John Crooker." John admitted later that he meant by the telegram that he intended to contact Norma's mother.

That same evening, Norma told a friend that "John"–she did not identify him further–had warned her "he knew enough about the law that he would kill her and get by with it. He said if Chessman could do it, he could do it." The reference here obviously was to Caryl Chessman, convicted of sex crimes six years before and still in death row awaiting execution. Norma's friend said that John "must be a psycho," and she replied, "Well, I really don't think he will do anything to me." As the friend explained later, "She was betwixt and between.

She ran hot and cold on it. One time she would be excited about it, and another time she would have confidence that nothing would happen."

On June 22, according to John, Norma told him for the first time that she had had an abortion. John immediately sent her flowers, a fact confirmed by the flower company. But the coroner who ultimately performed an autopsy on Norma testified that he found no evidence that she had recently undergone an operation.

On that same day, June 22, John called Norma's mother and asked to see her. But Mrs. Thompson was leaving on a trip with her husband the next day and was very busy. John said he guessed it would be too late when she got back.

In the meantime, he continued to call Norma almost daily, sometimes many times a day, pleading with her to come back to him. According to telephone company records, John made thirteen calls to Norma's house on June 22, six on June 23, seven on June 24, and nine on June 25.

Perhaps Norma's most significant conversations during this entire period were with a man named Fred Chell, who had gone to college with John and who had often double-dated with Norma and John. Norma told Fred that John was constantly calling and writing her and that she could not seem to make him understand their affair was over. She was afraid John would carry out his threat to expose their relationship to her parents. Fred called John and tried to dissuade him from this, pointing out how exposure would hurt not only Norma but his own career as well, but John seemed determined to take some drastic action.

John had in his apartment some mementoes that Norma had given him, including a picture, and Norma wanted them back. She asked Fred Chell to tell her when John was not in his apartment so she could go get them. Fred, however, indicated that if she would give him a list of the items she wanted, he would get them from John.

That was on July 3. Fred Chell never got back the mementoes, because on the morning of July 5, Norma was found murdered.

The police were able to piece together much of this information, and now John Crooker, later on the day of Norma's death, stood in his apartment in his plaid bathrobe and faced two officers with drawn revolvers.

Crooker appeared calm except for a faint twitching of cheek muscles. He seemed older than his age and was good-looking in a pale, brooding way so attractive to many women. His dark hair was short and began high on his forehead. His lower lip and chin receded in a barely noticeable manner, and his jowls were a bit heavy. Wary eyes were set below thin eyebrows, and the over-all impression was of a young and not-quite-so-handsome Robert Taylor.

Crooker was allowed to dress, and then the three men sat for forty-five minutes like awkward strangers in a European railroad compartment, each politely avoiding the one topic on all their minds. Noting several legal books on a shelf, an officer asked Crooker if he was studying law. Crooker said he was a student at Southwestern Law School and that a number of policemen were taking courses there in their spare time. The conversation continued in this vein, guarded and general.

Los Angeles officers finally arrived, took custody of the prisoner from their Hollywood counterparts, and told him they wanted to search his apartment. He protested that they would have to obtain a search warrant. An officer replied that Crooker was under arrest on suspicion of murder (Crooker did not ask whose murder) and that no warrant was necessary. The search was not very time-consuming; the apartment was a studio type consisting only of a living room, dressing room, kitchen, and bathroom. Crooker's clothes were examined unsuccessfully for bloodstains. Match folders discovered in his living room were compared with those taken from Norma's ashtray, but the comparison proved futile. No knife and no keys to Norma's apartment turned up, but the officers did find in the glove compartment of John's car a packet of letters and notes between John and Norma.

Crooker claimed later that while the officers were searching his apartment, he twice requested permission to call an attorney and that his requests were ignored. The officers said they could not remember any such request. Crooker also claimed that the officers questioned him about a picture he had of Norma and about a poem he had written called "Consummation," but for some reason the officers never mentioned these incidents. The poem, reprinted in the Los Angeles *Times*, read:

> *Darkness closes in upon my*
> *thought that you are gone;*
> *And then I try to see beyond but*
> *Beyond your life and love*
> *with me there lies a void,*
> *Beyond sight,*
> *Beyond love,*
> *Beyond life*
> *Or its proximity,*
> *and such darkness,*
> *Just in its thought*
> *consumes me now.*

Finally, at four fifteen in the afternoon, Crooker was taken to the photographic section of Los Angeles' Central Police Station where, for well over an hour, he posed for pictures by police and newspaper photographers. One of their purposes was to record scratches on his face and indentations on his fingers. Crooker said he had cut his face while shaving and injured his fingers trying to release two cars involved in an accident. Some of the pictures were taken while he stood nude behind a partition. When the photographers were finished, he was taken to the polygraph section where a technician explained the intricacies of a lie detector machine. Crooker commented that he had understood from a discussion of the lie detector in one of his law school classes that the results of such a test could not be admitted in evidence unless the attorneys so stipulated. In any event, he said, he would not take the test. The technician asked, "Well, if you have nothing to hide, why not take the test? Have you killed anyone?" Crooker simply changed the subject. The technician admitted later that Crooker "was talking about an attorney. . . . I know there was something about a former instructor or teacher of law of some type that he thought he would like to contact some place along there. . . ." But no facilities for contacting an attorney were furnished the suspect.

Officers who had left Crooker to go to supper now returned with a hamburger, a bottle of milk, and a cigarette for their harassed prisoner. He finished eating at 8:30 P.M. and was sitting alone with Officer Jack Gotch when he specifically requested the opportunity to consult a lawyer. Gotch asked whom he wanted to call. Crooker said he did not know. Gotch told him that after the investigation had been concluded, Crooker could call an attorney, and if he did not have funds the court would appoint a public defender to handle his case without charge. Crooker said he thought a friend of his named Simpson, who had instructed him at Pepperdine College, would probably handle the case for him.

Officer Gotch was joined by three other officers who questioned Crooker for an hour, the principal discussion centering about the suspect's refusal to take the lie detector test. About nine thirty, Crooker was transferred to the West Los Angeles Police Station, where he was interrogated by five officers from eleven o'clock until shortly after midnight. The nature of the questioning had radically changed. It was more direct, more pointed, more challenging. The side issues had faded, and the officers now wanted to know about this crime. Crooker denied any part in it. He was booked, examined by a police doctor, and then questioned again from one to two o'clock in the morning.

Crooker later swore that during this period, ". . . Sgt.

Hooper had taken over the questioning, and was questioning me, and jumped up from his chair over to my chair and banged his hand down on my knee. When he did so, I turned to Lt. Armstrong and said 'There, you see,' and Lt. Armstrong said, 'What do you mean?'

"And I said, 'They are going to use force to make me answer their questions before I have an attorney.'

"Lt. Armstrong didn't say anything and turned around and walked out to the outer office. At this point Sgt. Hooper said . . . , 'Look, you son-of-a-bitch. I have been in this work for sixteen years, and I am not going to let someone like you come in here and tell me he is not going to answer questions. You are going to tell us what we want to know, and you are going to tell us now,' and with that he hit me with his fist in my stomach. I didn't say anything. I went up like this. . . ." Here Crooker demonstrated by pulling himself up sharply in his seat. Hooper, he said, hit him again in the stomach and told him, " 'You are going to give me the answers that I want or I am going to take you out there and work on you like that for the rest of the night.' " All of the officers, including Hooper, denied that any of this occurred. One of them admitted he had told Crooker they were tired of his answers and wanted to hear the truth, but he also claimed, somewhat inconsistently, that he told Crooker he did not have to talk.

It was now after two o'clock in the morning, almost thirteen hours since Crooker had been apprehended in his apartment. He had been booked, photographed, examined, fingerprinted, and questioned for hours by squads of officers. He was desperately tired. The tension in him, like a fever in a deathly illness, seemed to have built over the hours to a shattering crisis, and then passed, and suddenly he went limp.

He said quietly, "Well, I will write it out for you." Sensing victory, the officers scrambled about and provided several sheets of yellow paper and a pen with red ink. For the next hour, Crooker sat at a desk and wrote:

I, John Crooker, on Monday, July 4, 1955, attempted to communicate with Norma T. McCauley to talk with her and discuss the reasons and feelings for her rejections of our close and intimate relationship of nearly two years standing. As exactly as I can recall the following facts constituted the sequence of events which culminated in her death. I left my place of residence at approximately 3:00 o'clock p.m. and drove toward her residence. I may have stopped for gas on the way and arrived at the entrance of Bel Air at approximately 4:00 o'clock. I drove directly up past her home, saw her car in the garage and saw her two eldest children playing on the neighbor's lawn. Realizing the futility of continuing my attempts to talk with her at that time, I drove back down past her house, by her parents' residence, stopped to note some activity of bathers at their pool, and then proceeding [sic] to a vantage point on that side of the canyon. From there I watched until she drove down the road toward her parents' home.

I then drove down to the Stone Canyon Drive entrance to Sunset, up the west entrance again and past her home again. I then drove down to the U.C.L.A. parking area and called a Yellow cab and was driven to her residence. I went around the house to the rear and entered by the door at the children's room. Then I waited until she returned with the children in the early evening hours. I hid in a closet in the children's room, waiting until they were asleep. Norma came home about 12:00 or 1:00 o'clock a.m. She was followed home by some other car. The other car's occupant waited until she closed her garage door and went around, opening her front door, and then drove away.

I waited in the children's room until she was in her own bedroom. Then I opened her door, which was ajar. Norma was stunned to see me but she remained remarkably calm and self-contained. I, on the other hand, was extremely nervous and generally unable to make myself realize that I was there in her room and had taken the means described to see her.

We talked for over an hour. Norma had been out, had some cocktails and felt sleepy. I tried again, as I had tried many, many times before by telephone and by letter to get her to tell me her reasons and feelings for leaving me. I told her that I could not believe that my threats were the answer. But Norma would not talk about it. I sat near her on the chaise lounge, smoking one cigarette after another and every few minutes going close to her to see whether or not she was really sleeping, and I think she was at least dozing. And I didn't know what to do. For days and days I had not known what to do. I had tried threats and coercion and profession of my feeling for her. She had rebuffed all my attempts and now she was going to sleep?

On the dresser by the door to her bedroom with a child's toy revolver and other things, I found a kitchen [sic] about ten inches long with the blade about six inches.

At this point a police officer, reading each page as Crooker finished it, pointed out that the word "knife" apparently had been left out after the word "kitchen." Crooker inserted the word. The confession continued:

I took the knife and went back to the chaise lounge. Then I put the knife in my coat pocket and knelt beside her for what seemed to be a long time. She was asleep. I took her throat in my hand and she awoke and started to scream. I heard the maid, so I reached the knife in my pocket while holding my hand over her mouth. Then I hit her with the knife and push and push on it but she still made sounds and struggled on the lounge. I choked her more with some clothes around her throat and after a long time she was still and the house was still, and I couldn't realize that Norma was gone. I took the knife, her car keys, and some money and thought I must take her car and go, but I walked and walked and walked. The dawn was coming when I reached my car, got in, drove home, took off my clothes and threw them into the incinerator. I went to bed and must have slept some because shortly before noon I couldn't sleep any more. I just waited for time to run out.

Somewhere along the way I must have thrown out her keys and the knife because I didn't have them in the things I threw in the incinerator. I took some money from her purse and her keys to her car and the knife with me.

John R. Crooker, Jr.

If Crooker thought this bit of catharsis would end the interrogation, he was sadly mistaken. The confession was no sooner completed than the officers drove him in the waning hours of the muggy July night to Norma's home for a re-enactment of the crime. He showed them how he had entered the house through the nursery door, which he said had been unlocked;

he pointed out Frank McCauley's closet where he had stood waiting for Norma; he led them to the bedroom where, less than twenty-four hours before, Norma had been murdered. Finally, at 5:00 A.M., the officers and their prisoner drove off along Somera Road, just as Melvin Rathmann had done at the same hour two days before.

Crooker was placed in his cell, and sleep came quickly. But the police work went on. Detectives returned to Somera Road in mid-morning and gingerly took from the top shelf of Frank McCauley's closet a glass partially filled with an amber liquid and three or four cigarette butts. The liquid they identified by its smell as urine. Quite inexplicably, they threw the entire contents of the glass down a toilet. When the surface of the glass was dusted, it fairly glowed with loops and whorls which were quickly identified as Crooker's fingerprints.

Other detectives drove to Crooker's apartment house and, in a thoroughly messy operation, sifted through twenty large barrels of ashes—the entire contents of the basement incinerator. They turned up melted keys, earrings, shoe soles, tin cans, zipper locks, and extraneous ragtag pieces of clothing, but nothing to connect John Crooker with the murder.

After lunch, the indefatigable police took a now refreshed Crooker to the office of Ernest Roll, the Los Angeles County district attorney, and asked him to repeat orally the substance of the confession he had already written. The prosecutor obviously was perplexed by some facts missing from Crooker's confession, including the whereabouts of the death knife. Crooker recited his story freely until he began telling about his entrance to Norma's house, at which point he balked. He insisted that he be allowed to speak with an attorney.

Roll asked him whom he had in mind. Crooker named Raymond Simpson, a Long Beach attorney who had taught him a history course at Pepperdine College and who had known him socially during law school days. Roll put through a telephone call to Simpson, explained that Crooker was under arrest, and allowed Crooker to take the phone.

Crooker told Simpson he had repeatedly asked for an attorney, he felt he needed counsel, and he hoped Simpson would represent him. He asked whether he was obliged to answer the questions of his interrogators—"Do they have the right to use any physical force to have me continue with the questioning?" Simpson said they did not. Crooker said, "I see. Well, probably they will attempt to continue with the questioning, and probably to avoid the force I will have to talk with them." District Attorney Roll, who was listening on an extension, broke into the conversation and told Simpson he had advised Crooker he did not have to answer any questions. When Crooker again referred to physical force, Roll broke in a second time and denied that any force was being used. Crooker told Simpson he had already given the police a statement in which he had "tried to express myself as well as possible. There are holes that I cannot fill and they insist that I fill them." Simpson made arrangements to see Crooker at the jail at seven o'clock that night.

After he hung up, Crooker continued to talk to Roll and his confederates at great length, reviewing essentially the same facts he had covered in his written confession. Finally, spent and nervous, the suspect was returned to his cell. As soon as he talked to Simpson that night, Crooker repudiated his confessions, asserting that they had been obtained against his will.

In the meantime, the Los Angeles papers were going out of their linotyped minds with the thrill of the whole performance. The murder and John's arrest were on all the front pages, and pictures of the participants, Norma's home, even her children, appeared in profusion. Neighbors, the Thompsons, Frank McCauley, John Baird—they were all interviewed. On July 7, the day Crooker talked to Simpson, the police revealed that Norma had given John a good deal of money, and the Los Angeles *Times* headlined across its entire front page in bold black type, SEE BLACKMAIL MOTIVE IN DIVORCEE'S MURDER. On the same page, but in smaller type, the newspaper told of another and an even more famous prison inmate: DEATH-CELL AUTHOR CHESSMAN GETS 7TH REPRIEVE. Mr. Justice Clark had granted Caryl Chessman another stay of execution.

Four months passed. Crooker was indicted for murder, pleaded not guilty, and obtained successively two new attorneys. The second, the man who would remain with Crooker through all of the grueling months to follow, was Robert W. Armstrong of Huntington Park, California.

Armstrong was thirty-two, a contemporary of Crooker's. The son of the former chief of police of Huntington Park, he was thoroughly familiar with police routine and practices. He received his education at Crooker's college, Pepperdine, and at the University of Southern California Law School, and decided early on trial practice as his particular specialty. He was a hard-hitting young attorney and made an attractive appearance before a jury, standing over six feet tall and well built, with a touch of gray appearing at his temples. The state attorney general, Edmund G. ("Pat") Brown, appointed two prosecutors to oppose him at the trial, Adolph Alexander and Allan H. McCurdy. These men, both in their late forties, were in many ways later editions of their opponent—forceful, presentable in appearance, and indefatigable.

The trial opened on November 17, 1955, in the superior court of Los Angeles County before Judge Stanley Mosk, and lasted seventeen trial days. It was brilliantly conducted. All three attorneys seemed thoroughly prepared, although Armstrong had been retained only a month before, and their questions were sharp and unrelenting. Their cross-examination of experts—the rarest form of successful questioning—was informed, rewarding, and productive on both sides. In one instance, Alexander, by means of a physical demonstration and by the sheer audacity of question-built-upon-question, forced an expert appearing for the defense to qualify his original testimony to such an extent that its effect was largely dissipated, a feat quite rare in the courtroom, where the expert normally is far better versed in his own specialty than his examiner.

Judge Mosk was brusque but fair. He listened to all pertinent argument, but as soon as he had ruled—and his rulings were incisively to the point—all argument ended and the trial proceeded. He allowed Crooker's confession to be read to the jury only after a thorough inquiry into how it was obtained and under careful instructions that the jury was to decide for itself whether, under all the circumstances, the confession had been given voluntarily. He allowed the jurors to look at most of the pictures taken by the police but excluded one close-up of Norma's body on the ground that it was too macabre and would only tend to inflame them. On another occasion, when the defense was attempting to introduce several of Norma's letters, the judge stated, "The Court has grave doubts as to the propriety of admitting this, but if we must err it must be on the side of admissibility for the defendant." He never lost his temper, but at one point he came very close. This was when the prosecution offered evidence of what Crooker had told the district attorney after his telephone conversation with Simpson. It developed that the district attorney not only had listened in on an extension and had interrupted twice with his own comments but had tape-recorded Crooker's part of the conversation. Judge Mosk fixed the two prosecution attorneys with a malevolent stare and ruled:

> Now the Court has always had high regard for the ethical standards of the office of the District Attorney. However, the conduct of the District Attorney, in listening to the defendant's conversation with an attorney, interrupting the conversation on an extension phone, is highly improper for a law enforcement officer who is a member of the bar. This Court cannot put its stamp of approval on this conduct by admitting the subsequent proceedings into evidence.

When Crooker took the stand in his own defense, he spoke very softly, sometimes coughed nervously, and quite often gave unresponsive answers. Judge Mosk admonished him on several occasions to answer the questions more directly. Armstrong came to the bench and expressed concern that the judge's impatience might indicate to the jury a disbelief in Crooker's story. The judge denied any such possibility but thereafter was more restrained in his attitude toward the defendant.

Crooker's story was simple enough. Certainly he had waited in the closet for Norma, had smoked the cigarettes, and had urinated in the glass. But that was July 3, not July 4; it was the night Melvin Rathmann had met Norma at the Thompsons', followed her home, and talked to her until five o'clock in the morning. Crooker said he had prearranged to see Norma after that party. First he waited outside her house, standing on a limb of the scrub tree in the back yard so he could keep an eye on Somera Road. He was watching a strange car stop momentarily in front of the house when he fell from the tree, and that was how he had scratched his hands. Then he went inside to the nursery through the sliding door on the patio which Norma had left unlocked for him. The three children were already asleep. He pushed one bed away from the wall and waited in the closet. Norma met him after Rathmann left, and the two of them talked in her bedroom. Norma told him that certain persons whom she refused to name had found out about her relationship with him and her abortion, and had threatened to ruin her if she did not give them a great deal of money. It was because of these people, she said, that she was trying to break off with him, to make him stay away. It was because of them that she wanted her letters and poems and pictures back, and not because she no longer loved him. He did not leave until six o'clock in the morning.

Crooker said that the next day, July 4, he left his car at the U.C.L.A. parking lot and called a cab to take him back to

Norma's house. This fact had already been confirmed by the cab driver, whose testimony, while helpful to the prosecution in the sense that it placed Crooker at the scene of the crime on July 4, also raised the question of why a killer would call a cab, give his right name, and be driven in style to the scene of his intended crime. Crooker's only explanation for his actions was that he was trying to find out who was threatening Norma. He went to her house "out of desperation more than anything else, to do something. I didn't want to just sit in my apartment with her being threatened in that manner."

Standing in the sub-structure of a new house being built across the street, he saw Norma bring the children home from the party and later saw the two cars pull up—John Baird with Norma and Bob Block with Pat Gallagher. He watched while Baird said good night. Then he walked to the kitchen window in time to see Norma answer the telephone. Thinking that she was now safe, he walked all the way back to the U.C.L.A. parking lot, picked up his car, and drove home. He insisted that at no time on July 4 did he go inside Norma's house.

Mr. Armstrong: "Did you kill Norma McCauley?"

Mr. Crooker: "No, I did not."

Mr. Armstrong: "Did you stab Norma McCauley?"

Mr. Crooker: "No, I did not."

Mr. Armstrong: "Did you tie a stole or scarf around Norma's neck?"

Mr. Crooker: "No, I did not."

Crooker said he wrote the confession because he wanted to get away from the police. He "didn't want to go on with this," and they told him that if he confessed, "they would leave me alone." He claimed that all of the pertinent facts recited in the confession had been supplied to him by the police during the previous hours of interrogation.

Alexander rigorously cross-examined the defendant. After reviewing in detail Crooker's relationship with Norma and the events leading up to her death, he read each sentence in the confession, one by one, and asked Crooker whether the sentence was in his own language, what part of it someone had told him to write, whether it expressed his own thought, and whether it contained the truth. When the prosecutor was finished, the net impression he left was of a document based largely on the defendant's own information, written almost entirely in his own words, and expressing a number of facts which he admitted were true.

A reconstruction of the crime itself came out largely through the testimony of the doctor who had performed the autopsy. Norma had died, he said, as the result of a massive hemorrhage due to stab wounds of the chest and strangulation. Of the eleven stab wounds, the second, penetrating deep into her chest, was the chief cause of death. About ten to fifteen minutes elapsed between the second and third wounds. One peculiarity of California trials is that the jurors may interrogate witnesses, and it was a juror who drew from the doctor this information that the stabbing was accomplished not in a flash but over a period of many minutes.

The doctor said that most or all the wounds preceded the strangulation, which was accomplished first by hand and then by wrapping the white stole tightly around her neck. She also had been hit on the head by a heavy object. Some of the wounds he characterized as "defense wounds," incurred during the course of a struggle. He estimated the death weapon to be a knife at least four inches long and about three-quarters of an inch in width.

The doctor could not estimate the time of death. He pointed out, however, that he found eight ounces of food in Norma's stomach, some of it identifiable as meat and peas, and that she must have eaten the food less than four hours—and probably closer to two and a half hours—before her death. He testified that while there was some alcohol in her blood, she had not been intoxicated. Neither had she been pregnant, and there was no evidence of sexual intercourse immediately preceding the crime. The good doctor, coldly methodical to the end, stepped down.

Despite an attorney's preparation and resourcefulness, even carefully laid plans go awry at a trial. The prosecution, in an effort to prove that no threats or force were used against Crooker, attempted to show that an intrepid newspaper reporter had crouched on a ledge below the window of the interrogation room at police headquarters and overheard the entire conversation leading up to the confession. Unfortunately, it developed that the reporter was vacationing in Mexico and was thus unavailable to testify, and his partner, attempting to demonstrate what had occurred, was hindered by a diagram of police headquarters which some hapless subordinate in the prosecutor's office had drawn completely backwards. The entire line of questioning collapsed.

Mrs. Thompson, a handsome woman with Norma's thin, sensual lips, made a devastating witness for the prosecution. She broke down at the outset of her testimony but quickly recovered. She told how John Crooker had called her less than two weeks before Norma's death and asked her to have lunch with him, and how she had declined because she was busy preparing for a trip. John had said, "Well, you know, I told you that sometime I would like to have a talk with you, and I feel this time has come; but, of course, you are going to be gone for two weeks, I guess it will be too late, anyway." The following night, said Mrs. Thompson, she told Norma about John's call and expressed concern that he might commit suicide. But Norma had replied: "Oh, Mother, don't waste any sympathy on him. He just wants money." When Mrs. Thompson repeated John's assurance that he had steady employment, Norma demurred: "Well, I happen to know he is out of a job. I told him to get out and hustle for a job, that a job wasn't going to come up and offer itself to him. Mother, he just goes around trying to get people's sympathy so that they will help him. It no doubt was money. . . . I am just avoiding him, and

I advise you just to do the same, just avoid him, because he is just no good, Mother."

McCurdy made the closing argument for the prosecution and gave no quarter to the defendant. He said this was a premeditated killing if there ever was one, and he demanded the death penalty. The motives, he argued, were revenge and blackmail. Crooker was "shaking down" Norma McCauley, threatening her constantly, obtaining over thirteen hundred dollars from her and another four hundred from her parents. Crooker, outraged when Norma tried to cut off both the money and her intimate relationship with him, deliberately murdered her.

The evidence against Crooker, said McCurdy, was overwhelming. The confession, spelled out in the defendant's own words, was corroborated by a myriad of facts, including the testimony of the taxi driver, the fingerprints on the glass in the closet, the urine in the glass, the injuries to his hands and face, the threats and calls recounted by Norma to her friends, the fact that Craig's bed was moved away from the closet, and Crooker's re-enactment of the crime at the scene. As to the voluntariness of the confession, McCurdy asked the jurors to look at all the circumstances: the police swore there was no violence, and surely if there had been, some of the newspapermen who were all over the police station would have heard of it. And certainly this Crooker, versed in the law, knew that he had a right to remain silent; his decision to speak must have come from a desire to tell the truth.

McCurdy pointed to various discrepancies in Crooker's story. For example, Crooker had tried to make the jury believe that his lovers' quarrel in late May had been patched up and that Norma still cared for him during June and early July, and yet his letters, phone calls, and threats, and Norma's entire course of conduct, showed that she was badly frightened of him. Then too, Crooker had given at least two different versions of how his hands were injured—first by disentangling cars and then by falling out of the scrub tree. Actually, said McCurdy, he had been hurt while struggling with Norma.

Derisively, McCurdy said that this man who pretended to have loved Norma McCauley had not hesitated to besmirch her name by testifying falsely that she had had an abortion. And in a bit of melodramatics which Armstrong would make him regret, McCurdy paraphrased Shakespeare: "Et Tu, Crooker, the most unkindest cut of all."

Crooker was thus painted as a cruel, vicious, blackmailing killer.

Despite the fervor of the prosecution's attack, Armstrong's counterattack was in no way apologetic. With imagination and skill, he incessantly picked away at every unexplained or conflicting piece of evidence until the entire mosaic of the prosecution's case looked flaky and pock-marked.

First, he said, there was the question of blood. There had been blood all around Norma, and even the police assumed that the killer had come away so covered with blood that he burned his clothes. If Crooker had been the killer, he might well have burned his clothes, but why was no blood found on the seat of his car?

The same police who had so carefully examined that car had neglected even to test the blood in Norma's room to determine whether some of it belonged to the killer. They assumed there had been a struggle, and some of the blood was so far up on the golden-brown drapes that it probably was not hers, and yet they had allowed the drapes to be taken out and cleaned before anyone could test them. Why?

Armstrong tried to turn to his own advantage Crooker's law school training, pointing out that with Crooker's intelligence, education, and brief introduction to the law, it was reasonable to assume that he had realized his need for counsel and had repeatedly requested it. When his requests were denied, Crooker was forced by means of threats and actual physical force to write a false confession. Armstrong made his point by comparing Crooker with Caryl Chessman, "the red-light bandit," whom Crooker allegedly had cited to Norma as proof that he could get away with murder. "Did John Crooker behave like a Chessman at any time? Did he take this arrogant attitude, 'I can be counsel by myself; I can be my own attorney; I can take care of my legal problems'? No! From the very beginning he refuted any notion that he was like a Caryl Chessman. He said, 'I need an attorney. I want an attorney. Won't you let me call an attorney?' . . . So don't ever make the mistake in this case of thinking that John is the type of person that is like a Chessman."

If the confession was voluntary and the police were not ashamed of how they had obtained it, why didn't they tape-record the entire interrogation, as they did when Crooker finally was allowed to talk to an attorney, demanded Armstrong. Moreover, parts of the confession simply made no sense. What was a large kitchen knife doing on the dresser in the bedroom, and how could Crooker have gotten a knife this size into his pocket? Remember, no knife was ever found. Moreover, John stated in the confession that he found and took a set of car keys, and yet John Baird saw Norma leave her keys on the kitchen bar, and Norma's brother discovered them there the next morning. Finally, some of the wording of the confession—such as Crooker's use of the wrong tense in some places—indicated he was in a semitrance by the time he wrote it. The entire confession, said Armstrong, was worthless.

Without the confession, he said, the state had no case. The police did not find the car keys or the knife referred to in the confession. They found no fingerprints at all except those on the glass, which were easily explained. The matches and the fingernail clippings had produced nothing at all. There were no bloody clothes and no bloody car. No eyewitnesses. The confession was all they had.

The young attorney ridiculed the state's theory of the motive. An extortionist does not kill his victim; he protects her.

If Crooker wanted to continue his relationship with Norma and to obtain more money from her, why would he end both the relationship and the money by killing her?

Armstrong had his own theory of what had actually happened. At first, said Armstrong, Norma gave John money because she loved him; later, she continued to give him money because she *had* loved him and did not want to hurt him; she wanted to let him down easily. During this latter period John could not believe that Norma would not change her mind and return his love; she had changed her mind so many times before. Regardless of what Norma thought, John was convinced that their quarrel did not signal the end of their relationship.

Armstrong theorized that Norma had white-lied to Baird. Because she respected and liked Baird and did not want him to think less of her, she made it appear that she had dated Crooker only a few times and that the former houseboy was now forcing his attentions upon her. Then when Norma was actually threatened by a third party and became concerned over the seriousness of the threat, she made arrangements to meet Crooker after the party on July 3 to get her letters back. She wanted to destroy all evidence of her relationship with him so that no one could blackmail her. Then on July 4, after coming home, she met her killer, left the house with him, ate somewhere, and returned home, where he murdered her. This, said Armstrong, was the only possible explanation of the crime, because on the Fourth Norma had finished dinner at the Thompsons' by 8:30 P.M., no one had seen her eat anything afterwards, and she took none of the leftovers home with her. She was alive at least until 1:15 A.M., when Jean Davis spoke to her on the phone. Yet the doctor had testified that the food in her stomach probably was consumed two and a half hours before she was killed. Therefore, she must have eaten with someone after she arrived home.

Armstrong never named his own candidate for the role of murderer. But he bluntly told the jury that the maid, Laurie

Dromtra, knew more than she was telling. Her story, said the attorney, simply did not stand up. For example, she testified that she never heard the telephone ring after she had gone to bed. Yet she admitted that the extension in the kitchen was easily heard in her room and that her door was slightly ajar. There was indisputable evidence from Jean Davis and George Fox that the phone rang not once but many times after Norma returned home. Could it have been that Laurie was a deep sleeper? Hardly, since the mere "fidgeting" on the part of Cinders easily wakened her. And, incidentally, if Cinders was so fidgety, why had he not welcomed his mistress when she arrived with John Baird?

Laurie also had claimed she heard no screams. But if ten to fifteen minutes elapsed between the second and third knife wounds, why didn't Norma scream? Moreover, if it was John Crooker in Norma's room, and Norma was so terrified of him, as the prosecution claimed, the confession certainly made no sense, because according to the confession, she talked to Crooker for over an hour and then *fell asleep*. If she was so frightened, why didn't she say something to Jean over the phone about her fright? Why didn't she call her girl friend and use the code which they had devised to ask each other for help?

Armstrong, the son of a police officer, was unremittingly caustic about the work of the authorities in this case. He called some of the officers "hoodlums," and he accused a jail attendant of outright perjury. Repeatedly, he made fun of the investigating officers who threw clues down the toilet and allowed bloodstained drapes to be sent to the cleaner's.

Wryly, Armstrong referred to McCurdy's use of Shakespeare. Mark Antony had indeed accused Brutus of "the most unkindest cut of all." But, Armstrong reminded the jurors, that was when Antony knew only half the case. "When Mark Antony knew the whole case, when he knew all the facts and circumstances of the case, and knew what Brutus really was, he stood over Brutus and said, 'This was the noblest Roman of them all. . . . His life was gentle, and the elements so mixed in him that nature might stand up and say to all the world, "This was a man!" ' "

Assistant Attorney General Alexander took over the rebuttal from his cohort, McCurdy. He told the jury it had heard "probably as vicious a tirade against public officials as any jury ever did." He ridiculed the theory of Crooker as a gentle man. Instead, Crooker had gone to Norma's house bent on murder and had carefully covered his tracks—"the Chessman brain." The prosecutor exhorted the jurors, "You know, you saw him on the stand; you heard him testify. I dare say you will never have the misfortune of seeing a shrewder, more cunning icicle than this defendant, Crooker. If there is such a thing as qualifications for being a killer, he has them all."

And so the case went to the jury of eight women and four men at 4:05 on the afternoon of December 8, 1955. An hour and a quarter later, the foreman sent a note to Judge Mosk asking whether the jurors could consider the confession if they found that Crooker had demanded and been denied the opportunity to consult counsel before writing it. The judge brought the jury back to the courtroom and reread his instructions on this point to the effect that the refusal to allow Crooker to consult an attorney did not in and of itself make the confession involuntary, but that such refusal could be considered by the jury along with all the other facts in deciding whether the confession had been given voluntarily or involuntarily.

The foreman then asked that the testimony of certain witnesses, including Laurie Dromtra, be reread. It was. The jury went to supper from 6:30 to 8:30 and then deliberated until 10:00 P.M. No poll was taken that evening, the jurors contenting themselves with discussing the facts of the case. The next morning, a Friday, they were up at 7:00 A.M., breakfasted until 8:00 A.M., and began their deliberations at 9:05. The first poll was taken at 11:30, and it was unanimous as to guilt. Two jurors, however, were undecided as to the degree of punishment. Lunch was sent in. Finally, at 1:47 P.M., after about seven and a half hours of actual deliberation, the jury returned its verdict of guilty of murder in the first degree, without recommendation of mercy. Crooker was thus doomed to death.

When Crooker was brought in for sentencing the following Monday, Armstrong told Judge Mosk that over the weekend he had discovered that at supper on the first evening of their deliberations, several jurors had consumed alcoholic beverages, and he moved that a new trial be granted, citing cases in which verdicts had been vacated when reached by intoxicated jurors. Judge Mosk called the foreman to the stand, who explained that eleven of the jurors had had one cocktail apiece before dinner. The foreman swore that no one had shown any effects of the drinks, and no vote on the case was taken until the following morning. Judge Mosk denied the motion for a new trial and sentenced Crooker to death.

It took almost a year for the case to work itself up to the Supreme Court of California. Armstrong argued at least seven different points to this august body, including the consumption of alcohol by the jury and the conduct of District Attorney Roll in listening in on Crooker's telephone conversation with his attorney. But Armstrong's two principal arguments were that Crooker had been denied due process of law by the refusal of the police to allow him counsel before he confessed, and that the confession itself had been coerced from him in violation of his constitutional rights.

The seven-man California Supreme Court, with one judge dissenting, turned down Armstrong's argument. The court ruled that the evidence was in conflict as to when and what Crooker requested in the way of legal advice and as to the circumstances surrounding the confession, and the conflict had been presented to and resolved by the jury. Moreover, to constitute a denial of due process, the lack of counsel must have so fatally infected the regularity of the trial as to result in a miscarriage of justice—which did not seem to have been the case here.

Judge Carter, the lone dissenter, disagreed with his brethren about the proper legal test to be applied. Once a suspect demands a lawyer and is turned down, the subsequent confession should be thrown out without any attempt to determine the exact amount of prejudice which might have resulted. "It appears to me," he wrote, "that if our constitutional safeguards are to be observed, they should be observed to the letter."

Armstrong sought and was denied a rehearing by the state court. But by now he had decided to ask the Supreme Court of the United States to review the case. He was encouraged by notice that the American Civil Liberties Union would file a brief on Crooker's behalf.

Undoubtedly, Judge Carter's dissent influenced at least to some extent the decision of the United States Supreme Court to hear Crooker's case. Theoretically, an important legal issue is either present or it is not, and the dissent of a state court judge should have little to do with whether that issue must be reviewed by a higher court. Actually, however, a dissent often is of great influence. The reason is twofold. First, a lawyer who argues that an important constitutional question is involved in his case often has a difficult time showing the facts of record that support the question. But when a state court judge (particularly one known and respected by the Justices) dissents on constitutional grounds, it means that at least one impartial arbiter has found the facts to support the question and has found substance to the question. Secondly, a judge often can articulate a viewpoint more accurately and persuasively than a lawyer, and he may thus ferret out and hold up for view serious points which otherwise would not sufficiently impress the higher court judges.

Armstrong presented a number of issues in his petition, but the Supreme Court limited the number it would hear to two: whether Crooker had been denied due process (1) by the refusal to allow him to consult an attorney when he demanded the opportunity, and (2) by the admission of the confession which was taken from him after he had been in custody for fourteen hours and had not been allowed to consult an attorney.

Like most of the constitutional problems to come before the courts, these two came not nakedly but with the gloss of prior interpretation. As Armstrong was well aware when he arose to argue his client's case on April 2, 1958, three previous cases decided by the Court bore directly on the problem before him.

The first was *Powell v. Alabama*, handed down in 1932. It involved seven illiterate Negroes convicted of raping two white girls. They had been unable to employ counsel and incapable adequately to provide their own defense. The Supreme Court reversed their death sentences, stating: "All that it is necessary now to decide, as we do decide, is that in a capital case, where the defendant is unable to employ counsel, and is incapable adequately of making his own defense because of ignorance, feeble mindedness, illiteracy, or the like, it is the duty of the court, whether requested or not, to assign counsel for him as a necessary requisite of due process of law. . . ." The Court also indicated that the defendants should have had the advice of counsel during the period preceding the trial.

In the second case, *Betts v. Brady*, the Supreme Court held in 1942 that in a *non*capital case, due process does not require the appointment of counsel, even at the request of the defendant, unless unfairness results from the refusal to grant the request.

The third decision was *House v. Mayo* in 1945. Here, a man in his twenties, uneducated and a stranger in town, hired an attorney who happened to be away when the defendant was required to plead guilty to burglary. The defendant's request for an opportunity to consult with his attorney was refused. The Supreme Court reversed the conviction, ruling that when the defendant was not afforded a reasonable opportunity to consult with his own attorney, he was denied his constitutional right to a fair trial.

But these cases, as close as they were to the matter at hand, did not really solve the precise problem presented by Crooker. When a legal problem is as amorphous as that involved in an interpretation of "due process," slight factual distinctions and variations can be decisive. Crooker had been represented by an attorney at his trial. He had even received legal advice from an attorney (Simpson) during part of the period preceding the trial. His claim was based upon the fact that during the crucial hours preceding his confession, he had been denied counsel. The Supreme Court had never decided whether a confession was inadmissible when obtained after a specific request for an attorney was made and denied. The Court had never defined "unfair treatment" when the man being denied an attorney is intelligent and educated. And, despite the general language in the Powell case, the Court had never held specifically that in a capital case a state must grant a defendant's request for an attorney during the period preceding the trial.

Armstrong, of course, argued that the general language in the Powell case and the spirit of the law expressed in the House case should be extended to Crooker's situation. In other words, the Court should rule that a defendant, particularly in a capital case, cannot be denied an attorney during his interrogation period if he expressly requests one.

On the other hand, William E. James, the deputy attorney general assigned to argue the case for the State of California, wanted the Court to extend the rule in Betts; he asked for a rule that even in a capital case, the denial of an attorney during the period preceding the trial should not affect the conviction unless the defendant can prove he was actually prejudiced by the refusal to provide counsel.

Through a concession in his brief, James was able to avoid a clash with the Justices. The California Supreme Court had held that the record was in doubt in regard to Crooker's request for an attorney and any resulting unfairness from his failure to have one. James, upon reviewing the record, could see that the prosecution's own witnesses had admitted that Crooker requested an attorney—perhaps not as many times as he claimed, but certainly one and perhaps two times prior to his confession. And so James conceded to the United States Supreme Court that Crooker had asked for counsel and been turned down. When James heard the Justices' questions at oral argument, he realized he had made a wise move, because most of them exhibited a thorough knowledge of the lengthy record. James was treated with courtesy, and the argument proceeded along strictly professional lines, with none of the rancor that marks some of the Court's sessions.

Perhaps it was confusing to those sitting in the courtroom that so little was said about the crime. But the question of guilt or innocence was no longer involved. The issue now was purely a legal one, having to do with the conduct of the California authorities after Crooker was in custody. It no longer mattered whether Crooker murdered Norma, and all the facts of their relationship so luridly detailed by the press were totally beside the point. All of the arguments about conflicts and inconsistencies in the record were part of the past, as was the evidence about unrequited love, threats, telephone calls, the abortion, and the rest. Even the truthfulness of the confession itself was not in issue. The question to be decided was what rule of law should govern; once determined, that rule would be applied without regard to the issue of guilt. In fact, only one aspect of the crime played a part—the fact that it was a capital crime. This was a death case. And in death cases, the normal rules do not always apply.

The arguments were completed, and the two attorneys flew back to California, the decision now out of their hands. During the following three months, while they waited curiously for the result, the Justices moved through the vital decision-making stage of their work.

First, a preliminary vote was taken at the weekly conference. Because Chief Justice Warren and Justice Black were both in dissent, the next senior Justice, Frankfurter, was called upon to assign the majority opinion. He selected Justice Tom C. Clark. Justice Douglas agreed informally to write for the dissenters.

After the case had been assigned, Clark conferred with his two law clerks. Ever since a wag commented some years ago that the Senate need not bother about the confirmation of Justices but should confirm the appointment of law clerks, the role of these shadowy figures in the work of the Court has been dubious if not downright suspect. Quite obviously, the use of law clerks depends upon the Justice to whom they are assigned. They are his to do with as he pleases, and some Justices use them more than others. Generally, however, the law clerk's duties fall into three categories.

The first is to condense to manageable proportions the mass of petitions asking the Court to hear cases. The clerks do not pass upon these petitions; they do not sift or eliminate. They merely distill facts, points of law, and authorities for their own Justice so that he will have time to pass upon each petition. It has been demonstrated time and again that if each Justice were to read every page of the mass of materials presented in all cases, he could devote only a few minutes to each case, including cases that are argued and decided. Therefore, some condensation is essential to the operation of the Court.

The clerk's second job is to work on the written opinions of his Justice. Sometimes a clerk is allowed to try his hand at a first draft, but more often than not the Justice writes the draft and the clerk checks authorities, fills in citations, etc. In no case is the clerk solely or even chiefly responsible for the finished product.

The third and most important task of the clerk is to act as a sounding board. Although the Justices do talk law informally among themselves, it is the law clerk—available nights, days, or weekends—who provides the Justice his most frequent opportunity to "sound off." And it is here that the clerk serves his most important and most delicate function. A good clerk will argue, cajole, deride, imagine new hypotheses, attack questionable assumptions—all in an effort not to make the Justice change his mind but to make him think through his decision. These sessions between each Justice and his clerks are sometimes heated, often lengthy, and almost always productive.

Justice Clark read the Crooker record and began the painstaking task of constructing an opinion. His nemesis on this particular case, Justice Douglas, roughed in his dissent. The majority opinion was printed in the basement of the Supreme Court Building by the select group of printers who devote their entire time to the Justices' opinions and speeches. It was then circulated among all nine judges. With the majority opinion before him, Justice Douglas finished his dissent, had it printed, and likewise circulated it among all the Justices.

As in a county pie-baking contest, the votes informally trickled in. A handwritten note, a formal letter, or scribblings on the back of the printed opinion—anything might serve as notice to the author that he has corralled the vote of such and such a Justice. The vote is not always as expected. A Justice who voted with the majority at the first conference may find that the reasoning he was employing, when put in cold print, simply will not hold up. Another Justice may agree with the entire opinion except for one phrase or sentence or paragraph with which he cannot honestly associate himself. The author then has the choice of changing the objectionable part to pick up a vote or of standing his ground. Among all the Justices, Clark was probably the most conciliatory and consequently enjoyed a high percentage of unanimous or near-unanimous opinions.

When a majority has finally joined an opinion, and the dissents and concurrences are all written, the decision is ready for delivery in open court.

The Crooker decision was rendered on June 30, 1958, the last day of the term. By a vote of five to four, the Court upheld Crooker's conviction.

Clark wrote for himself and Justices Felix Frankfurter, Harold H. Burton, John M. Harlan, and Charles E. Whittaker. Douglas dissented with Chief Justice Warren and Justices Hugo L. Black and William J. Brennan, Jr.—a quartet soon to become a familiar and cohesive dissenting bloc in due process cases before the Court.

Clark's statement of the facts was interesting. He emphasized that Crooker, "under sentence of death for the murder of his paramour," was "a college graduate who had attended the first year of law school." In telling the story of the crime, the Justice said that Crooker waited for Norma outside her house, watched her return home, and saw her talk on the telephone. This was the version Crooker gave at the trial rather than in his confession. It is not clear why Clark used these facts, particularly since he claimed to be relying only upon the "undisputed facts in the record," whereas this version was disputed by Crooker's own confession.

The Justice took up Armstrong's legal points in reverse order. First, was the confession coerced from Crooker? It was true that Crooker had been detained for fourteen hours prior to the confession and had not been taken "promptly" before a committing magistrate as required by California law. It was also true that the police had admonished Crooker to tell the truth. But these facts alone had never been held to violate due process of law. Thus, reasoned Clark, Crooker's claim of coercion rested almost entirely upon the denial of his request for an attorney. The Court, said Clark, had not previously decided this precise issue.

Of course, coercion seems more likely to result when a state denies a *specific request* for an attorney than when it simply fails to appoint an attorney, absent a request. But, wrote the Justice, the greater possibility of harm is not decisive:

It is negated here by [Crooker's] age, intelligence, and education. While in law school he had studied criminal law; indeed, when asked to take the lie detector test, he informed the operator that the results of such a test would not be admissible at trial absent a stipulation by the parties. Supplementing that background is the police statement to [Crooker] well before his confession that he did not have to answer questions. Moreover, the manner of his refusals to answer indicates full awareness of the right to be silent. On this record we are unable to say that [Crooker's] confession was anything other than voluntary.

Clark then turned to Armstrong's other point, that Crooker was entitled under the Fourteenth Amendment to the advice of counsel, which he was denied, and the refusal to grant him counsel made the confession inadmissible whether voluntary or not. Clark conceded that a defendant is constitutionally entitled to the advice of counsel during the period preceding the trial as well as at the trial itself. But he held that even in a capital case due process is not violated unless deprivation of counsel so prejudices the defendant that his subsequent trial lacks "fundamental fairness." Clark claimed in a footnote that he was not overruling the Powell case, because Powell involved a lack of counsel at *trial*, which is a more serious matter than lack of counsel during the pretrial proceedings. Technically, Clark was correct. But he was certainly overruling the dictum, or general language, in Powell, and he was also extending Betts to a capital case, as Douglas was to emphasize in his dissent.

Was Crooker prejudiced at his trial? Did the lack of counsel during the pretrial period deprive his trial of fundamental fairness? No, said Clark. And to make his point, he contrasted Crooker's situation with that in the House case, in which the defendant was in his twenties, a stranger in town, and uneducated. That was totally different from Crooker's case, where "the sum total of the circumstances here during the time [Crooker] was without counsel is a voluntary confession by a college-educated man with law school training who knew of his right to keep silent. Such facts, while perhaps a violation of California law, . . . do not approach the prejudicial impact in [the House case] and do not show [Crooker] to have been so 'taken advantage of' . . . as to violate due process of law."

Clark thus refused to adopt the stringent rule that, without regard to the circumstances of the case, a confession is inadmissible when counsel is denied. Instead, all of the facts must be reviewed to determine the basic question of fairness.

Essentially, Douglas dissented on the same ground adopted by Judge Carter in his California Supreme Court dissent. When the issue is as fundamental as the right to counsel, insisted Douglas, courts should not engage in nice distinctions about how much prejudice resulted from the denial of the right. Even assuming that Betts had been properly decided, it should never be extended to a capital case.

Douglas exhibited in this dissent, as he had done so often before, a genuine, deep-seated fear of coercive tactics by the police. He wrote:

> The right to have counsel at the pretrial stage is often necessary to give meaning and protection to the right to be heard at the trial itself. . . . It may also be necessary as a restraint on the coercive power of the police. The pattern of the third degree runs through our cases: a lone suspect unrepresented by counsel against whom the full coercive force of a secret inquisition is brought to bear. . . . The third degree flourishes only in secrecy. One who feels the need of a lawyer and asks for one is asking for some protection which the law can give him against a coerced confession. No matter what care is taken innocent people are convicted of crimes they did not commit. . . . We should not lower the barriers and deny the accused any procedural safeguard against coercive police practices. . . . The trial of the issue of coercion is seldom helpful. Law officers usually testify one way, the accused another. The citizen who has been the victim of these secret inquisitions has little chance to prove coercion. The mischief and abuse of the third degree will continue as long as an accused can be denied the right to counsel at this the most critical period of

his ordeal. . . . For what takes place in the secret confines of the police station may be more critical than what takes place at the trial.

Douglas scoffed at the majority's reliance on Crooker's intelligence and education. He quoted a prior decision by Justice George Sutherland to the effect that " Even the intelligent and educated layman has small and sometimes no skill in the science of law." Douglas made no direct reference to Crooker's one year at law school, but he did say that "No matter how well educated and how well trained in the law an accused may be, he is sorely in need of legal advice once he is arrested for an offense that may exact his life. The innocent as well as the guilty may be caught in a web of circumstantial evidence that is difficult to break. A man may be guilty of indiscretions but not of the crime. He may be implicated by ambiguous circumstances difficult to explain away. He desperately needs a lawyer to help extricate him if he's innocent." And he concluded: "The demands of our civilization expressed in the Due Process Clause require that the accused who wants a counsel should have one at any time after the moment of arrest."

Thus the essential conflict between the five-man majority and the four-man minority was one which arises time and again in the wide range of the Court's work. The minority thinks of the Bill of Rights as a set of rules, many of which are to be as strictly enforced against the states as against the Federal Government. If a state breaks a rule, the conviction cannot stand. Only in that way can the rules be effectively enforced.

The majority, on the other hand, sees "due process of law" as a phrase embodying mankind's basic concepts of justice and fairness. Due process depends not on a set of inflexible rules but on what the conscience of history regards as fundamentally fair. Thus, no precise formula can be applied to all cases; instead, the facts of each case must be weighed and measured until the court can finally say that the totality of what took place was, whether good or bad, not so outrageous as to shock the conscience.

And when all of the facts in Crooker's case were weighed, one fact alone seems to have been decisive to the result: Crooker's education, and particularly his one year at law school. None of the five Justices could bring himself to say that it was outrageous during an investigation to deny counsel to a law student—a man who had actually studied criminal law. It is a safe guess that if Crooker had been totally uneducated—and perhaps even if he had had only a college education—this decision might well have gone the other way. For John Crooker, a little bit of knowledge had turned out to be a very dangerous thing indeed.

Crooker, on death row, now had a complete nervous breakdown. He began experiencing delusions and hallucinations, diagnosed by the chief psychiatrist of San Quentin as schizophrenic reactions and conversion phenomena. Crooker was exhibiting a passive-aggressive personality, with partial or acute hysteria.

In the meantime, a three-man committee was taking a close look at Crooker's mental condition, as required of all condemned men by California law. Their report went to Edmund G. Brown, by this time Governor of California. On January 14, 1959, four years after Norma McCauley's murder, Governor Brown announced that he was commuting Crooker's sentence from death to life imprisonment without possibility of parole. Explained Brown:

> Following the historic policy of California Governors in all extreme penalty cases, I have carefully studied the reports submitted by the District Attorney, Trial Judge, Attorney General's Investigator, Neuropsychiatric Examining Committee, the majority and dissenting Opinions of the Supreme Court of California, and the majority and dissenting Opinions of the Supreme Court of the United States, in the case of John Russell Crooker, Jr. . . . Addi-

tionally, I have received special consultative advice from eminent psychiatric authorities.

The record clearly shows and I personally believe that Crooker is guilty of murder in the first degree; but his crime was caused by passion and emotional factors, and was not one committed for gain. His psychiatric reports reflect mental illness which undoubtedly contributed to his emotional blow-up. I also feel that had he pleaded guilty his life would probably have been spared, and in this connection I am impressed with the sentiments expressed by the Trial Judge, the Honorable Stanley Mosk, who stated in a letter to the Governor on January 9, 1957, that he would not object to a commutation of sentence from death to life imprisonment, and that " . . . this defendant's crime arose out of a relationship with the deceased under a set of circumstances that would not likely happen again. He is an intelligent young man of some cultural attainment and if personality defects could be cured or contained, he could in the distant future become rehabilitated and become a constructive member of society."

I have also considered Crooker's age, education, intelligence and general circumstances; the fact that he had never previously been in trouble, had no prior arrests, never exhibited any criminal tendencies, and had been honorably discharged from the Navy in 1946. . . .

Crooker was thus saved from the gas chamber and, just before his thirty-fifth birthday, was removed from death row and placed in a cell where he apparently was destined to spend the rest of his natural life.

He had one other strange and frightening experience as the result of being placed in death row with a man whom he had never met but whose name had figured prominently at his trial. The man was Caryl Chessman, the "red-light bandit." Chessman shared only one thing in common with Crooker —both had been principals in cases brought before the Supreme Court. Chessman was an instantly dislikable man, an aggressive egotist with few friends and many enemies. Sexually overstimulated, he sought homosexual experiences with his jailmates, and one of the men upon whom he attempted to press his attentions was Crooker. More than any other person,

Crooker was relieved when Caryl Chessman finally went to his death in the San Quentin gas chamber.

This, then, is the story of John Crooker from the cold record, from newspapers, and from those familiar with his case. But it leaves much unanswered. Did Crooker really murder Norma McCauley, and if so, why? Was Crooker the depraved killer painted by the prosecution, or the gentle, groping man pictured by Armstrong? If he killed, was he responsible? Are there lessons for society in his experience?

For answers, we turn to Crooker himself. At San Quentin, where he is serving his life sentence, Crooker wrote, for inclusion here, a brief history of his life. He composed it without reading what has been written above about his case. He did not write for money, for he received none, nor for mercy, for he was then serving a sentence without possibility of parole. Rather he has told his story in an attempt to understand himself and to throw light on the entire subject of crime and capital punishment. Dr. David G. Schmidt, chief psychiatrist at San Quentin, believes that what follows is a substantially accurate and truthful account of the facts as Crooker knows them.

Birth and Early Development:

I was born February 18, 1924, in a small town in Maine, the 3rd child and only male child of 7 children born to John R. and Pearl F. Crooker, Sr., and have been told by my mother I was a cyanotic infant, or blue-baby, but this is unverified. In my early years, I believe, I was somewhat coddled by my mother, as an only and much-wanted son, and by my sisters, as an only brother. However, at least by the time of early teens, I acted somewhat aloof from my mother and sisters, although my sisters were my main playmates until about age 12 when an influx of more readily available playmates among boys my own age came to the community.

Family History:

My father was born in Maine in 1880, and died in 1957 of natural causes, i.e., old age. My mother was born in 1896, also in Maine, and is still living. Both parents are of English extraction and have lived most of their lives in Maine.

My father came from a large family, had very little formal education (about 7 grades), and was disappointed because of insufficient education in pursuing engineering-type employment when he went to San Francisco following the catastrophic fire there. He returned to Maine, married, and became a carpenter and small building contractor and painter, and, after marriage, he purchased and operated a small general insurance agency with my mother.

My father was a respected, hard-working man before the community, but somewhat a tyrant at home. He was extremely autocratic, taciturn but authoritarian, and domineering, did not show love for his children or for my mother, and frequently practiced severe corporal punishment against us.

I vividly recall scenes in which my father inflicted corporal punishment.

For example, at an early age, probably not more than age 10, I was frightened out of an attempt to prevent my father from literally yanking, pulling and dragging and striking my mother with his fists, in taking her into the tool room where I witnessed my father throw my mother to the floor and beat her.

For example, my twin sisters were whipped unmercilessly on one occasion at an early age when, out of fear, they denied breaking an inexpensive little mirror which was discovered by my father.

For example, my oldest sister swore during some incident in the home and I witnessed my father take this sister bodily, force her down over a sink and repeatedly pour her mouth full of soapy water, while he cursed her for cursing and for her "tongue sucking," as he phrased her petting with a boyfriend.

For example, when I was about age 12, I was quarreling with my oldest sister and was observed by my father striking my sister. My father whipped me so thoroughly with an alder switch on this occasion that my entire right thigh was covered with deep, vivid black and blue scars, which I was then forced to exhibit for a week at summer Scout Camp which I pleaded not to attend for this reason.

My father was constantly bitter over economic costs and wastes in the home—not turning off lights, using too much water, scuffing shoes, using too much butter on bread, etc. The home was never open to gathering of youngsters and I believed this to be the main reason I was discouraged from, and later, was never invited to such gatherings in other homes.

When I was about age 17, a family bridge game one evening disintegrated into my father's severe chastizement of me. For some reason, I drew upon this occasion to stay up into the wee hours to write a lengthy indictment of my father's inhumanities toward his family over the years. The next day, my father seized upon the economic parts of this indictment and defended himself in great detail and at great length, in an account of real or imagined extravagance—as though it were embezzlement—by my mother in her handling of monies in the business and in the home.

At age 20, I interposed against my father when he gave signs of striking one of my sisters, and was told to leave home as a consequence, which I did and remained away, rooming in the community, about a year. When I returned home, just prior to entering the Service, my father accepted my presence without comment.

For some reason, unknown to me, my father refused all contact with his own family for the most part through the years, although he even had one sister living in the same community.

Something apparently obsessed my father, to such an extent that I recall, for example, my father once exclaimed in an argument with my mother: "If I had it all to do over, I never would get married! I'd take my business to a whore house." Once when my oldest sister accused my father of not knowing about love because he never loved anyone, tears immediately came to his eyes and he sobbed, and was very much depressed.

Shortly before his death, my father mellowed a great deal, according to reports, and showed that he seemed to realize that some personality problem had troubled him all his life—just as it had troubled his family.

My mother had a Normal School Education, taught school and played piano for silent movies before her marriage. She was instrumental in convincing my father to purchase the insurance business and was daily active in it, as well as in having borne 7 children and kept the home going with the aid of housekeepers during the day.

My mother was occasionally harsh in her treatment, particularly toward my twin sisters who, there is some indication, were not wanted by my mother. I recall occasions when my mother inflicted corporal punishment upon them, as well as one occasion when I prevented her from doing so. I also recall occasions when my mother's treatment of my enuresis was to rub my nose in my soiled bedding, as well as to insist I wash my soiled bedding daily before school.

My mother demonstrated affection for my father, hugging and kissing him frequently, which he would withdraw from and rejected. She constantly deferred to my father in all matters and developed a habit to a fault in keeping things from him which she felt would be upsetting to him.

My mother was a fairly demonstrative and affectionate and encouraging person to me. She was a "sweet," "kindly," and more or less retiring woman before the public, and a frequently "tired," motherly, somewhat martyrish woman in the home.

I have no memory or information of any unusual or significant illnesses, diseases, defects, accidents, or other difficulties among my sisters, with the following exceptions. One of my sisters developed a numbness in her entire right arm and hand during her teens, which was apparently psychosomatic and which disappeared after a period of time during which my mother apparently realized her treatment of this sister was having serious complications. Two of my sisters have used alcohol to excess. A fourth sister has had occasions of severe neurotic problems, including one severe emotional breakdown, and a fifth turned to the Baptist religion with great zeal.

I deferred to my father to an extreme, and was always acutely afraid of him physically, at least until my late teens. My father showed no warmth or affection toward me, as I recall. He evidenced pride in his son before others, while, at the same time, he was cold and demanding and frequently harsh toward me. Since leaving home and through the years, my attitude and feeling toward my father, at least consciously, has been one of understanding and sympathy, together with misgivings in not having been able to have a warm, affectionate relationship with him.

My attitude toward my mother has always been one of some affection, considerable admiration, some aloofness, and not enough objective criticism. I believe my mother's ill-advised handling of my father and her children may have contributed more to problems than I once thought. However, I feel very kindly and understanding toward my mother, and believe that I probably developed dependencies in relation to her, as well as in relation to other women, although with misgivings in not having had quite the warmth and affectionate relationship with my mother that I would have liked to have had.

My attitude toward my sisters has been one of reasonable friendliness and concern for their problems (which I continued to discuss with them, for example, all the time I was under death sentence) but not with a conscious feeling of deep affection, with the exception of my first younger sister with whom I have recently developed strong, affectionate and healthy ties.

My overall, conscious feelings toward my family I would describe as compassionate. I feel serious mistakes were made by my parents, for the first part, in having raised such a large family in a homelife wrought by real or imagined economic pressures, and rather extreme harshness, and so devoid of love and affection. I feel compassionate toward my sisters and their personality problems resulting in large part from my parents' mistakes which, in turn, to some extent, must reflect their own beginnings.

Emotional Development:

I heard much quarreling and saw much harshness in the home as a child; felt unhappy a good deal; cried rather easily; walked in my sleep as a child, and was a bed-wetter. There did not seem to be any available recourse to talk things over with my father, although there was at least surface recourse for doing so with my mother. I was surrounded by females, almost exclusively until about age 12, and more or less throughout my formative years—as an only son with six sisters. My father used to say such things as: "He's not interested in girls—are you?" And I was supposed to agree with my father and did so and developed a sort of aloofness (which I did not feel, and, in fact, probably felt an over-dependence upon women) toward females in the home and in general. But I believed my father considered this "aloofness" more manly and expected it of me.

My emotional development may be characterized by my having been a noticeably reserved, somewhat aloof, well-mannered, quiet, almost emotionless boy, who outwardly gave some appearance of emotional strength but inwardly was quite unhappy, thought of suicide, day-dreamed a good deal, and frequently cried, off by myself. My emotional development may also be characterized by my having been a boy who did not seem to have the ability of free and easy, unaffected, communications and associations with my schoolmates, seeming to be not quite in the group, a little apart, not quite accepted and not quite accepting.

An example serves to show another facet in my emotional development: When I was age 15 and was working with my father as a painter and carpenter's helper, I awoke one morning with a sharp pain in my right side, so sharp I was inspired to tell my father I simply could not work that day. But the next day the pain was somewhat abated and I went back to work because this was the expected thing for me to do according to my father's attitude. I worked all week, sanding floors on my knees, and on the way to a ball game on Sunday I limped down to the doctor's office—just to see what this pain was all about. Within the next hour, I was in a hospital and on the operating table and subsequently wore a tube in my side to drain off the poisons. My appendix had burst. The doctor who operated said I missed death only by a short margin. On this occasion my father held my hand for a brief moment there in the hospital—apparently for my show of what he considered to be my manliness. My father recovered, however, and felt it quite logical and fair that my wages for the summer's work be used to defray the hospital expense.

In short, my emotional development may be characterized as showing no disturbance on the surface of my five senses so as to cause my parents or others any concern. But, in retrospect, it is obvious that I was disturbed.

Sexual Development:

My sole sex instruction from my father consisted in my father's observation when I was about age 18 and when my mother discovered a contraceptive in my pocket: "You know, John, that thing between your legs can get you into a lot of trouble." This seemed somewhat nasty at the time, as I recall. Perhaps somewhat humorous now. And probably pathetically true.

My sex instruction came from my own later experience and from companions. I masturbated as a boy and into late teens and twenties, with fears and shame which diminished with time.

My first experience in sexual intercourse was at age 18 or 19, with a local girl a few years older.

Prior to this occasion, I was retiring almost to a point of prudishness around girls, as a result of ignorance, fear and shame. For example, a girlfriend of one of my sisters kidded me about this on one occasion when we were alone in the home and she stood before me, teasing me with her dress raised up to her navel, and I just turned my head away as though unimpressed, while, afterward, I used her as an image in masturbation for some time to come. Of course I was interested in girls, and, in fact, probably developed inordinate preoccupation about them, lacking in free association with them. I used to observe my sisters and their girlfriends, rather shyly and off to the side, as they began to develop physically.

But I recall a dislike for "dating" because of some notion the practice was flighty in matters of love which should, I thought, be grounded in deep feelings, not what I then felt to be mere social intercourse. My feelings made me unsuccessful with girls. I was infatuated by two or three of my high school teachers, young attractive women, fresh from college. I also felt I was in love with a little blonde schoolmate all through grade school and high school, and was very much preoccupied by her in my mind. But she was always "going" with one or another boy. She kissed me briefly on my 18th birthday and I recall how I treasured this kiss. After high school, this girl married and my feelings for her decreased with time, although I continued to have affectionate feelings toward her memory.

I was quite impressed by my first experience in sexual intercourse. But I was not emotionally attracted to the girl, and I had infrequent successes with other girls for whom I was either not emotionally attracted and not free and easy in pursuing them without emotional attachment, or was emotionally attracted but not able to attract the particular girl in the same way—which meant to me in either case that I could not be successful with them sexually. I never developed an affinity or ability—in fact, had distaste—toward pickups, or casual relationships through the practice of meeting girls here or there and enjoying them for an occasion or so.

I had infrequent outlets in sexual intercourse through about age 20. Then, I experienced a succession of strong emotional attachments, to the point of overdependence, with individual girlfriends, accompanied by apparent mutual sexual satisfactions. I fell in love with each in turn. However, I do not recall seriously, objectively considering marriage. In retrospect, it was as though I was subconsciously aware that I was unprepared for marriage, still in school, with only a vague Life Plan, and without a practicable conception of marriage as the normal, healthy and socially acceptable institution for sexual expression. In other words, there was no mutual emotional satisfaction in these relationships, except perhaps during the initial stages before my lack of emotional maturity probably became obvious to these girlfriends, although not to myself. And these individual attachments or dependencies, one after the other, with only some little promiscuous sexual experience in between, arose and ended, each time with more or less difficulty in my ability of acceptance of the termination of the particular relationship.

My sexual development and adjustments seem to have been late and poor in conceptual quality, and my accompanying emotional development also inadequate. I remained conceptually weak and immature, as shown by extreme emotional attachments or dependencies with a succession of individual girlfriends, without awareness of the obvious reasons these relationships were terminated, i.e., my lack of planning and providing for marriage, or the accompanying responsibilities.

Medical & Psychiatric History:

I had the usual childhood diseases; had no unusual or significant illnesses, diseases, defects, accidents, or other conditions, except those stated below; have developed into a 5′ 11½″ male with reasonably good physical health and no physical abnormalities; had an appendectomy at about age 15 with no subsequent complications; and had scarlet fever while in the Service with no complications.

My enuresis history should be noted.

Throughout my childhood from infancy, I voided in bed at night frequently, often every night through a week and usually upwards to five nights through a week. As a boy, I was taken to a country doctor who told me to avoid liquids in the evening, and to wear something wrapped around my waist with a knot at the back, so I presumedly would awaken before voiding in bed. I felt strong feelings of inferiority, because of this condition, at least in part; was embarrassed at Scout Camp by enuresis; was rejected for Service in 1942 because of enuresis; and in 1945, convinced my mother to state I was recovered from this condition and obtain a doctor's statement to this effect, so I could enter the Service; but during my time in the Service got up before others in my company to wash my bedding, to keep my secret of the continuing condition; was embarrassed in visiting the home of friends when I voided in their beds; was embarrassed and I embarrassed my first wife when I voided in our bed; and my second wife recommended a urinal to be worn at bedtime, which I used without success.

In 1953, I went to a urologist for treatment–urged by Norma McCauley. This treatment consisted of the insertion of an apparatus in the penis to stretch an opening connected with the bladder, etc., and continued over a period of some months. The doctor stated I did have or might have an inferior opening or valve connected with the bladder but, in any event, the treatment was unsuccessful.

Then, in 1955, and following commission of my crime, this enuresis condition vanished abruptly, and has never reoccurred, not even infrequently, not even once.

I was amazed and began to experience continually increasing feelings of greater manhood, stability and security in my personality—rather a great relief. At the same time, I was mystified by this abrupt disappearance of a condition which plagued me all my life, probably plagued me more than I realized; and since that time have read everything coming my way on the subject of enuresis, and have broached this phenomenon with my Psychiatric Therapist, as well as others, in order to understand it.

My attempted suicide should also be noted.

In 1949, my first marriage was deteriorating after a very few months of marriage. On the occasion of my wife's having ignored me over a period of time and having been absent from the home until the wee hours of the morning without explanations, one night, I went to a liquor store and bought a pint of whiskey, thinking I might be able to drink away my troubles, although I had never before attempted to drink away troubles. I brought the whiskey home, but did not drink any of it. Instead, I continued to brood and wait for my wife, and then, I took a vial of phenobarbital which was nearly full and which my wife used during menstrual periods, and I swallowed all the tablets, intending suicide.

I awoke the next day, about noon, found myself in bed where my wife had placed me the night before when finding me unconscious, and I stumbled out to the presence of my wife and stepdaughter, mumbling incoherently. Then, I stumbled back to bed, without the assistance from my wife I doubtlessly wanted; and awoke again about seven that evening, found my wife absent, took a razor and, still stupefied by effects of phenobarbital, slashed my left wrist, again intending suicide. Then I stumbled back to bed again.

I awoke again late that evening when my wife returned with

a young married couple of our acquaintance. My wife called police who came and escorted me to the hospital where my wrist was treated, and then escorted me home. My wife refused to stay with me and left with the wife of the couple while the husband stayed the night with me.

My wife continued to refuse to stay with me, stating that she would stay away until I left. She did take me to a doctor (psychiatrist?) attached to the Veteran's Administration for one interview. As I recall this interview, I was with this doctor in the presence of my wife for about 15 minutes, and was in a state of hysteria and effects of the phenobarbital (crying, somewhat incoherent, unstable on my feet and in speech, etc.—which lasted for several days) during this interview. At the conclusion of this remarkable session, the doctor diagnosed me on the spot to my wife and in my presence as a manic-depressive with whom she should no longer live and who, he would advise, she should divorce at once. My wife took me to a small hotel where she convinced me I should move, with $7.00 in my pocket for a week's rent. She deposited me there and left. She subsequently initiated papers drawn up by her attorney to declare me incompetent and to declare herself as my guardian, nearly convincing me to sign these papers ("I'll do whatever you want, anything for you"); but a friend did not approve of this action at the time and dissuaded me from signing such papers.

A period of rather severe hallucinations and general departure from reality during my incarceration should also be noted.

In 1956, while on condemned row and with some influence from others on condemned row, and my dependency complex, as well as the influence of having committed my crime and of being sentenced to death, I experienced a breakdown. I now have at least partial recall of this experience.

I recall believing officials of the institution were under the control of an inmate; that an inmate had or was going to take over the institution; that an inmate controlled a cult that was going to make a gas chamber of the entire institution and only those belonging to this cult would escape execution; and I heard voices, saw faces on the walls, and believed the milk was poisoned with cyanide.

I seemed to largely recover from this condition after a relatively short period of time, perhaps six weeks, but was isolated from condemned row at my request for a total time of about a year, with some supportive psychiatric interviews.

After about a year, I experienced what I term a sort of relapse in which I recall I drank an unusual quantity of water and then thought shortly afterward that I "recounted" my early childhood and background experiences, to a "voice" which I understood without having the impression the "voice" was audible at all—in a question and answer session in which I did not speak audibly either, and in the process of which I took everything down off the walls and shelves and packed them together and then became rigid in my legs and arms and unable to move about; and then, at the end of which, I "felt" a "grasp" on my right arm that "turned" me toward the front of my quarters, where I was observed by an officer in a state in which I could not move my legs or arms and could not speak and rolled my tongue uncontrollably around inside my mouth.

The next day after the above incident, and increasing thereafter, I experienced an elation, as though I were purged, cleaned out, relieved of a burden, by this experience, and I was quite inquisitive as to its cause.

After a short period of time, a few days, following this above incident, with only supportive psychiatric interviews, I requested to return to the population of condemned row and was permitted to do so. Thereafter, I continued to improve, and actually felt a strength of personality, stability and security of emotion and reason, greater than I had had in the past. I began to study the law pertaining to my case in earnest, continuously, and began to do a considerable amount of preparation of papers in my appeal proceedings, encouraged and advised by others.

During the entire course of my confinement, including this above incident, I have been either under the observation or the treatment of the Psychiatric Department at San Quentin Prison, limited to some supportive interviews and some medication while under a death sentence, and including Group and Individual Psychotherapy thereafter.

Military History:

I was inducted into the U.S. Navy about March, 1945; went through bootcamp training at Sampson, New York; was assigned to radar school and transferred to Point Loma, California; was then assigned to Treasure Island for a short time; and then shipped out aboard an armed-guard transport, sailing into the Philippines and back to San Francisco with a consignment of American soldiers who had been in Japanese prison camps; attained the rank of third class radarman; and upon my return to San Francisco, I was transferred to Boston, and then to New London to board a Patrol Craft going to Green Cove Springs, Florida for decommissioning. I was discharged in late 1946, receiving an Honorable Discharge.

It may be noted that my whole background previous to the time I entered the Service was confined to Maine. While I was in the Service, I was impressed by my first train ride, on the way to New York; then the train trip across the continent; and California, that State at the other end of the map; and then by going to sea; and visiting the Philippines, those dots on the map; etc.

Educational History:

I completed the public school system in Maine in 1942, obtaining about a B average in overall grades, enjoying English literature and composition and civic subjects most, and foreign language (French) least, and participating in sports a little, but more in journalism, debating, dramatics and the like. In my senior year in high school, I won an annual prize-speaking contest—with my version of Poe's Tell-Tale Heart. The principal and the superintendent thought I should become a lawyer, apparently because of my speaking and writing abilities.

After high school, I had no advice or knowledge of the many ways to go on to college without funds, although I wanted to go to college.

I did not start college for that reason until 1946 when I became eligible for benefits under the G.I. Bill. I entered the University of Maine, obtaining about a high C or low B average in my first year classes, entering into debate again, and playing the lead in a dramatic production. It may be noted that Professor Herschel Bricker, then in charge of Dramatics at the university, thought enough of my potential in acting to invite me to his home in an effort to interest me in a dramatic major and in pursuing acting as a career; but my background included the concept of actors as a somewhat irresponsible and unrespected group, and I consequently did not follow Professor Bricker's advice. At the end of my first year at Maine, I left college to help one of my sisters and, subsequently, I migrated to California.

It should also be noted that I did not have a clear Life Plan Goal of becoming an attorney, largely because of a notion that this was financially beyond my reach. But I took the Johnson O'Connor Aptitude testing, and aptitude testing at the university, both of which confirmed my aptitude for this profession. I felt an economic pressure in attending college with limited funds, and also seemed to feel what I vaguely termed to be "confined" by Maine's staid environment, during my time at the University of Maine.

Upon moving to California and marrying, I still had some eligibility left under the G.I. Bill; and entered the University of Southern California, did poorly in some of my subjects, and left college with only a few weeks remaining in a semester. It may be noted that I found U.S.C. to be somewhat of a mill, with too many thousands of students and too much an impersonal treatment of education, and that I sought the company of, and was dependent upon, my wife more than giving proper attention to my studies.

From the time I met my second wife and continuing at the time of our marriage, she encouraged me to return to college. She was familiar with Pepperdine College, a small Christian college in Los Angeles, and shortly after our marriage, in 1950, I entered Pepperdine and did quite well, with overall grades of about B average, with several A grades and some C grades and very few lower than C grades. I wrote for the college paper, a personal, human interest column; played the leads and other lesser parts in several dramatic productions; was very active in debate, and was ranked with my colleague as 5th in the nation in the National Debate Tournament held at West Point, New York, which we were selected to attend by open competition, and which was participated in by most colleges and universities in the nation; and placed 3rd in an annual local journalism contest among small colleges in the Los Angeles area; and was keynote speaker at the mock political convention held at Pepperdine just before the 1952 national elections and attended by over 1000 students. When my G.I. Bill eligibility terminated, I obtained a scholarship at Pepperdine for the remainder of my three years; and I graduated, in 1953, with a double major, a B.A. Degree in Political Science and Speech.

After graduation from college, my desire to study law had become clearer in my mind; I was without funds, was separated from my wife (with court action) and obtained employment placement with the McCauley family.

I obtained admission at U.C.L.A. Law School and enjoyed my classes and the prospect of becoming an attorney, which now seemed in sight. I believe I was doing well in my studies until I began to spend inordinately more and more time in a personal relationship which developed between myself and Mrs. McCauley.

At the end of my first year, I learned that my grades rendered me ineligible to return for the second year at U.C. L.A. [U.C.L.A. Law School reports that Crooker received two C's ("Introduction to Procedure" and "Criminal Law and Procedure"), three D's ("Contracts," "Property," and "Torts"), and one F ("Agency").] I obtained a transfer to Southwestern University Law School, obtained full time employment, and attended classes at night. My grades at the end of this repeated first year were about B average, with some A grades and some C grades. [Southwestern Law School reports that Crooker received two A's ("Introduction to Law" and "Criminal Law"), two B's ("Contracts I and II"), and two C's ("Torts I and II").] I took the "baby bar" examination required of students in non-accredited law schools, just prior to commission of my crime but have received no information whether or not I passed this examination. [Crooker passed the First Year Law Students' Examination with a grade of B.]

Employment History:

I worked with my father summers during high school, as a painter and carpenter's helper. After high school, in 1942, I worked for a short time in the local paper mill, and then went to work as a Stage Builder in a shipyard at South Portland, Maine, until I entered the Service in 1945. After the Service, in 1946, I worked weekends at the local paper mill, and was an agent with the Massachusetts Mutual Life Insurance Company, while attending the University of Maine.

When I moved to California, I tried unsuccessfully to sell life insurance again, with the Massachusetts Mutual Life Insurance Company, and feel I was unsuccessful largely because of lack of contacts in the Los Angeles area. I then entered

U.S.C. and worked nights at a service station as an attendant, on the corner of 8th and Soto Streets in Huntington Park, California. After I left U.S.C., I worked for a short time as a laborer at Truscon Street Yard in Maywood, and then went to work as a bus driver for the Los Angeles Transit Lines for about 9 months until I entered Pepperdine College.

I then obtained work on the campus at Pepperdine, doing the painting of its buildings and rooms and offices; and then obtained employment as a messenger with the California Bank, transporting interbank mail and non-negotiable securities, in an early morning and late afternoon run, and continued some painting for the college.

After college, I continued the bank employment through the summer and terminated this job at the beginning of Law School at U.C.L.A., when I obtained placement with the McCauley family in Bel Air, California. In June, 1954, I worked for a short time as a carhop at Truman's Drive-In in Westwood Village, and then obtained employment as a branch office clerk and then main office clerk with the Southern California Gas Company, being terminated for lack of sufficient dexterity in filing at the end of several months probationary period. Then I was employed as a Credit Clerk for Richfield Oil Company until just prior to the commission of my crime. Just prior to the commission of my crime, I was negotiating for a position with the Los Angeles School Board, as an inspector.

Marital History:

In the summer of 1948, my first wife, then single and about age 25, returned to Maine from California on vacation—later reported to me as being a trip to entice me into marriage in her spite over an unrequited love for another man. I had first known and had an intimate personal relationship with her in Maine, and then in California while I was in the Service. We renewed our relationship; I was thoroughly smitten and made plans to follow her to California where we planned to marry; and I did so in the fall of 1948, with $60.00, two suits of clothes, and a set of new luggage, to take up responsibilities of a wife and an 8 year old stepdaughter by my wife's former unsuccessful marriage.

We lived in my wife's trailer home, with the stepdaughter sleeping in the house of the family in whose yard the trailer was parked; we honeymooned in the San Bernadino Mountains, to which we drove in my wife's little 1938 coupé, and where we stayed in my wife's friends' cottage; and there we spent a blissful week, blissfully unprepared for the responsibilities of a healthy marriage.

My first wife was and had been for some time a hard-working girl, working in a Goodyear rubber plant to buy her trailer home and car and to support her daughter and herself. To this I added the pittance of some $25.00 a week as a service station attendant. My wife's childhood had been unhappy; she came from a broken home; and she had an extremely unhappy first marriage. My wife and I were sexually well-mated, but emotionally mismated—I was still immature emotionally and overly dependent. My wife wanted a home more than anything, and she needed a man—not an emotional boy—to care for her and her daughter. The glitter of our sexual attraction wore off, at least as far as she was concerned, and my experience in terminated relationships was repeated again. When this happened and affected my wife's treatment of me, I reacted this time by my attempted suicide. This marriage was terminated and divorce action was instituted by my first wife.

When I had recovered somewhat from the experience of my first marriage, and had gone to work as a bus driver, and, except for a very few female acquaintances, had little sexual outlets, I met my second wife. I met her at the home of a family I used to visit. She was about 12 years older than myself—I am not sure exactly because she never revealed her true age—and she was a rather plain but somewhat cultured woman, who had attended U.S.C., majoring in Fine Arts. She was an almost totally inexperienced woman in sexual matters and in a great many of the social intercourses as well. She was sheltered and was somewhat oldfashioned in her ways and in her thinking. She seemed attracted to me, with the help of our mutual friend, the wife in the family I visited. We began to visit places such as Huntington Museum, and concerts at the Hollywood Bowl and plays at the Biltmore Hotel Theatre, and Griffith Park, and Balboa Art Festival—all entirely new experiences for me. She started to teach me to play the piano —which I had wanted my mother to do when I was a boy, but which my mother never seemed to have time to do. She encouraged me to return to college and appealed to my vanity by seeing a potential for accomplishments in me. Eventually, our relationship included sexual intercourse, although I was consciously aware I was not even physically attracted to her, let alone emotionally attracted or suited to her. But my inability in seeking and obtaining sexual outlet was still operative, doubtlessly, and there were these few occasions of intercourse with her.

Then one day, she called me on the telephone and informed me she was pregnant.

My first words to her were: "Well, fine. Don't sound so worried. It's not the end of the world, you know—and I have always wanted a son." That was the substance of the words which came immediately to my mind.

I married my second wife. I obtained an annulment of my first marriage to make this possible, through the help of my second wife in the selection of an attorney able to do this, and through her small bank account to finance it.

We honeymooned at Yosemite. I recall that very first night, when I realized so acutely how little physical or emotional or any other kind of compatibility I had with this unfortunate, totally inexperienced, trusting woman I had married. But I thought I was pursuing the only proper moral course in marrying her under the circumstances. And the honeymoon was not entirely unhappy, perhaps because of the novelty and especially in the beautiful surroundings of Yosemite.

We obtained a little apartment in a court operated by friends of my wife; I continued working as a bus driver and then entered Pepperdine College; our son was born and I was overjoyed with him, helping my wife care for him and loving him; and I began to be something of a family man in many ways, in decorating our apartment, caring for my wife and son, and working and attending college.

But our basic incompatibility and my emotional immaturity asserted influence almost from the beginning of this marriage.

I was attracted to one or two other young women and had an occasional extramarital sexual experience with them, which my wife suspected and reacted strongly against—moving back to her mother's home without a word. I did not pursue her but moved into campus housing at the college. Then when I was visiting our son, it was decided between my wife and I to try again and we took up house-keeping in a campus apartment—I began to act like a more or less mature married man, painting and papering the apartment, buying furniture, working and going to school and caring for my wife and son.

But again, our basic incompatibility and my immaturity asserted influence.

I moved out of the apartment in 1951, and we remained separated. I visited my wife and son when my wife moved back to her mother's home again; and I took our son on outings. Prior to our second separation, my wife again became pregnant, and at the time our daughter was born, I attended my wife, at the home, in the hospital, at the time of the birth, and at home afterward. But we did not live together again.

While I was in law school and during my relationship with the deceased Norma McCauley, I continued to visit my children, taking them on outings and to Norma McCauley's home to play with her own children.

At times during this marriage, I have sought divorce, and my wife has refused to grant me divorce; at times the reverse was so, in that she sought divorce and I have contested it. We are still married. I was and am adamant that my children not spend their formative years in a home environment of unhappy parents, much less harsh parents, such as I myself experienced. I am satisfied that my marriage to my second wife would not have been happy, and, to that extent, my children may be better prepared to face life than if I had actually maintained this marriage—and I have discussed this with my second wife, during and after the time I lived with her.

Social History:

I had absolutely no juvenile record or criminal record; was 31 years of age at the time of commission of my crime, and never had committed a crime and never had been arrested previously. As regards thought of consequences, it is more accurate to say I never even thought of crime, or penalties, never even read crime news, lived in Los Angeles at the height of the Barbara Graham case and the Chessman case, for example, but remained unaware, as far as I recall, not only of the existence of these cases but also of the existence of the death penalty in California. These things were simply outside my purview and interest, as far as any practical application is concerned although I seem to recall having discussed capital punishment as a student at some time and to have had an opinion against it—and, now that I think of it, had criminal cases in law school. But I never thought of consequences of crime because I never contemplated or thought of crime in relation to myself, not at any time, including prior to the commission of my crime.

My social attitude, as a personality, may be fairly described as evidencing a reasonably strong and responsible social consciousness and conscientiousness, with liberal social views, but with a history of an academic experience and frame of reference, perhaps significantly without adequate practical experience or applications for a person my age.

I have had several normally healthy identifications in my background; joined the Boy Scouts and became a Life Scout; joined the Congregationalist Church along with some of my schoolmates, although I was not especially impressed by this church and have been most impressed by the Unitarian Church with which I had some contact while in college, and my conceptions of fact and reason and emotion do not seem to permit me to have any strong religious affiliations—although I feel imbued with Christian tenets of morality to a large extent and have a personal philosophy of life which I feel is healthy for myself and for my society and which is presently clear, although not entirely clear in the past; and I was also accepted into the Masonic Order, in the local Lodge in my hometown, shortly prior to moving to California; and my family identification has always been quite strong, although probably not as healthy as could be.

I have always tended toward a selected, perhaps relatively few friends; as a boy I had pals with whom I played ball and went swimming and skating, and later developed the more friendly ties with a few friends, and some of my friends as a young man were somewhat older, businessmen.

In my hometown, my social activities were necessarily confined almost exclusively to school activities and local dances and movies, except, of course, some sporting activities, swimming, camping, and the like. In California, with my first wife, the level of social activities was occasional cabaret night life, movies, and beach parties, but, of course, this marriage was short in duration. As heretofore stated, the level of my social life was higher during my second marriage, because my wife introduced me to many advantages that were unavailable in Maine—concerts, legitimate theatre, museums, places of scenic interests, etc., with few movies, and with some picnics, etc.

My social activities with the deceased Norma McCauley

were of a level comparable to that with my second wife, but on a somewhat higher economic level because of the deceased Norma McCauley's circumstances, and included more mixed social occasions because I had developed lasting friends in California by this time.

I notice a remarkable lack of good reading throughout my early life and extending until the time of my incarceration. Most of my reading was in academic texts. A whole new world of books was revealed to me during my incarceration. Before that I even had a mistaken concept resulting in distaste for fiction, and during my incarceration I have read a great deal of fiction, historical fiction, etc., as well as some documentary volumes and texts. I recall no real awareness of the existence and value of such reading in my background, and I feel this may be of some significance in my personality formation and problems, limited as I was to my own background and experience, without the broadening instruction and association found in good literature.

Similarly, my awareness of painting and classical and semi-classical music seems to me to have been extremely limited and, in my early background, even nonexistent. I discovered considerable appreciation for these art forms after incarceration, in reading lives of painters and studying some of their works to some extent, and discovered also that, even in listening to radio recordings of classical and semi-classical music, without technical knowledge, I far preferred this music.

Television, at this point in its development, stinks! And I have spent very, very little time with it, even when it was and now is readily available.

During some periods in my background—in Maine, and at times in California—I have spent too much time on movies, which are, admittedly, pretty poor for the most part, even as entertainment.

I have never used alcohol to excess, and might be called a social drinker—that is, one who has four or five cocktails in the course of an evening at a party, and never spends time in bars, daily or even occasionally, just drinking. I have never used any type of drug. I smoke a pack of cigarettes a day and have done so for the past 16 years or so, although I now intend to stop this habit.

I am quite interested in politics and social issues, and have always followed national politics and my own local politics quite closely, as well as having done some little grass roots footwork during one campaign.

I also like to write.

Background to Crime, the Crime, and After:

In July, 1953, I obtained placement in the McCauley home, in Bel Air, California, after an interview by both Norma McCauley and her husband. The arrangement, a common one in the area, was for me to obtain board, room and a small stipend while attending U.C.L.A. Law School, in return for my services in everything from baby-sitting to bartending.

Norma McCauley was the daughter of a local contractor. She had one brother and no sisters, and she was close to her parent family. Her parents approved my placement in her home.

Norma McCauley's husband was a former Major in the U.S. Air Force, and they were married during the war years when he was still a dashing young officer, about age 33, who came from Michigan and had previously attended that State's agricultural college. Upon his marriage to Norma McCauley, her father took him into the contracting business, apparently in the thought of and with high hopes of providing for his daughter and her anticipated children in this manner.

The McCauleys had three boys, ages 8, 5, and about 10 months. My role in my placement appeared to fit well into the McCauley home. By consensus of opinion, I was capable in managing and caring for Norma's children, and actually developed a healthy mutual affection with them, and was considerable help in this respect, because Norma McCauley's husband was, in many ways, not an entirely mature man—again, by consensus of opinion. I was well-liked by Norma's parents, her brother, and by various friends who visited the home on social occasions. For an example of how I was accepted in the home, some of the guests who were attorneys gave me assurance of help and placement when I took the bar. Another example, along these lines, I was invited to take off my white jacket and participate in the dancing and the conversations during parties and was always invited to take cocktails in the course of such evenings.

Norma McCauley was a rather attractive, quiet, unpretentious, friendly, sweet dispositioned, socially very active woman, 31 years of age. Her parents were wealthy and she was accustomed to wealth and its material advantages, and had the frame of references most common in one born and raised in wealth. As a young girl and a young woman in competition for attentions of males, she was never overly selfconfident, even had some selfconsciousness and inferiority feelings from such things as having red hair which, as a young girl at least, she thought was unattractive. She said she was swept off her feet by the dashing young Air Force Major, and they were married after a very short courtship.

She and I were attracted to each other at once, to the extent that we seemed to have much to talk about and spent hours and hours together over coffee or while performing some household task. As she developed confidence in me as a person, she revealed that her marriage was not and had not been happy. Through our long conversation around the home, Norma and I discussed the substance of difficulties in her marriage. And in general, we became personally well-acquainted with each other.

Then two things happened.

One, Norma and her parents began discussing in earnest the prospect of her divorcing her husband. And two, one night, after a party in the home, Norma and I were cleaning up after the party; her husband had long since retired; and when we were finished we sat down in the living room before the fireplace, having coffee and talking; and then we began to dance together; and finally we kissed each other–literally like two school children in a newly found first love. We sat there and held hands and talked and literally quaked in feelings for each other and, also, in the thought of having such feelings and having kissed while she was married and her husband was there in the home. In recounting this scene I have been careful to avoid overdramatizing, and may be underdramatizing the extent of Norma McCauley's and my own emotions (however immature we both were) on this night when our relationship began to be intimately personal.

Our relationship progressed rapidly from that night, and divorce proceedings against her husband also happened to be just as rapidly instituted–within something like a week as I recall. I helped Norma move in with her parents with her children for a few days, stayed there myself, and acted as a liaison between her home and her parents' home, to report when her husband had moved out of the home. When he did so and Norma moved back into the home, I continued to live there for a few months, part of which time Norma's girlfriends also lived there for appearances. After this period, through her parents' suggestion, I slept at their home and commuted the five minutes' drive between their home and Norma's home, where I spent substantially all my non-school hours and into the early morning hours.

During this period, which lasted until around late February or March, 1954, Norma and I spent many hours together, in a homelife not much different in substance from that of man and wife, caring for her children, attending parties and lectures together, and other affairs, including outings at her parents' home. We spent long hours together in the daytime hours, as well as the nighttime hours. It would be only fair to say here that I jeopardized my first year at law school by the time and energies I took away from studies in this immature and overly dependent manner.

With Norma's friends—who were also friendly with her parents—my presence and our relationship was kept clandestine and explained on impersonal grounds whenever we were together among such friends. When we were with my own friends our relationship was well-known.

We talked of our eventual marriage, more than planning for it. Norma's divorce action took a year in its initial stages, due to a claim against her father's business involving the community property. I made overtures to my wife for divorce.

Norma's mother, through Norma's suggestion, made two loans to me to help me in law school expenses, etc.; and Norma also helped me financially to some extent. We discussed these financial aspects of our relationship quite frankly, and mutually agreed these arrangements were investments in our future together—and if, in any event, our future together did not materialize, any financial help from her would be treated as a loan, just as such help from her mother was already being treated by me. But Norma felt we should enjoy the advantages which her circumstances offered to us, e.g., her home, her car, her membership at a beach club, etc.

About February or March, 1954, when Norma became more embroiled in the contest in the divorce proceedings, through her parents' suggestion I stayed and worked at her parents' home, where Norma frequently visited with her children and alone. We also continued our clandestine hours together, daytime and nighttime hours, in her home, in her parents' home on occasions when they were absent, and away from home at various night spots and out-of-the-way places.

In June, 1954, just at the time of my finals at law school, Norma's father discovered our relationship, threatened to disown his daughter and vehemently chastized me and discharged me from the home. Nevertheless, we persisted in our relationship. For a short time, I worked in the Westwood area and lived nearby and we continued to see each other in her home and go out more frequently in the evening. Then, I obtained other employment and also obtained an apartment in Hollywood. I had transferred to Southwestern University Law School, was going to classes at night, and was working during the day.

Most of our time together was then spent at my apartment and out together in the evenings, although I still visited her in her home. In many ways, the apartment was our home together—we entertained friends there, etc.

In late May or early June, 1955, something happened to change our relationship. I am not sure of either the extent or the cause of this change.

The one thing I know did happen may be the entire explanation or only a part of the explanation. Norma informed me she had become pregnant and had just had an abortion, the circumstances of which she described to me in some detail and with considerable understandable emotion, and she also discussed it with a mutual friend who, in turn, discussed it with me. During the period of a few weeks before and a few weeks after this abortion, our relationship deteriorated.

Norma never did flatly tell me our relationship was ended; and in fact, she was somewhat evasive, sometimes warm and sometimes cold and distant—particularly so, disturbingly so, as affected myself.

We saw each other, in my apartment, in her home, and elsewhere, on occasions during this period of about a month and a half. But we were both greatly disturbed. Norma was distressed by something, whether solely the experience of the abortion, or the fact, as she later revealed to me, that someone knew of it and of our relationship, or whatever else. I was equally or more distressed by Norma's evasiveness about what was distressing her and my feelings toward the possibility of our relationship ending. I did not know what to believe, and my anxiety built up during this period before my crime into what can only fairly be described as an agony for me.

I could not study–despite my "baby bar" examination in June. I could not sleep; could not eat; cried a good deal; and on one occasion, literally ran away from a young couple who were closest friends to myself and Norma and well-acquainted with our relationship–and I ran away from them when I met them in a public place, crying uncontrollably and not feeling able to face them or anyone. I seemed to be, as I recall in retrospect, disintegrated emotionally, without control of myself to the point where I could not stop thinking of my love for Norma and the puzzle of what was distressing her, and the unbearable prospect of an end of our relationship–but I recall no conscious animosity, or hostility, no conscious wish to harm her, or physical aggressive feelings toward her–and, to the contrary, felt I loved her, wanted her, needed her, ached for her, and felt an utter despair in trying to repair our relationship.

These events and emotions resulted in my going to Norma's home in the evening of July 3, 1955, the evening before the night of the crime.

By prearrangement with Norma, I entered her home and waited for her that evening and talked with her. During this conversation, she told me that someone knew of the abortion and our relationship and had threatened her for money. She asked me to promise to stay away from her until the situation was over, and I did promise to do so.

The following day, July 4, 1955, I was as disturbed, confused and distressed, as I was during the preceding weeks, despite my promise to Norma. In fact, I was more disturbed; not seeming to be able to stop thinking about her and what was happening more intensely than before–was distraught in thinking someone was threatening her, but also because she had wanted my promise to stay away. Any doubts I may have had of what she had told me, which I seem to think in retrospect that I did have to some extent—even though a plot by others which threatened her children after her death was actually uncovered subsequent to my crime—and although I do not seem to be able to clearly reconstruct my thoughts, feelings and actions during this emotional period, I am quite certain, did not result in any conscious feelings of resentment toward Norma, *at any time,* before, during, or after commission of my crime. The feelings I do recall having at the time of my crime are three: love for Norma; concern or worry (and perhaps some doubt) over someone threatening her; and intense despair. Of these three feelings, I seem to think in retrospect, what I term to have been despair predominated at the time of the actual commission almost exclusively—not only despair about our relationship, but about "everything," as though I were irreparably broken apart and without hope.

I spent the day of July 4 around Norma's home, and in the early evening, before dark, about 6 o'clock, I took a taxi to her home, after leaving my car at the U.C.L.A. campus, and entered her home. This was without prearrangement with Norma, but, in all respects, was not an unusual occurrence in our relationship, because we had frequently done such things in this clandestine relationship.

When Norma came home, around 12:30 A.M., as I recall, she was somewhat surprised to see me and somewhat disturbed that I had not kept my promise to stay away. But no argument or harsh words or the like occurred between us, never had and did not at this time.

We were in Norma's bedroom, as I recall.

I have difficulty stating the facts that I recall of the actual crime—difficulty in stating I could have had the capacity to do a violent act to take Norma McCauley's life (or anyone's life)—and my having done so is extremely repugnant and repulsive and reproved in my thoughts and emotions, and seems to me to be so entirely foreign to my makeup and my past and my present experience.

Nevertheless, I was in Norma's bedroom with her; tried to talk with her about our relationship, etc.; and we were there for some period of time, perhaps two hours or more; and evidence of the lack of argument, harsh words or the like is found in the fact of the telephone call received by Norma during this time, in which she talked freely; but she seemed unwilling or unable to talk with me about our relationship or the things she had told me were happening, as I recall; and I can only give my present impressions of my feelings at that time in a general way—I seemed to feel as though everything was hopeless and useless and extremely, agonizingly, endlessly wearisome in a way that was like a continuing, gnawing pain on nerves which cannot be reached to ease such pain.

After some time and while I was trying to talk with Norma, as I recall, I have the impression she was lying on the chaise longue with her eyes closed—perhaps dozing or asleep—and I have the impression that I sat there in silence, with an intense despair seeming to close in on myself—and the next moment that I had struck Norma with something, I do not know what, although the evidence would seem to indicate not a "ten inch kitchen knife" because of the length and other description of the wounds at trial. I have the impression that Norma may have raised her arm or turned off the chaise longue and made some sounds, and I have the impression of having put something around her throat—what, I do not know. And I have the impression that I sat on the chaise longue beside her for what seems to me to have been a long, long time, but I do not know this, although I do have the impression of walking down the road from her home; and the impression that I must have wandered for some time on the roads in Bel Air, because when I reached the boulevard leading to the U.C.L.A. campus where I left my car the previous afternoon, as I recall, it was light or nearly daylight, and I have the impression of coming out an entrance from Bel Air that was not familiar to me.

I would describe my conscious feeling following this crime

as a numbness. I have the impression of having felt while I was driving on the way to my apartment (about a 25 minute drive) that it was taking a long, long time and that I could not seem to drive faster or hurry. I have the impression of entering the apartment building (in daylight) and my apartment, noticing my clothes were all soiled and throwing them into the incinerator and going to bed. But I recall this feeling I describe as numbness during all these actions.

When I awoke a few hours later, I realized that I had hurt Norma—but did not know she was dead—and felt appalled and afraid and wishful that nothing like this had happened to her; and tried to proceed as though nothing like this had happened; made coffee, got out some bills and wrote some checks; and I recall how these simple operations seemed to take a great deal of time.

The next thing, as I recall, two plainclothes men (officers) burst into my apartment with drawn guns pointed at me.

The men searched me, allowed me to dress and handcuffed me behind my back.

Then, two more plainclothes men (officers) came in; and then two more and then two more—altogether some 6 or 8 men, including the Assistant District Attorney who subsequently prosecuted this case at trial; and I recall now how melodramatic (in the C-grade movie sense of the term) these men appeared, walking in, walking slowly by me seated handcuffed in a chair in the corner, staring at me as they passed, circulating through the apartment, returning, staring at me again, and sitting silently there in the apartment.

I asked to call an attorney and was refused.

The men questioned me; I gave some answers and refused to answer other questions, and continued to ask for an attorney.

My person, apartment and personal effects, and my car were examined; and by the time I was taken from my apartment (after the arrival of these men about noon) it was around

4:30 P.M. and television crews were conveniently set up in the foyer of the apartment building to take pictures of me as I was taken from the apartment building.

I was taken to Central Station, stripped and photographed (with and without clothing); then taken to the Polygraph Room where a man started to administer the polygraph test, which I said I wanted to take only if they let me call an attorney—which was refused, both tacitly and in so many words—and it may be noted that I did subsequently take the polygraph test at the request of my attorney and with permission of the Los Angeles Superior Court.

I was then informed that Norma was dead and that it was thought by these men that I had been "shaking her down" and had killed her; the interrogators swearing and cursing me and about me in the process of telling me this terrible news; and this period of questioning, with some answers and requests and refusals of requests for an attorney, lasted until about 9:30 P.M.

When I was taken from Central Station it was with a thinly veiled, nebulous threat of taking me "down by the sea, with no turning back then," and with my feeling alien to these plainclothes men (officers) and their hardened approach, and with my physical fear of them.

I was taken to West Los Angeles Station, where questioning was resumed; first by one plainclothes man (officer) and then another, and another, and then in groups. I kept asking to call an attorney and was refused and ignored; the questioning continuing while I got more and more tired and weary. At Central Station, I was given a cold hamburger which I could not eat and did not eat, and a half pint of milk. I had had no breakfast and extremely little sleep in more than four days, and about this time was barely able to hold my eyes open, and I recall I felt more tired than ever before in my life, except perhaps at the time of my crime.

A big plainclothes man (officer) hit me in the stomach with

his fist at this point, twice, and threatened to "work like that on me the rest of the night" if I didn't tell them what they wanted to know.

It was more than enough of their treatment of me at that time; and I told them I would tell them anything they wanted me to tell them, if they would leave me alone.

I wrote a so-called confession of my crime.

I still call it a so-called confession, because it was not a free and voluntary statement, and it was written in what can only fairly be described as a daze, and it is filled with particulars of half-truths and confusion and untruths and it is a rambling statement by a totally inexperienced, fearful, extremely weary and emotionally disturbed person, at three o'clock in the morning, after I had committed a terrible crime, as distressing to myself as to society, and had been subjected to the police conduct described.

After the so-called confession, I was fed and allowed to sleep—at 5 or 5:30 in the morning—after being taken to the scene of the crime and being unable to shed light on the obvious holes in the so-called confession.

The next day, I was taken to the District Attorney's office where I again renewed my request for an attorney and, only after considerable persistence on my part, was finally allowed to call an attorney, who was only allowed to see me some hours later in the West Los Angeles Station.

Then, a few hours later, in the West Los Angeles Station, the same plainclothes man (officer) who struck me in the stomach the night before and denied hurting me while in the District Attorney's office a few hours earlier and questioned about it, now talked of the gas chamber, ominously—talking about the gas chamber in my presence, with references to me, in a way that I would be sure not to miss the point. I would get the gas chamber.

Through my attorney, I then repudiated my so-called confession, was subsequently arraigned at a preliminary hearing, and was bound over to the Superior Court for trial.

I was extremely fortunate (for which I am very grateful) in that a friend obtained an attorney to defend me and stay with me throughout trial, appeal in the California Supreme Court, and review by the United States Supreme Court, and subsequent proceedings, including the Commutation Hearing before Honorable Governor Edmund G. Brown—for which I am, again, very grateful and cannot say enough to express my opinion of the high ethical, professional and humanitarian qualities of such men.

Suffice it to say, my attorney approached this case with a trial date set only a month away and with extremely limited funds, and from the point of view of the position I presented to him.

I could not admit my guilt—emotionally could not, either from the inability to accept the fact of my having taken a person's life or from the threat of the gas chamber by the plainclothes man (officer). At the same time, prison to me was a terrible, gruesome, dark, foreboding place—much as I suppose prison is generally conceived to be by those without any experience with prisons or with persons who know about prisons. Just as I could not admit my guilt, I could not think of going to prison.

My attorney has told me that an offer of Second Degree was made prior to trial, but the fact remains that I simply would not and was in no emotional state to consider such an offer. Under such conditions, this case went to trial.

By the time of trial, despite the reported offer of Second Degree, the death penalty was vehemently advocated. In hindsight, I feel that I should have and, except for my emotional condition, undoubtedly would have made such a plea; and realize that such a disposition would have intelligently avoided the long, costly appellate proceedings for all concerned.

However, as the trial proceeded, the first and largest single issue was whether my so-called confession was free and voluntary. I feel my attorney did remarkably well, all things considered, in bringing out the facts in support of the contention that it was not free and voluntary; and feel that the Honorable Stanley Mosk, who conducted the trial, ruled preliminarily on this issue with good conscience, according to his view of the divided law pertaining to this issue; and in fact, I was impressed by Judge Mosk throughout the trial and afterward.

But I feel with justification that some prosecution witnesses definitely did not possess a healthy predilection for the truth; that their untruths and half-truths on this issue of the so-called confession was poor instruction to me, in my only appearance before a court of law on a criminal charge, when I testified subsequently on other issues. I cannot excuse myself for any fabrications on my part, but neither do I feel that these others (with as great or greater responsibilities for the truth) should be excused, much less encouraged in their fabrications.

For a wealth of reasons, I feel a man needs and should be allowed to have an attorney upon his arrest on a serious criminal charge. I needed an attorney; and feel I should have been allowed to call one when it was admitted that I asked the officers to permit me to do so. Here too I feel the long, costly trial and appellate proceedings in my own case might well have been intelligently avoided, had I been allowed to see an attorney at this time. Reading case after case on this point of the right of counsel convinces me even further, that our system of justice and our prosecution of crime would actually be enhanced if this right were extended to State jurisdictions as it is in Federal jurisdictions.

I feel I had a fair trial (except that, honestly, I was so hungry at times during the long days in court from the inferior food in the county jail that I had real difficulty at times in expressing myself and thinking properly!) On the basis of the position I presented to my attorney, my attorney defended me with great energy and with several examples of unusual ability, and established the legal basis for appeal.

As it happened, when the verdict was returned my attorney was personally greatly disturbed, right along with me.

I arose when everyone in the court arose, as the time came for the verdict to be read. My knees were rubbery and I felt as though my whole system had paused for this moment, as though I were not breathing, my heart not pumping blood through my veins, and my mind—all thoughts—were arrested, still and waiting. But nevertheless, my eyes followed that piece of paper from the hand of the foreman to the hand of the Judge who read it and passed it back. Then, the death verdict was read and my breath came in short bursts and my blood raced and, in my mind, it was as though I had just been completely rejected by all mankind, my fellow human beings—called dog, scum, worthless thing to be destroyed—and I could not seem to bring my eyes up to face my peers for several moments. But while they were being polled, I did so, and I saw some stare at me with what I felt was hate as they answered yes, and others with tears, and others appearing stone cold. I could not look at them any longer and I stared down at the top of the counsel table, seeming to see nothing, hearing little, until the proceedings were ended and the jurors filed by the table and were gone.

Then, my sister was beside me, so I felt a need to be strong, to turn to her and tell her not to worry, to go back home, that there was nothing more to do. And when she had gone my attorney was beside me with tears in his eyes, so I felt a need to be strong a little longer, to turn to him and tell him not to worry, not to feel badly, that he had done all he could do and had done it well. And finally, I had to be taken back to jail, so I felt the need to be strong still a little longer. But then, at last, I was alone in my cell and my tears gushed to the surface, and I was not and could not be enough alone, with cells filled around me, and I even asked to be taken where I could be entirely alone—because this is the feeling, this is what it is like to hear a foreman pronounce a verdict of death: I felt utterly rejected. I had been called waste. I needed to be alone because I felt that nobody realized—except myself, inside myself—I was still a human being, still had some human value. Nobody—except myself, inside myself—seemed to realize I would not have done what I had done, would not have committed this crime, and would erase it and wanted to erase it long before this verdict—but of course could not, and did not know what else to do, except to now accept this desolate, complete rejection by my fellowman.

On a cold night in December, 1955, I arrived at prison in tears, and walked down that long, foreboding looking, closely guarded row of condemned men's cells. It was late but I was hungry and was fed. Then I made my bed and laid down to sleep among the doomed.

But when I awoke and as time went on I began to learn that these doomed men *are* human beings, were not and are not monsters like I and they have been called. And I learned also that much invaluable research material was and is being wasted, snuffed out, in a gas chamber because there were and are causes for the crime of every condemned man and society obviously did not and does not know these causes—if society did know these causes, it would strive to eliminate them and might, in time, be successful to a large extent.

And I also began to learn that my legal case was not unique in having involved a serious legal issue. For some reason, it almost seemed that a man could not be condemned to death without one or more serious legal issues arising out of the proceedings at his trial. Was this a subtle phenomenon which gave credit to my peers, the men and women who are jurors? Do they perhaps—and perhaps United States Supreme Court Justices, too—subconsciously resist against a verdict of punishment of death so much in their minds and hearts that prosecutors and judges fight too hard for such verdicts and in their own zeal create these legal errors, or at least serious legal issues to be resolved in such cases?

In my case, I know from my own experience, with all due respect to the majority opinion in the decision of the United States Supreme Court, that my age, my experience, and my education did not protect my rights at the time I needed and requested and was refused the opportunity to call an attorney.

I was 31 years of age, but like a child as far as concerned my fear of a ring of detectives around me. My experience did not include any experience with the situation I was in at the time I needed and requested counsel. My education, which, by the way, only included the bare first year, three hours of criminal law and no constitutional law, which, as any lawyer knows, is absolutely no training for police interrogations, much less an intelligent personal judgment in such an emotion-packed situation, was helpless in this situation.

I have been asked what it is like to wait to be put to death.

On death row, you never escape the thought of death.

It is there in your mind, day after day, while you eat, while you play, while you bathe, while you walk down among the living for a visit, while you glance or stare out a window at the open sky, when you hear the sparrows chirping and see them gather around a window and fly out into the air, and while you watch one after another of your fellowcondemned, your fellowman, escorted by your cell, down toward the gas chamber, to be put to death. You never escape the thought—until months and months later, when the relieving gas rises to destroy your thought, and all of you.

You awaken from the shock of the death verdict, unless you are one of those too sick in your mind. You begin to resist death, study your legal case, listen, talk, read this thing—the law—which has ordered you to be put to death. Day after day you do this, constantly, hour after hour. You learn something about this thing—the law: that it is not a fine, straight line from crime to trial to punishment; that it is a broad, waving line, where similar or worse crimes of the same type do not lead to the same punishment; that it is also a line of several links, in which each link has the power over the preceding link—only if you, yourself, usually poor and ignorant and friendless, can reach that next link, to seek to exert this power, by appeal, which is the link to life.

You are one who never even thought of crime, much less punishment, and still less capital punishment, until after your crime. Or you are one who knew of the gas chamber and subconsciously sought its relieving gas. Or you are one who knew of the gas chamber and consciously sought this way of suicide. You are probably one of those three, because condemned men who knew of capital punishment and calculated the gas chamber as a risk of their crimes, before their crimes, are relatively very, very few.

You relive your crime many times, or approach near to it in your thoughts and then back away from it in horror, appalled by it. You would turn backward. You would show your remorse—as condemned men sometimes do, one to another—the remorse you hide with your fear in your heart and mind you would show to the one with the power and the given promise to understand and not condemn you, to the one you cannot find, unless perhaps you are a person who finds him in God.

Waiting to be put to death is like having a charge of electricity attached to your limbs—not a big charge, but a small irritant charge to the nerve endings—constantly there and needling at any moment of the days or the nights, no matter what you are doing, even awaking you from your sleep.

It is like being immersed in water and taking an eternity to drown.

That is what it is like to wait to be put to death—not just to me—but, I believe, it is to a large extent an unexaggerated statement of what almost all condemned men feel, whether or not they can express their feelings in so many words.

Except among those who are too sick in their minds.

And even those who are too sick in their minds experience much of what it is like to wait to be put to death, except that they do not resist death; or they welcome death; or they run and hide from it in dreams that do not last long enough; or they blindly curse themselves or their judges or their juries or their victims or their families or their societies or their worlds; or they fly through the windows with the sparrows and are gone long before the gas takes away their breath.

That is what it is like to wait to be put to death.

The day I was taken from condemned row, when I walked unescorted down among the living, rode in a bus along the highway, saw the open sky, the green grass and flowers, the men and women and children, the homes and places of business along the way, and breathed a relatively free air again—can only be described with accuracy as somewhat of a resurrection for me—an opportunity to begin now to build a life of real understanding of myself and other human beings, training myself, with the help of psychiatric and other professional staff members to live a healthy way of life in this new life given to me.

That is Crooker's story. Either directly or by implication, it answers most of the questions about his case. He did kill Norma McCauley. As to why he did it, members of the psychiatric staff at San Quentin draw certain conclusions from his story and from their exhaustive examinations of him. Crooker, they say, grew up feeling rejected. As the only boy in a virtually all-female family, and as the object of his father's cruelty and contempt, he defended himself by withdrawing from reality, by spending hours in daydreams which often were more real to him than his actual experiences. Immature, confused, and emotionally unstable, he passed from school to school and from woman to woman in an ever increasing spiral of rejection. When he met Norma McCauley, she quickly became the center of his life. His desperate need for love was satisfied by her warmth and attention, until finally she too rejected him. This was the most humiliating experience of all, a rejection so serious that he was mentally, emotionally, and physically unable to cope with it. Like a child, he fought her decision in every way he could—with love, entreaties, threats of suicide, threats of murder—until finally, when nothing else worked, he completely broke under the strain and killed the person who represented the ultimate rejection of his entire life.

It is interesting to compare this diagnosis with Crooker's own description of his feelings when the jury pronounced him guilty. ". . . [I]t was as though I had just been completely rejected by all mankind, my fellow human beings—called dog, scum, worthless thing to be destroyed—and I could not seem to bring my eyes up to face my peers for several moments."

In a few jurisdictions, such as the District of Columbia, John Crooker would never have gone to trial but instead would have been certified as of unsound mind and transferred to a mental institution. But because the test of insanity in California is a strict one, based upon the age-old (and outmoded, say psychiatrists) theory of "adherence to the right," Crooker's mental state was never raised at trial and never presented on appeal. Despite the extreme complexity of his crime, when viewed against his background and state of mind, the only points decided by the Supreme Court of the United States dealt with a bare fragment, an episodic interlude, in the whole range of facts that made up this crime. There is a lesson here for those who think that the Supreme Court is merely another trial court deciding guilt or innocence, and that justice will necessarily prevail once the high tribunal agrees to hear a case. To the contrary, the Court is often faced with quite narrow points of law that have little or nothing to do with guilt.

Crooker's story fails to clarify one aspect of the case—the instrument used to kill Norma. As loquacious as Crooker was with the police after the crime, he repeatedly drew a blank when asked for a description and the whereabouts of the knife. He genuinely seemed not to know. And when he wrote his confession for the police, he made the Freudian slip of leaving out the word "knife" until reminded of the oversight by an officer. Now in his latest story of the crime he questions whether he used a knife at all, despite the fact that Norma was stabbed eleven times. What is there about a knife that Crooker cannot face, cannot even acknowledge? Is the knife a symbol, perhaps a phallic symbol, of the source of all his difficulties as he sees them? This question remains unanswered.

What was the prognosis for Crooker's recovery from his mental difficulties? Excellent, said Dr. Schmidt, who had treated him at San Quentin. Not only was Crooker in charge of the prison's electroencephalograph, but his fears were breaking down and he had begun normal socializing among his fellow prisoners. This prognosis proved accurate. Today, Crooker seems entirely normal.

His case, however, illustrates the quixotic nature of the law, for the majority's legal rationale has been rejected by later decisions of the Court. If Crooker had waited a few years to commit his crime, his conviction would have been reversed out of hand and his confession never allowed in evidence.

One of Governor Brown's last acts before leaving office was to commute Crooker's sentence to life imprisonment, as opposed to life imprisonment without possibility of parole. The parole board has once refused to release him. Unless it changes its mind, the law student who knew just enough law to demand an attorney will remain a prisoner to the end.

6

Portrait in Yellow and White

A shot! It seemed incredible.

Broad daylight on a Saturday morning, and Peters Street, winding its way through a busy commercial area near downtown Atlanta, teemed with shoppers. Cars and trucks roared along the four open lanes or backed carefully into the metered zones bordering the curbs or simply double-parked while passengers, with surreptitious glances here and there, hurried in and out of shops. Pedestrians crowded the sidewalks, made difficult for walking by surfaces of imperfectly fitted, octagonally-shaped cement blocks, and children scurried from sidewalk to street and back in a flanking maneuver around their envious and wistful elders.

At the precise moment of the shot, the sidewalk in front of Simon's Liquor Store was miraculously clear, like a sudden silence at a crowded party, but beyond the walk a ton-and-a-half Chevrolet truck was being angled into the curb. The four stovewood peddlers in the truck—Mr. Derrick, his son, and two helpers—looked up unbelievingly. Their penumbral experiences, without excess or intensity, had left them totally unprepared for a pistol shot in the daylight of a downtown street.

When they all looked up, the inside of Simon's Liquor Store was plainly visible. The building was only thirty feet across, its entire front façade taken up with two large, square windows that flanked glass double doors. An unpaved, cluttered alley, no wider than a truck, skirted one side of the store; Jacobs' Department Store bordered the other. They saw a single room with innocuously plastered walls ringed on three sides by rows of shelves carrying whisky and wine. A counter ran from front to back, its only ornament a cash register at the far end.

Two men stood, one on each side of the counter—a white man whom one of the peddlers recognized as the manager, Harry Furst, and a Negro. The Negro wore brown khaki pants with large pockets on the sides. He held a pistol in one hand and was reaching toward the cash register with the other. As the Negro scooped out the contents of the drawer, Furst began sliding down behind the counter, gasping in protest and pain and fright as he went.

The men in the truck were too astonished to react. But next door, Sidney Jacobs came to life like a threshing machine. He heard the "explosion" from the back of his department store, ran out to the sidewalk, looked in at his neighbor just in time to see the Negro with his hand in the cash register, and ran back into his own store. The dutiful audience of stovewood peddlers in the truck continued to watch as the Negro finished rifling the register. They saw him swing around and dash out to the sidewalk. He turned right, passing directly beside the truck, and turned immediately to his right again, and into the alley.

The elder Derrick came to life to the extent of hopping out of his truck and squinting at the figure retreating in a peculiar fashion up the alley. Jacobs ran out of his department store for the second time, screaming "Stop that man." Since no one seemed to be taking this plea very seriously, he entered the liquor store and looked at Furst behind the counter. Jacobs was too excited to tell whether the liquor dealer was alive or dead; all he comprehended was the blood on Furst's chest, just above the stomach. Jacobs yelled, "Mr. Furst," but got no answer.

Almost at once, Jacobs was joined by a breathless Seymour

Zimmerman, the owner of the liquor store, who had seen the commotion from a block away. Jacobs hardly had time to observe superfluously that Furst had been shot when Zimmerman, thinking he might apprehend the thief, dashed out of the store and up the alley for a short distance. He caught a glimpse of a fleeing figure but immediately lost the trail. Jacobs, left behind, pulled the burglar alarm.

In the meantime, the thief, confused, frightened, his senses all converged on the one thought of escape, was running with a peculiar effort, part skip, part stride. He covered the length of the alley in seconds and dashed out into Walker Street, where a car careened to avoid hitting him. He cut diagonally across to a filling station and passed within four feet of a merchant who was standing on the sidewalk. The merchant had seen people run through the alley before and paid no particular attention until he noticed that this man was holding a pistol in his right hand. He watched the man turn into Loew's Alley.

Loew's Alley began its tortuous, unpaved route beside the filling station. What had been a busy commercial area with thriving streets abruptly sloped off by way of this alley to become a borough of small, wooden, unpainted, dilapidated Negro houses, each surrounded by a cluttered and forsaken yard. On one barren plot stood a broken chair, listing badly to one side and nostalgically rocking in the gentle wind, while on another lay three tires rotting in the dirt. Bedraggled roosters squawked and strutted from one side of the alley to the other, seemingly homeless and yet perfectly at ease. Tin cans and broken glass littered the area, and a screen door hung loose from a post.

This was the path which the thief chose, dodging past the debris, scattering the roosters, trying to gauge his footing on the craggy, hard-mud surface. But he was still dangerously out in the open. As soon as he could, he abandoned the alley.

An elderly railroad worker standing on the back porch of

his house on Trenholm Street saw the thief running toward his house. The thief, his face pinched with fear, slowed to a fast walk, not unlike the disjointed swagger of a foot racer near the end of a marathon. He jumped a ditch and skirted the house.

Two men and a girl were standing across Trenholm Street, chatting amiably in the noon sun, when they saw the Negro approaching. Something about his appearance suggested to the girl that she ask him what he was doing, but then she noticed the handle of a pistol sticking out of his right trousers pocket, and she decided not to bother him. He passed between two houses in the direction of Hills Avenue.

The thief emerged on Hills Avenue and turned right, loping along the sidewalk. As he came into view of Number 317, a single-story frame house with a screen porch across its front, he was observed casually by a Swift & Company employee who sat on the porch. The interloper turned left beside an abandoned church and disappeared in the direction of McDaniel Street.

The character of the neighborhood was changing. The houses, though still small, were more individualistic and stylized, and some were newly painted. A few blocks away was a better-class Negro development with two-story, four-family stucco houses, and still farther along behind Northside Drive were four Negro colleges.

The thief approached McDaniel Street on a line between Aunt Fanny's Bargain Store and McCord's Sandwich Shop. The latter was a tiny whitewashed affair with a counter, two booths, and the inevitable Coca-Cola signs in the window. Willie McCord, the proprietor, relaxed and rangy, generally bestowed his slow smile and inert speech on customers from a stool beside the ice-cream receptacle. On this particular morning, however, Willie had roused himself and was taking a smoke out back of his shop when he saw the thief approach from Hills Avenue and watched him pass within a few feet of the sandwich shop. On McDaniel Street the thief disappeared.

Thus, from Simon's Liquor Store to McDaniel Street six blocks away, the thief's circuitous route of escape on this bright, busy Saturday morning in October, 1952 had been literally cluttered with witnesses.

By now, an ambulance had arrived to carry away to a funeral home the remains of Harry Furst. In death he looked pathetic. He was only five foot five and in his early sixties. His horn-rimmed glasses sat askew on his nose, and his partially bald head gleamed white in the sun. He left behind a wife and two children.

Detectives had converged on the scene and were asking questions. They wanted to know from Zimmerman how much money was missing, so the liquor store owner extracted the tape from the cash register and began calculating. He had only casually checked the register earlier that morning, because the job of making an actual acount was normally saved for Thursdays and Mondays, and this was only Saturday. But by comparing what was now in the register with what had been there on the previous Thursday, and by adding the amounts shown on the tape, he estimated that $868.73 had been stolen.

That same Saturday afternoon, sometime between one and three o'clock, the proprietor of a pawnshop on Decatur Street in Atlanta was confronted by a man who wanted to pawn a .32 Colt revolver. The proprietor asked for identification, was shown a Social Security card bearing the name of Irvin Washington, and made a fifteen-dollar loan on the pistol. When the man had left, the proprietor inspected the revolver and found one shell missing. With that suspicious turn of mind begotten by years of trading, the pawnbroker called the police. Two detectives arrived and took possession of the revolver. At the Atlanta Police Station, sufficient comparisons were made to establish a tentative relationship between the revolver and the Furst killing, and soon the revolver, with a

Western .32 shell found in the liquor store, and the bullet taken from Furst's body were all mailed for further tests to the Federal Bureau of Investigation in Washington.

Eighteen days passed with no new developments in the case except the offer of a reward by the Liquor Dealers' Protective Association.

Then, at 6:26 on the morning of October 17, a Negro named Aubry Lee Williams was brought into the Atlanta Police Station and booked.

The details of his arrest are not known, but a Social Security card bearing the name Irvin Washington was found in his trousers. Five members of the police department talked to him in jail, and in short order Williams admitted he had participated in the robbery of Simon's Liquor Store. However, he placed the blame for the actual shooting on a man named Robinson who was already in jail on another charge. When the police confronted Williams with Robinson, Williams admitted that Robinson had not been involved and that he himself was entirely responsible for the shooting. He claimed that during the holdup he had held the pistol in his hand but had rested his hand on the counter; when he leaned over to scoop the cash out of the register, the pistol had gone off accidentally.

Four days after his arrest, Williams was indicted for murder, the charge being that on October 4, 1952, he "did unlawfully, with malice aforethought, kill and murder one Harry Furst, by then and there shooting him with a pistol, contrary to the law of [Georgia], the good order, peace, and dignity thereof."

Every story, real or fictional, should have a hero. This is a rule of writing, of the stage, and of common sense when people's emotions are at stake. We are most stirred when clear good is pitted against clear evil, and when right and wrong are easily discernible. But only a social psychologist could have found in Aubry Williams' sordid, twisted career the seeds of virtue. Certainly his appearance offered nothing of interest.

He was a twenty-seven-year-old, light-skinned Negro with scars running diagonally across a broad, sullen face. A small mustache cluttered his lip. He was of medium height and medium build—essentially a nondescript man, neither weak nor strong, neither intelligent nor stupid. He was the antithesis of his address, for he lived on Penelope Street.

His record was eventful but disreputable. He had been arrested at least fifteen times between 1942 and the Furst shooting in October, 1952, although he had worked during the war years for the Navy and War Departments and for the Civil Service Administration. In fact, he had already spent about six and a half years of his life in prison. His crimes included such diversified and far-flung operations as larceny, reckless driving, and wife-beating. No, Aubry Williams was no hero, even to his wife, and his barren existence would have passed largely unnoticed had he not become involved, quite unintentionally and through the most haphazard of circumstances, in a legal tangle involving the Constitution itself.

Four months passed after his arrest. Christmas and the new year came and went, and Williams sat passively in jail, awaiting trial. Finally, on February 18, 1953, the jury panels which would serve in Atlanta's civil and criminal cases during the week of March 9 were chosen. A regular ritual accompanied the selection of panels.

The ritual took place in the courtroom of the presiding judge—in this instance Judge Jesse M. Wood, a short man in his early eighties; a man of medium build and of bright blue eyes. His courtroom was on the fourth floor of the Fulton County courthouse in downtown Atlanta. The judge's dais was raised but a few inches off the floor, so that those in the last of the eight rows of spectator benches could see him only by raising themselves in their seats and peering over the heads in front of them. The ceiling of the courtroom was high and the acoustics poor. The tone of the room was mahogany, with heavy wooden tables, seats, benches, and jury box filling most of the available space. The flags of the United States and Georgia stood solemnly and unrifled behind the bench, on either side of a framed portrait of a former judge.

But the most striking feature of the courtroom was its green lamps. They stood everywhere—on either end of the bench, on the clerk's desk, in double pairs at the counsel tables—like monstrous green toadstools. Undoubtedly relics of the days when an object's beauty was gauged by its sensational effect, these lamps had all the gaiety of giant eyeshades, and they turned everything above chin level into an eerie verdure.

A small wooden box with two compartments stood on one of the counsel tables. Judge Wood successively drew from one compartment more than a hundred and twenty tickets, each containing the name of a citizen of the State of Georgia. These tickets had been made up by jury commissioners from Atlanta's tax records.

White tickets were used for the names of white citizens, and yellow tickets for the names of Negroes.

The judge handed each ticket to a deputy sheriff, who in turn gave it to the deputy clerk for listing on a long sheet. The tickets were then returned to the judge, who placed them in the box's second compartment. Some time later, the petit jurors whose names had been listed were summoned to the courtroom and questioned. After a number were excused, the remaining ones were organized into panels, six of which were assigned to the criminal calendar. Four of the one hundred and twenty jurors thus selected were Negroes.

On March 9, the day before Williams' trial and over five hundred miles away, the Supreme Court of the United States was taking action in another Atlanta case involving a Negro named James Avery, a strong handsome young man with as unsavory a past as Williams'. His trial for rape revealed that while drunk, he had gone to the home of a white woman who was alone with several small children, dragged her out into the yard, and forcibly had intercourse with her while she screamed and struggled. Her fourteen-year-old son and a man had come upon them while Avery still had the woman on the ground, and Avery had gotten up and run. Arrested that same night, he had been positively identified by the woman as her assailant. Avery was convicted of rape by a jury chosen in precisely the same manner as the jury in the Williams case, except that no Negroes at all turned up on the panels. Prior to trial, Avery's attorney had objected to the impaneling of the jury on the ground that the use of yellow and white tickets to distinguish Negro from white jurors violated Avery's rights under the Equal Protection Clauses of the Georgia and Federal Constitutions. The Georgia Supreme Court, with one judge concurring and two dissenting, condemned the use of yellow and white tickets but held that there was no constitutional violation because the officials who had drawn the tickets testified that no actual discrimination had been practiced. Now the United States Supreme Court, on the day before Williams' trial was to begin, announced that it would hear argument in the Avery case.

The trial of Aubry Williams lasted one day. Since Williams had no money, the court appointed Carter Goode, an Atlanta attorney, to defend him. Goode was a thick-set man of one hundred and eighty pounds with a firm voice that left no doubt of his southern origins. A graduate of the Woodrow Wilson College of Law in Atlanta, he was just turning forty at the time of his appointment.

The first order of business was to select a jury from the various panels already drawn. Forty-eight jurors (again including the four Negroes) were "put upon" Williams—that is, tentatively chosen as the group from which his jurors would be selected.

They were again questioned. Thirteen, including three of the Negroes, were eliminated by the judge "for cause." All of the remaining jurors were technically competent, from the court's viewpoint, to try Williams. But the state and defense counsel were allowed a number of peremptory challenges—that is, vetoes without the necessity of stating a reason—and as soon as the name of the one remaining Negro juror was called, the state exercised its first peremptory challenge and eliminated him from the list. Williams' jury thus evolved into an all-white group of twelve Georgians. Williams' attorney, Carter Goode, made no objection to the selection, drawing, or empaneling of the jury.

Twenty-three witnesses testified for the state, and Williams appeared briefly, though unsworn, in his own behalf. Keeping a firm hand on the proceedings was E. E. Andrews, whose official title was "Judge, Fulton Superior Court, Atlanta Judicial Circuit." He was a temperamental and fiery man; his short, fat body exuded boundless energy and an overpowering confidence. In his late fifties and with hair already grey, this judge left no doubt as to who was in charge of the trial. He sat like a robust Buddha on a dais in a courtroom which, except for a few less toadstool lamps and a different judge's portrait, was virtually a replica of the one where the jury panels had been drawn.

The first witness was Mrs. Furst, who briefly identified her late husband as the victim of the shooting. She was not cross-examined.

Mr. Derrick, the stovewood peddler, nervously took the stand and told how he had witnessed the crime. But he said he could make no identification because when the man who had done the shooting ran out of the store, "he had his arm over his face." He was just "a medium-built skinny fellow" who "kind of crow-hopped as he went down towards Walker Street." Derrick's son could not identify Williams either ("it has been such a long time . . ."); one of the two workers with the Derricks told the same story; and Mr. Jacobs, the department store owner, testified that he saw the killer but could not identify him "because of the shock of it." The merchant who had stood by the filling station said he too could not identify Williams; ". . . I didn't see him in the face because it didn't excite me until I saw the gun and I didn't notice him."

The testimony of Mr. Zimmerman, who ran the liquor store and who had seen the thief only fleetingly, was concerned principally with the amount of money which had been stolen. Goode objected strenuously on the ground that the cash register tapes had not been checked immediately prior to the shooting, but Judge Andrews allowed the testimony and the tapes to be introduced into evidence.

Thus, the first six witnesses who had seen the killer of Harry Furst all failed to identify Aubry Williams, lounging at the defense table with a cocky smile. He kept looking at Mrs. Furst, who remained at the prosecution table throughout the proceedings, until finally Judge Andrews told him to keep his eyes to the front.

Now Williams' luck failed. The elderly railroad worker took the stand and told about the man he had observed first from his back porch. He had never seen the man before but would know him if he saw him again. Had he seen him again? The witness leaned forward and pointed at Williams. "I see him sitting over there."

Goode rose in wrath to cross-examine. He brought out that the witness had been at least twenty-five feet away from the man he was identifying as Williams, that he had no idea where the man had been coming from, that other people cut across his back yard from time to time, that he had no idea what kind of a pistol the man had held, and that he had not spoken to the man or tried to stop him. Pressed as to whether he could really be sure he had seen Williams, the witness at first could only reply, "if he wasn't the man he looks like the man and he had to be a man because he couldn't have been a woman." But then, gathering his strength, he stoutly asserted, "I see him now. I see him over there now."

The girl and one of the two men who had stood chatting

in front of the railroad worker's house each took the witness chair in turn. The girl said she could not identify the man she had seen, but her companion stated flatly, as he nodded at Williams, that the man he had seen "was the same man who sits over there at the table today."

The Swift & Company employee could add little to the prosecution's case, nor could Willie McCord, the sandwich man. Willie admitted that some time after the Saturday of the shooting, the police had brought a Negro to his back fence, and that the Negro had confessed to the crime, but Willie could not say whether Aubry Williams was the man he had seen. Goode objected to references to a confession, but Judge Andrews overruled the objection, subject to the confession being "connected up" by the police officers later.

There then appeared an important link in the state's chain of evidence in the person of one Harris, who had been a taxi driver on the day Furst was killed. Harris had been parked in a driveway at the corner of Maher and Fair Streets at about eleven o'clock in the morning when a man approached Harris's taxi and asked if he was going "into town"—meaning the mid-downtown section of Atlanta. Harris said he was, and the man asked if he could have a lift, since he wanted to get a haircut and a shave. He said his sister knew he was in town, and he wanted to get cleaned up before he visited her; he was from Florida. Harris told the man he could ride with him, and the two of them apparently understood this to mean a free ride, since the rider did not offer, and Harris did not demand, a fare. Harris deposited his passenger in front of a café on Decatur Street.

Harris definitely identified Aubry Williams as his passenger. And he pointed out, under careful questioning from the prosecutor, that the intersection where he had picked up Williams was only about four blocks from Willie McCord's sandwich shop on McDaniel Street.

Near the café on Decatur Street where Harris had left

Williams was a little shelter from the heat of the sun known affectionately and euphemistically by its habitués as Shy's Place. The name of its proprietor, Joe Shikaney, had been shortened by some tortuous and inexplicable process over the years to "Shy." The establishment, to Shy, was a beer and wine shop, and he loved it as a mother loves her child. To Maggie Jones, who worked there, it was a beer joint.

Maggie took the stand with sauce and flip. She explained that on *some* day—she thought it was a Saturday but she could not further identify the day, the month, or the year—her friend Aubry Williams had come into Shy's Place while she was sweeping the floor and said, "Hey, Maggie," and she said, "Hey, Aubry," and he said, "Lend me a quarter," and she laughed and said, "I haven't got nothing," and he pulled out a big stack of money and said, "If I needed money I wouldn't be here." The stack looked like five- and ten-dollar bills. She said, "Give me a dollar to get some stockings," and with that Williams ran out the door.

"Shy" testified that one Saturday Aubry Williams shot dice in the back of his beer and wine shop—and lost his shirt. Shy had passed back and forth behind the players several times, stopping only long enough to win about forty dollars from Williams. Williams' principal opponent in the game was a man named Bell.

Bell swore that on some Saturday afternoon ("I don't remember when that was; I don't know the exact date now. . . . I don't remember what month it was. I think it was the Saturday afternoon that Mr. Furst was killed. . . ."), he had rolled dice with Williams in the back of Shy's Place, shooting about twenty or thirty dollars a roll. Bell won over five hundred dollars from Williams. When the game broke up, Williams was so broke that Bell had to lend him ten dollars out of his winnings. Williams, said Bell, carried a pistol while they were playing.

The pawnshop proprietor told how the defendant Williams

had entered his shop, shown him the Social Security card of Irvin Washington, and pawned a pistol for fifteen dollars. The proprietor said his records would show that the pistol Williams pawned had the same serial number as the pistol in evidence as State's Exhibit 3.

A special agent of the Federal Bureau of Investigation assigned to the FBI Laboratory in Washington, D. C., identified the .32 Colt revolver, its cartridge, and the bullet, all sent to him by the Georgia police. He had run various tests and concluded that the bullet could have been fired from the revolver and cartridge. However, approximately two-thirds of the sides of the bullet had been mutilated so that he could not make a positive identification. The director of the Crime Laboratory of the State of Georgia, who had performed an autopsy on the body of Harry Furst, was similarly hazy about whether the bullet he had taken from Furst's body had been fired from the pistol which Williams had pawned.

Goode objected when an officer in the robbery squad began to testify about a statement Williams had given the police. Goode pointed out that no one had shown what had happened to Williams for the first hour and a half after his arrest, and there was no evidence as to whether threats or offers had been made during that period which induced him to give the statement. But Judge Andrews overruled these objections, and the officer related Williams' oral statement and then presented a written statement which the defendant had made about seven o'clock in the evening on the day of his arrest. The written statement read in part:

On two Saturdays ago I went to a mans house they call Cat Hill who lives on Larchwood and Whatley. I got the gun off the bed in the middle room. A man by the name of Junior Griffin, Willie Bevins and Cat Hills was there. I left from there and went home. I left home and went down there and got a bottle of beer, this was somewhere in Dixie Hills. It was somewhere around about 9:00. I left from there and went on up the road and caught a trolley. I caught the trolley at Battle Hill at the end of the line and got off on Peters St. at the corner of McDaniel St. When I got off the bus at Peters St. and McDaniel St. I went to the Blue Ribbon on McDaniel St. and got a pitcher of beer and drank it. I left from there and went on up Peters St. on across Walker St. to the liquor Store above the alley and went in the whiskey store and had the gun in my front right pocket. I pulled it out and told him to open the cash register and had the gun resting on the counter with the gun in my hand. There was a white man behind the counter and I hit my hand and the gun went off while I was getting the money out of the cash register. The man hollered OH when I shot him. I then run out of the store and turned back into the alley. . . .

The statement went on to tell of the flight through alleys and across yards, the cab ride to a "restaurant" where he lost all his money, and the pawning of the pistol. With the money from the gun, he bought a jacket, a pair of pants, and a pair of shoes, and then he went home and took a bath. In a sudden switch from this rambling, ungrammatical style, the statement concluded: "I have made this statement freely and voluntarily and understand from the officers present who have told me of my rights that anything stated herein may be used against me in any court of competent authority and do hereby agree to such procedure and that this is the truth the whole truth and nothing but the truth so help me GOD."

The state rested its case. The entire defense consisted of the following statement by Aubry Williams: "The only thing I know about this case is what the officers told me. I was on that side of town that morning, and when I signed the papers I was afraid. I did not do it and don't know who did it."

The jury was out less than one hour. Its verdict was foregone: "We the jury find the defendant guilty." Since there was no recommendation of clemency, the sentence was also foregone. The very next day, Judge Andrews intoned it out in a voice of doom: Aubry Williams was to be taken from the common jail of Fulton County to the Georgia State Prison in Tatnall County and there to be electrocuted seven weeks hence, on May 1, 1953, between the hours of 10:00 A.M. and 2:00 P.M.—"and may God have mercy on your soul."

Within two weeks, Carter Goode filed a lengthy motion for a new trial, alleging numerous errors during the conduct of the trial. He argued, among other things, that Judge Andrews' charge to the jury had been prejudicial, that Williams' statement of the crime should not have been used against him, and that the amount of money missing from the cash register was never established. But nothing was said about the yellow and white tickets used to select the jury. Judge Andrews took the motion under consideration.

A month after Williams' motion was filed, the Supreme Court of the United States heard argument in the Avery case, and the following month it reached its decision. The use of yellow and white tickets to choose jury panels violated the Federal Constitution, and Avery was entitled to a new trial. Mr. Justice Reed and, to some extent, Mr. Justice Frankfurter based their opinions upon the small percentage of Negroes who appeared on jury panels in Atlanta despite a twenty-five per cent Negro population, but the five-man majority decided the case squarely on the *use* of the tickets and the *opportunity* thus allowed for discrimination. The reasoning was clear. The different colors were not accidental; they had a purpose. What purpose, if not to make discrimination possible by the avoidance of Negro names or the deliberate choice of white names? And if Negroes were purposely excluded from the jury, Avery, a Negro, was discriminated against because of his race in violation of the Constitution. Once the tickets were used, the burden was on the state to prove that no discrimination had in fact been used.

On June 29, Goode filed in the Georgia trial court an amendment to his motion for a new trial, but again nothing was said of yellow and white tickets. The trial court overruled the amended motion the same day it was filed.

Summer gave way to fall, and a chill crept into the Atlanta

jail. The railings of the cot which had offered Williams a welcome coolness against his skin during the heat of summer were now almost turgid with the chill of the coming winter. Shadows moved into the emptiness earlier in the afternoons. Williams watched them and waited, glad to be alive. He read no books, he wrote no letters, he lived no memories. He just waited. A more intelligent man would have gone mad. The utter boredom, combined with a certain suspense, the confinement, the drab, gray surroundings all would have eaten away the senses of someone with more awareness than Aubry Williams. But Williams' past had been on a par with this very type of existence. Bleak and useless, he had whittled away twenty-seven years in waiting—often for nothing.

In mid-October the Georgia Supreme Court affirmed his conviction, ruling that there was no error in any part of the trial. The execution, which had been stayed during the appeal, was reset for December 11.

And now, on the first day of December, over six months after the Avery decision and almost nine months after the Williams trial, Goode filed an "extraordinary motion for a new trial" alleging for the first time that Williams' constitutional rights had been violated because of the use of yellow and white tickets in the selection of the jury. This motion was accompanied by two affidavits, one signed by Williams and one by Goode. Williams declared that he did not raise the objection earlier because he had no information as to how his jury had been selected. Goode's affidavit stated that prior to trial he had not known the facts about the jury selection and he could not have discovered them in the exercise of ordinary diligence.

The motion was denied by the trial court, and again Goode took the case to the Georgia Supreme Court. But soon after the advent of the new year came the announcement that the conviction would stand. The court said the very sequence of events in the Avery case showed that Goode, contrary to his affidavit, could have discovered the facts if he had used due diligence. Referring to the use of different colored tickets, the court ruled: "Defendant in his motion sets forth a practice which has been condemned by this court and the Supreme Court of the United States. However, any question to be considered by this court must be raised at the time and in the manner required under the rules of law and practice and procedure in effect in the states. . . . When this defendant failed to raise this question when the panel was put upon him, he waived the question once and for all." In other words, under Georgia practice, certain objections had to be made at certain times, or they were considered waived and could not thereafter be raised at all. By failing to object to the use of yellow and white tickets prior to trial, Williams and his attorney had lost the right to object at all.

Of course, there are sound reasons in the law for rules such as this. If lawyers could raise objections at any stage they cared to, they would simply save their contentions until long after trial—after they had seen what the result would be—and then raise all manner of objection which, if presented earlier, might have stopped the proceedings in their tracks. Without such rules, there would be no end to litigation. On the other hand, some objections are so important and so basic to a man's constitutional rights that often he is allowed to raise them at any time.

The Georgia Supreme Court chose to enforce its rules. An objection of this type must be raised before trial or not at all. Avery had raised it in time; Williams had not. Avery's conviction was reversed; Williams' was affirmed. Williams would go to his death.

There seemed to be only one other means of redress, and Goode promptly filed his request for the Supreme Court of the United States to hear the case. In his petition, he argued that for him to have challenged the jury when it was "put upon" Williams would have been premature and useless, because "only when counsel for the state, having the first jury challenge, peremptorily challenged the one remaining Negro juror was the end of the discriminatory process reached." In other words, there were no Negroes on the panel which faced Avery, and so he could object at any time, but since there was still one Negro on the panel which confronted Williams, the discriminatory process was neither complete nor obvious, and there was no point in objecting. Goode did not say, however, why he had not objected after the final Negro juror was challenged. Perhaps his theory was that even an objection at that time would have been too late, since the panel had already been "put upon" Williams.

In any case, the Supreme Court, at its second session of the term after its return from the summer of 1954, announced it would hear arguments in the Williams case.

As was his usual custom, the clerk of the Supreme Court wrote to the attorneys on both sides—Goode and the attorney general of Georgia—informing them of the date of oral argument. In this case it was March 3. Less than three weeks prior to that date an assistant attorney general of Georgia wrote the clerk that in all probability Goode would not participate in the oral argument. The clerk immediately wrote Goode and asked him his plans. Goode replied:

"At the present time, it does not appear that I will be able to come to Washington to present oral argument in the above case. I have little or nothing to add to the brief. . . .

"I am assuming that if events take such a turn that I am able to come to Washington, I will be permitted to make a short oral argument."

The clerk showed the letter to Chief Justice Warren and, as a result of their conference, wrote back to Goode:

"I have spoken to the Chief Justice about the oral argument in this case and of the probability that you would not be present.

"He asked me to inform you that the Court would appreciate your presenting oral argument if at all possible, particularly in view of the fact that this is a capital case."

Two days later Goode replied:

"I am in this position about this case: I originally entered the case by appointment, before our General Assembly enacted legislation authorizing the payment of appointed counsel from the treasury of Fulton County. This petitioner [Williams] has no money. His family have made contributions which have in part paid actual expenses. At the present time, they have only paid one-half the cost of printing the brief, and in this situation, it appears that any expense connected with a trip to Washington will be out-of-pocket to me.

"In addition, I am sole counsel in a suit in the Superior Court of Polk County, Georgia, on the calendar of that court for trial during the present week where my absence for any cause will have the result that payment of temporary alimony to my client will not be continued, which in turn, will have the result that I will lose the client.

"I have appeared in the Supreme Court of Georgia twice in this case and have pursued it thus far in the Supreme Court of the United States at a considerable sacrifice. It has been my intention to present oral argument if at all possible. In view of the foregoing, however, it simply does not seem that I will be able to. If I can try the case in Polk Superior Court tomorrow (March 1st), there remains a possibility that I will be able to appear before the Supreme Court. I do not, however, believe such will be the case and for that reason, I cannot plan on going to Washington."

This letter necessitated another conference between the clerk and the Chief Justice. Obviously, someone would have to be appointed to argue the case for Williams, and just as obviously the argument would have to be put over until a later date so that the appointed attorney would have time to become acquainted with the facts and to submit his brief. The Court decided to name Eugene Gressman, a Washington attorney, to present the argument on Williams' behalf. Oral argument was reset for April 18, allowing Gressman five weeks' preparation.

Gressman thus had the pleasure of arguing before the Court on his thirty-eighth birthday. A Phi Beta Kappa from the undergraduate and law schools of the University of Michigan, Gressman was no stranger to the Supreme Court. For five years, from 1943 until 1948, he had served as the only law clerk to Mr. Justice Murphy and in that capacity had participated in the Willie Francis case involving the faulty electric chair. Since leaving the Court, Gressman had coauthored a standard text on Supreme Court practice. He was a dark young man, quite thin, and younger looking than his actual age. He spoke quietly, precisely, without anger and without any real flair. One tended to listen to him because he sounded as if what he had to say was important. In the Williams case, he had real problems.

It may come as a shock to many, but the Supreme Court does not have jurisdiction to decide all constitutional issues presented to it. In a case coming from a state court, the issue must be raised at the proper stage of the proceedings as established by state law. Of course, a state cannot be arbitrary or discriminatory in applying its rules, but assuming that the rule is applied fairly, the Supreme Court simply has no power to decide an issue which the state court declares was improperly raised. The saving grace, however, is that when a constitutional issue is presented, the Supreme Court itself decides whether the state rules have been equitably and fairly applied and thus whether the issue is properly before it.

Goode had largely ignored this jurisdictional problem. His brief went straight to the use of yellow and white tickets and presented the case as a parallel to Avery's. But the attorney general of Georgia, Eugene Cooke, argued in his brief that the Supreme Court was without jurisdiction because the constitutional issue had not been raised in time; and in any event, he added, the appearance of Negroes on the jury lists rebutted any presumption of discrimination even though it so happened that none appeared among the twelve jurors who tried Williams.

Gressman realized that his principal problem was the jurisdictional one. He had to convince the Court that it had jurisdiction and could decide the case on its merits. Otherwise, the Court would simply dismiss the writ of certiorari as "improvidently granted"—that is, admit that it had no power to decide the constitutional question and that it should never have agreed to hear the case in the first place. This is a more common occurrence than laymen may suspect.

Gressman faced up to this dilemma by arguing two principal points. First, for Williams to have asserted his rights prior to trial would have been a futile gesture. The entire procedure in the Georgia courts at that time, including the continued use of yellow and white tickets after the Supreme Court of Georgia had condemned them, demonstrated that the constitutional objection would have been ignored. The law does not require the faithful observance of futile gestures. Secondly, in a capital case a constitutional right should not be considered waived unless for substantial and compelling reasons—reasons which were wholly lacking in this case.

The oral argument was held on April 18, 1955. Gressman spoke for one hour and in his deliberate way ticked off the points in his favor. The attorney general of Georgia sent two of his assistants, E. Freeman Leverett and Robert H. Hall, to argue on behalf of the state. Leverett was in his late twenties and Hall in his early thirties, and both glowed with the confidence and attractiveness of youth. They divided their time between them. Without rancor, they struck again and again at the theme that no properly raised constitutional issue was before the Court.

The Chief Justice sat silent for much of the argument. But toward the end of Leverett's presentation he leaned forward slightly and cleared his throat. He spoke in a slow, persistent, methodical way; once he began pursuing his subject, Leverett had as much chance of shaking him loose as a possum has of unclamping a bulldog from his throat.

Warren drew attention to the argument in Leverett's brief that no discrimination had been practiced. Wasn't it true, asked Warren, that precisely the same system of yellow and white tickets had been used to select the Williams jury as had been condemned by the Supreme Court in the Avery case?

Yes, admitted Leverett; basically the same system had been used.

And wasn't it further true, Warren pursued, that the Supreme Court had held that the use of yellow and white tickets was itself a constitutional violation, regardless of whether actual discrimination was proven?

Well, replied Leverett, the Avery opinion did refer to the fact that no Negroes appeared on the jury lists, whereas here four Negroes turned up.

True, said Warren, but wasn't the Avery opinion based upon the *opportunity* which yellow and white tickets afforded for discrimination rather than upon proof of discrimination itself, and therefore it was the system of selection which was unconstitutional?

Yes, conceded Leverett, the opinion seemed to rest on that ground.

Warren went doggedly on. Doesn't it follow, then, that there *was* a violation of the Constitution in Williams' case, since exactly the same system of yellow and white tickets had been used to select the jury?

Leverett protested that constitutional rights must be asserted; here, Williams had waived, or forfeited, his constitutional rights by failing to assert them at the proper time.

Warren said he appreciated that argument. But what he was trying to get at was this: regardless of whether the rights were properly asserted, didn't the method of jury selection violate the Constitution under the Avery decision?

Leverett hesitated. He knew it was an important question, and he knew he had been maneuvered into a position where there was only one answer. Pointing out again that Williams' constitutional objections had not been properly asserted, he agreed that had they been properly asserted, they would have been valid.

Warren leaned back in his seat and reassumed his inexpressive pose. He had obtained an admission that the Williams jury had been unconstitutionally impaneled. The important, the vital remaining question was whether the constitutional issue had been properly raised. If it had not, the Supreme Court had no jurisdiction over the matter and was powerless to act.

To probe a man's mind is surely a hazardous business. We know so little. Warren's expression was set, carved, tight. It said that for him the case was over. If so, was Leverett's admission really the deciding factor for Warren, or had he been unalterably set on his course before the argument began? It is like asking whether you would have liked a book quite so much if you had not heard in advance that it was a great book. We suspect the answer, but we do not know. We grope and feel among the pathways of the mind, but can we really come to a legitimate conclusion about it? Looking at Warren, one could as easily see in that stolid face a cold, unfeeling, narrow consciousness as one could detect a gentleness and warmth, and yet the man could not be two people. Or could he? How do we account for the way his mind functioned and how it reached the results it did? Although less intellectual than Frankfurter, Warren surely was more difficult to explain. Everything about Frankfurter's past, his religion, his contacts, his appearance, his perceptions cried out for the paths he followed. But Warren could have gone either way. Some say that his father's murder had a profound effect upon him. It may well have, but who could have said in advance *what* effect it would have? That Warren would become a champion of liberal causes and that he would allow little to stand in the way of just results as he saw them was more obvious after the fact than before.

The argument was held on a Monday. On the following Saturday, the Court met for its regular conference to act on the week's business.

Tucked into the back recesses of the Supreme Court Building is an awesome, chandeliered room seldom seen by the public. It is the room where the conferences of the Court are held, where the cases are discussed, the votes taken and tentative results reached. Perhaps by objective standards the room is not awesome at all, rectangularly angled as it is into the east corner of the building, with windows overlooking an unexceptional view of street and homes. But this room brooks no objectivity; it is a subjective room, a personality room. Although quiet, it is a room with a purpose. It breathes suppressed controversy from the pores of every stiff-backed chair, ranged around the black oblong table like nine jealous show dogs. At one end of the room is a fireplace and a mantelpiece, commanded by a grave portrait of John Marshall, staring with candor upon the scene he has wrought. Next to the fireplace is the entrance to the office serving the Chief Justice's law clerks, so that when tempers rise during the sacrosanct conferences, the gist of the argument filters through to fascinated ears. On the opposite side of the room is an entrance, normally unused, which leads to the Chief Justice's office. But the main exit from the room is through a corridor which empties into the hallway behind the courtroom. The corridor is used in part as a robing room. Thus, the Justices, when they leave the bench, stride across the hallway and into the corridor where they leave their robes with their messengers, and from there go either directly into the conference room, into the office of the Chief Justice's two secretaries, or out into the hallway to their own offices. But for most of each week, the conference room is deserted. It seems to be lying in wait for great events. Like the ballroom of a country club, it sits lonely for most of the week only to burst into life on the weekends. Today, conferences begin on Friday and only on occasion run over into Saturday, but in 1955, Saturday was conference day, and the ordeal usually lasted the full day.

A negligible amount of ceremony accompanies these meetings. No matter in what recriminations the day ends, it begins in decorum and fellowship, as the Justices shake hands, each with the other, as they enter and take their seats. They have been preceded by their messengers, who have rolled carts into place behind the chairs. The carts contain the petitions for certiorari and other briefs and papers upon which the Court will vote during its conference. When all the Justices have arrived, everyone else leaves the room, and the doors are closed. No secretary, no law clerk, no clerk of court, no messenger is allowed to enter after the session has begun, and if some urgent message has to be relayed in or out, the junior associate in point of service—at the time of the Williams case, Mr. Justice Harlan—must leave the conference table and shuffle to the door like a page boy. This duty had been particularly hard on Mr. Justice Minton, who walked with difficulty on a bad leg, and he had happily turned the chore over to John M. Harlan when the new Justice took his seat exactly three weeks before the Williams argument.

The Chief Justice led the discussion, taking each case in turn, summarizing the salient facts and arguments, expressing his own views of the applicable law, and then turning the discussion over to the next senior Justice, Mr. Justice Black of Alabama. After eighteen years on the Court, Black looked tanned and fit as the result of his regular tennis matches with friends and law clerks. His eyes reflected determination and an iron spirit. The discussion passed to bald and gaunt Mr. Justice Reed. Sitting low in his swivel chair, he spoke in moderate tones and with a slight accent that barely betrayed his Kentucky upbringing. Next was Mr. Justice Frankfurter, the Viennese immigrant with the extraordinary memory; the man of many questions. Small and quick, he epitomized the law he expounded. He passed to Mr. Justice Douglas, the controversial world traveler and book writer. Still a young man—he was only forty-one when appointed to the Court—his face was misleading. He looked like a weather-beaten cowpoke, a rather naive Midwesterner, but this exterior concealed a brilliant, impatient mind. Like a sphinx farther along the table was Mr. Justice Burton of Ohio. Quiet, dignified, attentive Burton, never vituperative, never rankled, a study in judicial temperament. Next senior was Mr. Justice Clark, the kindly former Attorney General. Gray and relaxed, he sat listening with his head slightly to one side and, when it was his turn, spoke softly and with some hesitation. Then the bulldog, Mr. Justice Minton, whose face, as rough and as stony as craggy cliffs, belied a keen love of baseball and a delightful sense of humor. And finally the tall, attractive, freshman associate, Mr. Justice Harlan, whose grandfather had sat at a similar table and thrashed out similar constitutional problems long before the Supreme Court moved from the Capitol to its spacious new quarters.

The vote was taken in reverse order, the junior associate voting first. The theory is that by voting in this order, the newer associates are not overawed or intimidated by their seniors. Actually, of course, the voting is little more than a formality, since each Justice generally has made his position clear by the time the vote is taken. Moreover, the vote is only tentative; each Justice will in effect vote again when he approves or disapproves the written opinion, and even then he may change his mind any time up until the decision is actually rendered from the bench.

To its newest members, perhaps the most surprising thing about the Court is that it acts less as one institution than as nine. Each Justice is a temple unto himself, and only on occasion is there a real effort toward an accommodation of views. Unlike jurors in a criminal trial, who must agree or be dismissed, the Justices can and do maintain their own individual positions as long as they like, no matter how arbitrary, no matter how ill-founded these positions may seem to their brethren. The Court could easily have grown up differently, with the chief emphasis on joint action and with individual views subjugated to the group will, but from the beginning it was felt that the strength of the Court lay in its nine independent judgments, independently expressed, no matter how diverse, no matter how obstinate.

This independence manifests itself at conference. On a difficult case the gentle flow of the discussion can quickly turn to argument, and the argument to sharp defiance. On occasion, things are said which had better been left to intuition.

As the result of the Court's conference on April 23, Mr. Justice Frankfurter was assigned by the Chief Justice to write for the majority. Justices Clark and Minton began working on their own opinions. All in all, it took seven weeks for the various views to be put in writing, printed, circulated among the Justices, approved or disapproved, re-edited, and reprinted.

On June 6, 1955, the Justices filed to their places, and the ritual of delivering opinions began.

For some reason buried in history, the Supreme Court renders its decisions not only in print but verbally. In 1955, Mondays were decision days, and spectators, then as now, flocked to hear the learned judges expostulate the law.

As each case is reached, the Chief Justice turns and nods to the author of the majority opinion. The Justice nods back and is on his own. He can read his entire written opinion, as was usually the custom with Justice Harold Hitz Burton; he can give a brief synopsis of the facts and law, as Mr. Justice Douglas generally does, or he can render in effect an entirely new opinion which sometimes exceeds in length and complexities what he has written. This last method lay almost exclusively in the personal domain of Mr. Justice Frankfurter. A rather slow starter, he calmly launched into an extended discussion of the facts, problems, and issues involved. As he progressed, he warmed to his subject. His body stiffened; his voice became vibrant, raspy, and even strident; his thin lips quivered, and the blood vessels stood out on his head. His chair began to vibrate like a Relaxacizor, as he bobbed and weaved in tune to the delivery. He was incensed at the dissenters, protective toward the majority, and stricken by the delicacy of the questions presented and by the balance required to be drawn between the competing rights. It was always a fine performance. And it came from the heart.

On this Monday in June, the Chief Justice nodded to Frankfurter, and the seventy-three-year-old Justice delivered the majority opinion for the Court. He recounted all of the facts leading up to the present posture of the case, including the letters which had passed back and forth between Goode and the clerk of the Supreme Court. He pointed out that the State of Georgia, through its assistant attorney general, had conceded "with commendable regard for its responsibility" that the use of yellow and white tickets violated the Constitution. The only remaining question, said the Justice, was whether the Supreme Court had jurisdiction to review the decision of the Georgia court.

If Georgia invariably prohibited the raising of constitutional questions at late stages of the case, said Justice Frankfurter, that would end the matter. The Supreme Court could do nothing further. But a state cannot cut off the Supreme Court's jurisdiction by allowing constitutional questions to be raised late in some cases and not in others; it cannot allow its courts discretion to decide these questions in some instances and then arbitrarily refuse to consider them in others. The Justice then proceeded into a discussion of the law of Georgia, in an effort to determine whether motions such as Goode had submitted for Williams after trial were ever granted in that state. Frankfurter's written opinion cited thirty-four decisions by the Georgia Supreme Court. These decisions, while not entirely consistent, added up to the fact that while Georgia did not favor motions which raised questions at late stages of the case, such motions were granted on occasion. Or to put it another way, the Georgia courts did not invariably deny such motions; they had discretion to grant them or not as they saw fit. "We conclude," wrote Justice Frankfurter, "that the trial court and the State Supreme Court declined to grant Williams' motion though possessed of power to do so under state law." Therefore, the Supreme Court of the United States had jurisdiction to decide the constitutional issue raised by Williams.

Those listening to Frankfurter's rendition relaxed. It seemed clear that the Supreme Court, having gotten over the procedural barrier in the case, would reverse. They were startled to hear the Justice's next sentence: "But the fact that we have jurisdiction does not compel us to exercise it."

There was precedent, he said, for simply returning the case to the Georgia court for further consideration. After all, the state's representative had not conceded to the Georgia court, as he had to the Supreme Court, that Williams' constitutional rights had been violated, and the Georgia court might well want to reconsider its decision in the light of the assistant attorney general's admission.

Frankfurter's opinion concluded with a highly unusual paragraph. It acknowledged that a "death" case was in a class by itself—a case that may call for special consideration and special treatment. And the Justice virtually pleaded with the Georgia court not to allow Williams to go to his death. Wrote Frankfurter:

> The facts of this case are extraordinary, particularly in view of the use of yellow and white tickets by a judge of the Fulton County Superior Court almost a year after the State's own Supreme Court had condemned the practice in the *Avery* case. That life is at stake is of course another important factor in creating

the extraordinary situation. The difference between capital and non-capital offenses is the basis of differentiation in law in diverse ways in which the distinction becomes relevant. . . . We think that orderly procedure requires a remand to the State Supreme Court for reconsideration of the case. Fair regard for the principles which the Georgia courts have enforced in numerous cases and for the constitutional commands binding on all courts compels us to reject the assumption that the courts of Georgia would allow this man to go to his death as the result of a conviction secured from a jury which the State admits was unconstitutionally impaneled.

Justices Reed, Clark, and Minton dissented, each of them joining in two separate opinions—one written by Clark and one by Minton. All three men wanted to dismiss the writ of certiorari as improvidently granted and thus leave the Georgia courts to their own devices. Justice Clark's opinion was the most reproachful. He began, "To borrow a phrase from Mr. Justice Holmes, the opinion of the Court 'just won't wash.'" He said that the majority had misinterpreted Georgia law; Georgia allowed late objections only to individual jurors and not to an entire jury panel. There was no attempt by Georgia to "evade" the Supreme Court's jurisdiction. And regardless of what the Georgia law was or what the Georgia court had done, Goode had never proven that he had used "due diligence" in discovering and raising the point about the jury panel in the first place. Minton's briefer dissent was based entirely upon his interpretation of Georgia law.

And so it was that the Williams case, through a seldom used procedure, was sent back to the Georgia court for another round. The Supreme Court accomplished this result by picking up a point barely mentioned at the end of Gressman's brief, looking for itself at the Georgia law, and reaching its own middle ground, short of outright affirmance or reversal.

Two weeks after the Supreme Court's decision, the state attorney general, Eugene Cook, filed a brief in the Georgia court asking it to reaffirm its original decision. He said that the Supreme Court Justices had misinterpreted what had been told them during oral argument. Leverett had not meant that Williams' constitutional rights had been violated, but rather that *if* Williams had raised the issue in time, he would have been entitled to a reversal. Since Williams had not raised the issue in time, he had "waived" it. And a right which is waived is not subject to being "denied." Cook also argued that the Supreme Court had completely garbled the Georgia law; there were important differences between the types of motions which the Georgia courts allowed to be filed late in the case and those which were always denied.

Without calling for further briefs, and without hearing oral argument, Georgia's highest court, less than a month later, reached its decision. The brief opinion, rendered in the stifling heat of Georgia's mid-July, was perhaps the most sharply worded document ever issued in the court's history. In its entirety, the opinion read as follows:

By the Court:

Duckworth, Chief Justice. "The powers not delegated to the United States by the Constitution, nor prohibited by it to the States, are reserved to the States respectively, or to the people." Constitution of the United States, 10th Amendment; Code Sec. 1-810. Even though executives and legislators, not being constitutional lawyers, might often overstep the foregoing unambiguous constitutional prohibition of Federal invasion of State jurisdiction, there can never be an acceptable excuse for judicial failure to strictly observe it. This Court bows to the Supreme Court on all Federal questions of law, but we will not supinely surrender sovereign powers of this State. In this case the opinion of the majority of that court recognizes that this court decided the case according to established rules of law, and that no Federal jurisdiction existed which would authorize that court to render a judgment either affirming or reversing the judgment of this court, which are the only judgments by that court that this court can constitutionally recognize.

The Supreme Court undertakes to remand the case for further consideration, and in its opinion has pointed to Georgia law vesting in the trial judge discretion in ruling upon an extraordinary motion for new trial, and apparently concluded therefrom that this court should reverse the trial court because that discretion was not exercised in the way the Supreme Court would have exercised it. We know and respect the universally recognized rule that the exercise of discretion never authorizes a violation or defiance of law. In this case, as pointed out to us, that law is that the question sought to be raised must be raised before trial and not otherwise.

Not in recognition of any jurisdiction of the Supreme Court to influence or in any manner to interfere with the functioning of this court on strictly State questions, but solely for the purpose of completing the record in this court in a case that was first decided by us in 1953, and to avoid further delay, we state that our opinion in Williams v. State, 210 Ga. 665 (82 S. E. 2d 217), is supported by sound and unchallenged law, conforms with the State and Federal Constitutions, and stands as the judgment of all seven of the Justices of this Court.

Judgment of affirmance rendered May 10, 1954, adhered to. All the Justices concur.

This remarkable document not only told the Supreme Court to mind its own business but virtually told it to go to hell.

The statement in the opinion that the Supreme Court had recognized its own lack of jurisdiction was directly contrary to what Justice Frankfurter had actually ruled: namely, that the Supreme Court had jurisdiction but chose not to exercise it. And the statement by the Georgia court that it was acting "to avoid further delay" seemed to Gressman particularly callous in view of the irredeemable effect upon Williams of rushing the case along. No mention at all was made in the opinion of the fact that the procedure used to select Williams' jury violated the Constitution. And there was only the most oblique reference to the various types of motions which the Georgia courts had discretion to grant.

Goode and Gressman immediately set in motion the procedure for having the Supreme Court of the United States again review the case. Their petition for certiorari told the Supreme Court that the Georgia court in effect had refused to review its prior decision and instead "openly flouts the jurisdiction and authority of this Court." Such a "flat defiance of this Court's ruling," they said, "raises a most basic question as to the supremacy of this Court over state courts on issues arising out of the federal Constitution." They asked the Supreme Court to take jurisdiction and reverse the conviction.

Perhaps to the layman, the Supreme Court's duty seems clear; perhaps the quandary in which the Justices found themselves seems more verbal than real. But a quandary it really was. Only soul-searching of the deepest sort could produce an answer.

On one side, of course, was the indisputable fact that the Williams jury had been selected in violation of the Constitution, and that the failure to raise the point at the outset of the trial was not the fault of Williams himself; if the Williams jury had been "challenged" as the Avery jury had been, this conviction would have been reversed summarily. There was the further fact that the Georgia court had blatantly challenged the authority of the Supreme Court and could be said to have "reconsidered" its prior decision only under the most liberal interpretation of that word. And then, too, there was the fact of death—the inescapable, brooding presence of the penalty—which permeated even the legalistic arguments about "jurisdiction" and "discretion" and "extraordinary motions" and the like.

But on the other side was the stark realization that in order to reverse this conviction, the Supreme Court had to make liars out of the learned judges of Georgia's highest court. Those judges had now stated unequivocally that as a matter of state law, an objection to the jury panel "must be raised before trial and not otherwise." If the objection is raised *after* trial, the Georgia courts cannot even consider the objection; they have no power at all to grant relief. Williams had not raised his objection before trial. The Supreme Court, if it reversed the conviction, would be saying in effect that the statement of the Georgia court was not true, that the Georgia courts really have discretion to grant or deny objections to jury panels even when made after trial, and that the Supreme Court therefore had jurisdiction to decide the case on its merits. A proper respect for the delicate balance between the state and Federal systems was inextricably involved in whatever the Supreme Court now decided to do.

On January 16, 1956, the Supreme Court turned its other cheek. It issued an order which read: "No. 328 Misc. Williams v. Georgia. Supreme Court of Georgia. Certiorari denied." These words, which Williams probably could not even understand, meant that the Supreme Court was refusing to hear the case further. It thus bowed to the interpretation of state law rendered by the Georgia Supreme Court.

Gressman was horrified. Fully aware both of the technical problems involved and of the delicate balance between state and Federal jurisdiction which the Supreme Court must constantly attempt to maintain, he nevertheless could not bring himself to concede that Williams would be executed in the face of what Gressman considered an illegal jury panel.

He set in motion several courses of action.

First, he and Goode wrote a "petition for rehearing," asking that the Supreme Court reconsider its decision and decide the case on the merits. This the Supreme Court refused to do. However, Marvin Griffin, the colorful, compassionate Governor of Georgia, granted a thirty-day reprieve so that all avenues of appeal could be exhausted. Gressman next urged Goode to file in Georgia a "petition for a writ of habeas corpus" which, if granted, would have allowed Goode to argue the illegality of Williams' detention because of the white and yellow tickets. Under rather complicated rulings by the Supreme Court, a Federal district judge may sometimes grant a writ of habeas corpus even after the Supreme Court has refused to act, if constitutional issues are involved. Gressman, in order to spur his cohort on, arranged to place at Goode's disposal the services of Morris Abram, an attorney with the

American Civil Liberties Union. Goode said that he would prepare the necessary petition immediately.

But on March 28, 1956, Goode wrote to the staff counsel of the American Civil Liberties Union in New York:

> After much research and some soul-searching, I have reached the conclusion that any further efforts in behalf of Williams would be of no benefit to him and almost surely be detrimental to me. Williams, of course, is in a situation where nothing that is done can be of detriment to him. Upon this conclusion, I went to the Georgia State Prison at Reidsville, Georgia, and told Williams of my conclusion. While he is most anxious that anything be done which might save his life, he has recognized that when the Supreme Court failed to do anything for him on the last petition for certiorari, he was pretty well through. I had prepared a petition for writ of habeas corpus, and arranged with the United States Judge for the Southern District of Georgia to present it today, but after conferring with my client advised the judge and the Assistant Attorney General who has been in charge of the case for the state of Georgia that the petition would not be presented.
>
> Two factors compelled the decision, first the law, as in *Jugiro* v. *Brush*, 140 U.S. 291, *Wood* v. *Brush*, 140 U.S. 278, *Darr* v. *Burford*, 339 U.S. 200, and *Brown* v. *Allen*, 344 U.S. 443.
>
> The second factor was the feeling that from this point on I would be putting myself in a position to receive a rather well-founded accusation of seeking to obstruct the processes of the Georgia courts by frivolous proceedings.
>
> I am most grateful for your offer of assistance, but believe that our efforts will be better spent in other and more hopeful causes. I am forwarding copies of this letter to Messrs. Abram and Gressman.

Copies of the letter were received at the American Civil Liberties Union and by Gressman two days later, March 30.

On the same day, Williams was taken from his cell at the Georgia State Prison at Reidsville and marched down a short corridor to a smallish, rectangular room. He was strapped into the electric chair and blindfolded. There was a brief pause before the executioner threw the switch. Williams almost spun in his seat, restrained only by the straps. In a few moments the current was turned off, and it was all over for Aubry Lee Williams. The Sovereign State of Georgia had exacted its due, and Harry Furst was avenged.

Suppose the question of the yellow and white tickets had been raised prior to Williams' trial as it was in Avery's. Would it really have made any difference to Williams? Would he not have been retried, reconvicted, and then finally executed anyway? We have no way of knowing, except perhaps by the example of Avery himself. Avery, who also had been sentenced to death, was allowed to plead guilty after the Supreme Court reversed his conviction. He received a sentence of twenty years, and he sits today in a Georgia prison.

Tickets are still used to select juries in Atlanta. But they are all the same color now. The yellow tickets died with Aubry Williams.

Conclusion

Death, for all the attention its majestic presence usually commands, has no guaranteed admission to the Supreme Court. Even a man condemned to death must establish a clear claim to be heard. It takes a magic combination of attributes and circumstances for him to be recognized by—and to prevail before—the highest court in the land. What constitutes this extraordinary combination?

First in importance are the character, ability, imagination, and perseverance of the condemned man's attorney. Not one lawyer in a hundred would have had the imagination to develop the legal theories that freed Everett Green, and not one in five hundred would have dared pursue them. No one at Green's first trial realized that he could not be guilty of second degree murder—that it had to be first degree or nothing. The reasoning employed by George Blow to reverse the second degree conviction was so logical that one tends to forget he was the first to think of it: if Bettie Brown died as the result of a fire, and Green set the fire, Green committed a felony (arson) and necessarily was guilty of first degree murder under the "felony murder rule" in effect in the District of Columbia. Nor was it obvious, as Blow was successful in making the Supreme Court decide, that the jury at the first trial found Green not only guilty of second degree murder but by implication not guilty of first degree murder, so that prosecuting him a second time for first degree murder constituted double jeopardy. Green walked out free because he was willing to gamble his life and because his attorney, though young, was superior in every respect.

The unhappy truth is that for every defendant who has had his case reversed by the Supreme Court, there are scores whose cases could have been reversed if their attorneys had recognized or ferreted out important legal questions, raised those questions at the proper stage in the proceedings, and adequately researched and presented the questions on appeal. The disparity of representation in capital cases raises doubts about capital punishment itself, which has been abolished in only nine states. If a James Avery can be saved from electrocution because his attorney made timely objection to the selection of a jury by the use of yellow and white tickets, while an Aubry Williams can be sent to his death by a jury selected in precisely the same manner, we are imposing our most extreme penalty in an uneven fashion.

The problem of proper representation is not a problem of money, as some have claimed, but of a lawyer's ability, and it is not true that only the rich have able lawyers. Both the rich and the poor usually are well represented—the poor because more often than not the best attorneys are appointed to defend them. It is the middle-class defendant, who can afford to hire an attorney but not a very good one, who is at a disadvantage. Certainly William Fikes, despite the anomalous position in which he finds himself today, received as effective and intelligent a defense from his court-appointed attorneys as he would have received from an attorney his family had scraped together enough money to hire.

And it is not only a matter of ability. An attorney must be found who is prepared to spend precious hours—the basic commodity he has to sell—on a case that seldom fully compensates him and often brings him no fee at all. The public has no conception of the time and effort devoted by attorneys to indigent cases. And in a first-degree case, the added responsibility of having a man's life depend upon the outcome exacts a heavy toll.

One would think that any attorney who argued before the Supreme Court would of necessity be well qualified. Not so at all. The Court listens to some atrocious arguments, and a number of attorneys would be shocked to see the comments made about them in notes passed from Justice to Justice. But when there is a fine argument—articulate, lucid, precise, knowledgeable—the enthusiasm and gratitude of the Court are unbounded.

The frustrating part is that there is so little the Court can do about a defendant's legal representation. In extreme cases, it can hold that the defendant was denied the effective assistance of counsel and thus denied due process of law. But most cases are not extreme—they simply have about them a certain stickiness, a suggestion that perhaps the attorney was not all he might have been. The Court cannot act as second-guesser when the attorney might well have made tactical and strategical decisions which only later, because of circumstances beyond his control, turned out to have been unfortunate.

Because the Supreme Court decides only those cases it wishes to decide, the next factor that comes into play is the importance of the legal issue presented by the case. For the statistically minded, during a typical term the Court was asked to review over 2000 cases, of which forty-two involved the death penalty. The crimes were murder (sometimes entailing an additional crime such as rape, robbery, sodomy, or kidnapping), rape, and burglary with intent to steal and ravish. The attorneys in these cases gave credence to Mr. Justice Fuller's observation in 1895, "It is natural that counsel for the condemned in a capital case should lay hold of every ground which, in their judgment might tend to the advantage of their client. . . ." Among their arguments, for example, were these:

—The defendant was convicted without proof that he was

guilty of the crime or that the crime had in fact been committed.

—The police extracted a confession from the defendant, an illiterate Negro, after sustained interrogation, punctuated by beatings while a sheet was placed over his head, after he was held incommunicado for four days.

—The defendant's attorneys wilfully and knowingly neglected to represent him properly.

—The trial judge communicated with the jurors about the penalty outside the presence of the accused and his attorneys.

—The defendant was convicted even though eight of the twelve jurors had stated prior to being sworn that they thought the defendant was guilty.

—The trial court appointed one attorney from the courtroom at arraignment who served under protest, appointed another attorney for the preliminary hearing who failed to appear, appointed two other attorneys from the courtroom for the preliminary hearing who consulted with the accused only a few minutes and then waived the preliminary hearing, and finally at the arraignment appointed still another attorney with less than sixty days' experience to represent the accused at trial.

In fact, all of the allegations in these capital cases were so serious that the Supreme Court might have felt compelled to decide each and every one of them. Yet, of the forty-two, the Court refused to hear argument in twenty-nine, returned two to a lower court for further hearings, and listened to argument in only eleven (six of which were subsequently dismissed because the facts turned out to be quite different from those originally alleged). Five convictions were reversed. Thus, while it can be generalized that it is far easier for a condemned man to have his case heard than for the average litigant, whose chances are one in twenty, the fact remains that out of every four condemned men only one receives a hearing.

How does the Court separate the wheat from the chaff?

More often than not, a simple investigation of the briefs and records when the cases are first presented suffices to show the Court that in most instances, the allegations were not properly raised in the courts below, are not supported by evidence, or, at best, are too unclear or disputed to warrant review. There must be a factual basis for the presentation of a constitutional question.

The issues which do warrant review are not necessarily related to guilt or innocence. That is the business of the jury, applying legal tests under the instruction and direction of the trial judge. Once the trial is over, and the case passes to the appellate level, the entire complexion changes. More often than not, the issue on appeal is not whether there was sufficient evidence of guilt, but whether the procedural safeguards which the law accords every man have been followed. These safeguards are often referred to in newspapers as "technicalities." They are nothing of the sort. The English-speaking world has found through bitter experience that a fair trial is guaranteed and justice best served when government is made to follow prescribed standards regardless of the seeming guilt of the accused. Once an appellate court begins disregarding these standards because it believes an accused to be guilty, it invites short-cuts by the officials who enforce the law in the first instance. And when the application of civilized standards of justice depends upon the whimsy of minor police officials, society has ceased to live under law and is instead proceeding on a *sui generis* basis that protects no one. The purpose of so-called "technicalities" in the law is to protect us all—from overzealous, arbitrary, inefficient, or corrupt people, wherever they may be, whatever their position.

We must remember this when we review a case like Everett Green's. We are tempted to say that the Supreme Court "let him off scot-free." The truth is that if anyone erred, it was the prosecutor and the trial judge, not the Supreme Court. Green's first jury should never have been instructed on the issue of second degree murder. It was too late, once the erroneous instructions were given, to alter the chain of events that led to Green's release. This is not to say that in the Green case the appellate courts rendered the only decisions open to them; the closeness of the votes indicates otherwise. But those votes dealt with intricate and difficult questions of law, not with guilt or innocence, and, once decided, the law was applied without regard to the verdict of any jury.

It can be argued, of course, that an appellate tribunal such as the Supreme Court should consider guilt or innocence and should reverse a conviction only when, in its opinion, an innocent man has been wronged. But the Court simply is not equipped to make such determinations. It does not see or hear the witnesses and cannot measure their honesty from a cold, written record. The Court has neither the time nor the clairvoyance to decide each case *de novo*, as if a jury had never been impaneled. The Supreme Court is at its best when it decides the narrow problems before it and then applies the appropriate legal standards to guilty and innocent alike.

This is not to say that the "flavor" of guilt or innocence surrounding a case does not have its psychological effect. Not infrequently, a Justice himself will read, or have his law clerk read, an entire record to determine whether a defendant seems to have been "railroaded" or deprived of rights in addition to those claimed in his briefs. But such concern cannot be legitimatized into a rule applicable to all cases.

Once the issues have been properly raised, the Court has agreed to decide the case, and the attorneys have presented their arguments, the critical decision-making process begins. Most capital cases do not require the Court to construe a statute or regulation; most involve instead the application of nebulous constitutional concepts such as "due process of law" and "equal protection of the law." Starting with certain basic standards of fairness evolved from the British system of jurisprudence, the Supreme Court has built up over the years a whole series of interpretations of due process and equal protection, so that each decision is related to and, at least to some extent, dependent upon the other. There are few cases the Court can approach completely afresh, as if nothing had gone before. Instead, the Court is continually restrained by its own precedents. An example is the John Crooker case. Crooker was intelligent and educated, and he had briefly studied law. When he was arrested for the murder of his mistress, he demanded and was denied the advice of counsel before he confessed. He might have won a reversal if his had been the first case of its type ever to reach the Supreme Court. But the Court had already used language in analogous cases indicating that a defendant's intelligence and education are factors to be considered on the issue of due process. With this precedent established, it was difficult for judges like Clark and Frankfurter to rationalize how Crooker was injured by lack of counsel. Perhaps if they had had the advantage of Crooker's full story, as he has given it here, and had been aware of the mental deterioration he had experienced prior to his arrest—a deterioration that may have sapped his will to resist questioning—his situation would have been sufficiently distinguished from prior cases and a different result engendered.

Precedents are important, but they can go only so far. At some point in most proceedings, after the precedents have been exhausted and the Justices still have found no answer to the precise problem before them, they must turn to some inner light for guidance. It is here that they begin to draw upon their experience, their judgment, their training. For the constitutional problems they are called upon to solve are not black-and-white problems. What is cruel and unusual punishment? How cruel? How unusual? What is double jeopardy? To what extent and under what circumstances is an accused entitled to the advice of counsel? Does it make any difference that he asks for counsel? When is a confession coerced? The myriad questions that arise under the four-thousand-word Constitution and its few thousand words of Amendments seem endless—and unfathomable. Those who treat the Constitution as a static instrument and who act as if all the Justices need do to decide a given case is to lay the facts and the issue beside the Constitution and there find the necessary result would do well to look again. The "felony murder rule" in the Green case, the faulty electric chair in the Francis case, the yellow and white tickets in the Williams case—none of these complications was envisaged by the makers of the Constitution. The application of constitutional principles is an evolutionary process precisely because no two cases are exactly alike and because the degree of difference between them is so difficult to measure.

And so a majority of the Justices has repeatedly turned to the basic concept of "fairness." Due process is violated, they say, if the conduct of the police, the prosecution, or the court has been so unfair as to shock the conscience of mankind. The difficulty, of course, is that what shocks one man's conscience may not shock another's. The week-long incommunicado detention of William Fikes shocked the conscience of Earl Warren but not the conscience of John Marshall Harlan. The refusal to grant John Crooker's request for an attorney shocked the conscience of William O. Douglas but not the conscience of Tom C. Clark. In due process cases, we find ourselves more and more delving into the subconscious motives of each Justice. I imagine the Senate would welcome a conscience-shocking test for the Justices it is called upon to confirm. How interesting to know in advance, if the test could be devised, whether a new Justice, faced with the Fikes case, would start from Warren's premise or from Harlan's. How interesting to know where his sympathies and his prejudices lie, how empathetic he is, how swayed by emotion. The difficulty is that once the Senate had all this information, it probably would split squarely down the middle in deciding what the information meant and how to apply it, just as the Court does on the meaning of the Constitution itself.

The power wielded by the Justices is great, particularly where the legal standards they apply are as vague as "due process of law." Our system of government is unique in allowing the judiciary to declare void an act of the President, the Congress, the highest court of a state, and the legislature of a state. But the power is not as awesome in practice as it seems in theory. There are limitations to it.

Some of these limitations are self-imposed. Most members of the Court are acutely aware of the distrust and distaste with which many state courts look upon the exercise of Federal authority in the field of criminal law, and these members attempt whenever possible to practice judicial self-restraint in their approach to criminal cases. Even though some police tactics sanctioned by state courts are personally obnoxious to these members of the Supreme Court, they wisely recognize that the states were deliberately left much leeway under the Constitution to deal with criminal matters as they see fit. If the Court had the same "supervisory" power over the state courts that it has over lower Federal courts, the percentage of reversals in capital cases would rise precipitously. There would be more opinions like that in Baxter Griffin's case, where the Court exercised its supervisory power over the District of Columbia Federal court to remand a case not because of some constitutional infirmity but solely because a penknife had been found in the dead man's pocket and had not been revealed at trial. It is a recognition of the role of the states under our constitutional system that prevents so many capital cases from being reversed.

This problem of how much power to wield in cases coming from state courts is an ever present one. A case in point is that of Aubry Williams, whose jury was chosen by yellow and white tickets already condemned by the Georgia courts but whose attorney did not raise the point until long after trial.

Critics of the Supreme Court argue that sending the case back to the Georgia courts was an overreaching of authority and a gross abuse of power. The Georgia Supreme Court said as much. My own view is that the case represents not an abuse of power but a classic instance of judicial self-restraint, because the Court, after holding that it had jurisdiction to reverse, refused to do so even after the Georgia court had defiantly challenged the Supreme Court's authority. If I am wrong, and the remand to the Georgia court was an abuse of power, it probably can be explained in very human terms. Six Justices simply could not believe that the State of Georgia would put Williams to death under the peculiar circumstances of his case. They believe it now.

There are other important limitations on the Court's power which are not self-imposed. The case of William Earl Fikes is an example. Convicted first of rape and given a life sentence and then of burglary with intent to ravish and given death, Fikes appealed only the second conviction. The Supreme Court reversed because of a confession coerced from Fikes at the same time and in the same manner as a confession admitted at his rape trial. Yet the Supreme Court has no authority to bring up for consideration Fikes's conviction for rape. Fikes's attorneys must file appropriate papers in the appropriate courts and move the case along until jurisdiction finally lodges in the Supreme Court. This they will not do, and for a very good reason: a reversal and new trial would mean almost certain death for Fikes as long as the victim of the rape is alive to identify him. It does not matter a tinker's damn what the Supreme Court thinks of the situation; the Court is powerless to act.

Another very practical limitation on the effectiveness of the Court is the number of hours in the day available to consider and decide cases. With over two thousand cases being filed each term, the Court is precluded from taking action in as many matters as it might like. Mr. Justice Jackson once estimated that if each case on an average list to be decided by the Court were actually considered at conference, that case would receive only thirty-three seconds of discussion from each Justice. What happens in practice is that some cases are so obviously frivolous that the Justices agree not even to discuss them. However, I have never known a capital case to be treated in this manner. On the contrary, the Court overcomes all kinds of difficulties to devote to such cases a disproportionately large amount of time. Most capital cases involve indigents, and their appeals come to the Court *in forma pauperis*—that is, without the ordinary expenses involved in presenting an appeal. Thus, instead of filing forty printed briefs and records, the attorney for an indigent files only one. Sometimes the petition is in the defendant's own handwriting—ungrammatical, barely legible, and wild in its accusations. The single copy is circulated among all nine Justices, accompanied by a memorandum prepared by one of the Chief Justice's law clerks. Nevertheless, despite these unpropitious circumstances, each Justice gives meticulous attention to the file when he sees the label "capital case" printed in red on the outside cover. In fact, the capital case receives more attention than any other class of cases coming before the Court.

After the precedents are all considered and the Justices have searched their souls for the right answers, still another element often plays a part. That element is luck—or fate, if you are a romanticist. How else can we explain that Baxter Griffin, awaiting execution, became acquainted with an attorney who was himself accused of a crime, who subsequently was released on bond, who found a morgue attendant responsible for the discovery of an open penknife in the murdered man's pocket, and who caught Chief Justice Vinson at that precise moment in time when he was in a mood to grant a stay of execution?

The Court's history is filled with little-known instances of luck, of coincidence, and of hair-breadth timing. Perhaps one of the most dramatic involved Joe Vernon, sentenced to death in Alabama for killing a young college student during the course of a robbery. In 1940, not long after Mr. Justice Frankfurter had become an Associate Justice, the Supreme Court refused to take Vernon's case, and it denied a petition for rehearing. On the evening Vernon was to die, his attorney called the Supreme Court and asked for Justice Frankfurter. The Court gave the attorney the number of Philip L. Graham, who was then the Justice's law clerk and who years later was to become the publisher of the Washington *Post and Times Herald*. Mrs. Graham answered the attorney's call and told him her husband was working at the Justice's home in Georgetown, but that she would telephone him there and give him a message. She did, and Graham immediately called the lawyer back and put the Justice on the line. The attorney was able to persuade the Justice that even though the Supreme Court had already twice refused to hear the case, a stay of execution should be granted to enable him to file still another application to the Court. Frankfurter, new to the bench, was not certain as to his authority. He called Edmund Cullinan, the Court's deputy clerk and an old hand at the Court's procedures. Cullinan assured the Justice he had the requisite power to act. "All right," said the Justice. "Stop the execution."

This proved easier in the saying than in the doing. With only half an hour to go, Cullinan telephoned the warden of Vernon's prison and told him Justice Frankfurter had issued a stay. The warden replied tartly that he took orders from the governor and the attorney general but not from some stranger over the telephone. Frantically, Cullinan put through a call to the attorney general of Alabama, who fortunately remembered the deputy clerk from a previous visit to the Court. The attorney general contacted the warden, and the execution was halted with only minutes to spare.

Vernon's case was subsequently heard—and reversed—by the Supreme Court.

Mr. Justice Brennan still shudders when he recalls another,

more recent case. He was vacationing in a remote mountain area near Aspen, Colorado, when he suddenly received word that his son, who was in military service, was about to arrive in Aspen after a long cross-country trip. The Justice rushed off to Aspen to meet him. While he was waiting at an inn, a waiter asked him, "Aren't you the judge?" Brennan replied that he was. The waiter told him that a package had been waiting for him for several days. The Justice secured the package, and inside was the application for a stay of execution from a man scheduled to die the next day. By phone, the Justice stopped the execution. The New Jersey Supreme Court, learning of Brennan's action, then granted the man a new trial.

These are dramatic examples, and they illustrate the role that chance can play in even so important a matter as a capital case. But these examples also illustrate another phase of the Court's work, because each involved purposeful delay in the final disposition of a criminal case. Delay haunts the American judicial system like a specter. Before the beginning of the twentieth century, substantial delay between trial and execution was almost unthinkable, in part because of the wear and tear on the defendant. As one lawyer put it in 1774: "The cruelty of an execution after respite is equal to many deaths, and therefore there is rarely an instance of it." But today, respite after respite is common. In the six cases covered in this book, the time periods from arrest to final disposition by the courts ranged from two and a half to four and a half years, with an average of three and a half years per case. The ordeal of Caryl Chessman—eleven years on death row—was not as exceptional as we would like to believe. Stays of executions have become almost automatic, so that defendants are subjected to the imminence of death, the hope of reprieve, desperate disappointment—all repeated many times over. John Crooker suffered a nervous breakdown from this treatment. Willie Lee Stewart, convicted of murder three times and sentenced to death each time, weighed a hundred and seventy pounds when he entered death row. Seven years later, he weighed two hundred and sixty-five pounds, an increase which prison doctors attributed to the tension he was constantly under. Undoubtedly, many of the four to five hundred prisoners now awaiting execution had similar traumatic experiences.

But stating the problem is one thing; suggesting an answer is another. The fact is that a Justice of the Supreme Court will delay an execution any time he has reasonable grounds to believe that the condemned man has not received every safeguard the Constitution demands. Life is precious and sacred, and the state undertakes no more awesome a responsibility than when it deliberately sets about to excise the life of one of its citizens. Every protection must be accorded innocent and guilty alike, regardless of delay, lest a mistake be made for which there can be no remedy. As terrible as life imprisonment would be for an innocent man, nothing transcends the horror of a life wrongly taken—not in the heat of passion, not in a haze of alcohol, not through provocation or hatred or revenge, but coolly, deliberately, by society itself. Because of this possibility, doubts are resolved in favor of the accused. Rules are stretched. Some bad law is made. And all because there are no second chances once the penalty has been exacted.

It is my own belief that many delays, many votes, and many decisions in these cases can be explained only in terms of the schizophrenic situation in which the Justices find themselves—compelled to recognize and even enforce a penalty they abhor: the death penalty. Their quandary is epitomized by the plight of Willie Francis, brought to the brink of death and allowed to hang there because of a faulty electric chair, peering over the edge into eternity, and then given a brief reprieve before the state went through the whole process again. Here was a case in which four Justices were willing to reverse on an issue having nothing whatever to do with guilt or the processes by which the accused was arrested, tried, or sentenced; in which four other Justices could not bring themselves to overrule the highest court of Louisiana but nevertheless expressed their distaste for what they were doing, and in which the ninth Justice, caught between personal revulsion at the outcome and his belief in judicial self-restraint, tipped the scales to execution.

Those who have watched the Court at work know the burden that each Justice carries in a death case. It is the one case in which he feels the full impact of both his responsibility and his fallibility. It is the case he takes to meals and to bed; it is the case that lingers on in his mind long after it is decided. It finally drops away only because another death case, equally troublesome, has taken its place.

Because the Justices generally write in restrained, unemotional terms, it is difficult to document their concern. Nevertheless, there is an undercurrent running through their majority, concurring, and dissenting opinions over the years, no less discernible because guarded and judicial in tone. Statements such as these:

Mr. Justice Miller (1890): "Nor can we withhold our conviction of the proposition that when a prisoner sentenced by a court to death is confined in the penitentiary awaiting the execution of the sentence, one of the most horrible feelings to which he can be subjected during that time is the uncertainty during the whole of it, which may exist for the period of four weeks, as to the precise time when his execution shall take place."

Mr. Justice Black (1940): "Due process of law, preserved for all by our Constitution, commands that no such practice as that disclosed by this record shall send any accused to his death."

Mr. Justice Frankfurter (1948): "The statute reflects the movement, active during the nineteenth century, against the death sentence. The movement was impelled both by ethical and humanitarian arguments against capital punishment, as well as by the practical consideration that jurors were reluctant to bring in verdicts which inevitably called for its infliction."

Mr. Justice Reed (1948): "In death cases doubts such as those presented here should be resolved in favor of the accused."

Mr. Justice Frankfurter (1952): "Even though a person be the immediate occasion of another's death, he is not a deodand to be forfeited like a thing in the medieval law."

Mr. Justice Jackson (1953): "Vacating this stay is not to be construed as indorsing the wisdom or appropriateness to this case of a death sentence."

Mr. Justice Clark (1953): "Human lives are at stake; we need not turn this decision on fine points of procedure or a party's technical standing to claim relief."

Mr. Justice Black (1953): "This would be a strange argument in any case but it seems still stranger to me in a case which involves matters of life and death. . . . I cannot believe . . . that if the sentence of a citizen to death is plainly illegal, this Court would allow that citizen to be executed on the grounds that his lawyers had 'waived' plain error. . . . I have long thought that the practice of some of the states to require an automatic review by the highest court of the state in cases which involve the death penalty was a good practice."

Mr. Justice Douglas (1953): "It is also important that before we allow human lives to be snuffed out we be sure—emphatically sure—that we act within the law. If we are not sure, there will be lingering doubts to plague the conscience after the event."

These are voices of deep concern. They spring from men not likely to change their minds and to begin sanctioning executions on faulty records. What, then, is to be done? Of course, an obvious solution would be for the various states or for the Court itself to eliminate the death penalty, as surely it will be eliminated in time; the inexorable trend in our country runs directly contrary to that in the Soviet Union, where the death penalty is now being broadened to encompass more and more crimes. Although the number of persons awaiting execution in this country is slowly growing, the number of persons actually being executed is being dramatically reduced. For the last few years we have executed only one or two a year.

But an immediate and far-reaching solution would be for our state authorities to begin taking a stringent look at their own processes. The criminal law, after all, is primarily a state rather than a federal responsibility. It is almost incredible that until recently we were still executing citizens in some states without any transcript being made of their trials. And it is still true in far too many instances that police interrogate almost at will, that homes are broken into without judicial authority, that minorities are kept off juries, and that medically insane defendants are put to death.

Today, when state courts refuse to act, the Supreme Court of the United States stands as a last bulwark against many such outrages. And its task in due process cases is exceedingly complex; it cannot simply apply rigid standards and mechanical rules. As extraordinary as it may seem in this age of centralization and collectivism, of wars and threats of wars, of population explosions, breakaway science, and the emphasis on social utility—in this frightening time of cheap life—the fact is that an active ingredient in the workings of one branch of the most powerful government on earth is compassion. Compassion for the fate of solitary people, of desperate, lonely, untutored, and disturbed people. Compassion for human life regardless of its extrinsic worth.

Is this feeling, shared in varying degrees by all members of the Supreme Court, merely "some fastidious squeamishness or private sentimentalism"?

I think not. I think that in the long pull of humanity, one of the phenomena most proudly recorded will be this extraordinary attempt, hardly articulated and yet forcefully manifest, to enhance human dignity through the protection of human life.